The Hike to Eternity

A Practical Manual for the De-churched

Christer Thomas

The Hike to Eternity
A Practical Manual for the De-churched

© 2020 by Christer Thomas

ISBN: 978-1-7347270-0-5

COVER NOTES
The map under the compass is a welcome map of the 230 acres of the woods and wetlands of Washington Park Arboretum, Seattle, Washington, where the first hike took place.
The compass was a gift from the author's children.

PHOTOGRAPHS
With the exception of Discovery Park in Seattle, Washington, the photographs in the book were taken by the author.

First Printing May 2020.

DEDICATION

MY WONDERFUL WIFE has been my greatest support and encouragement. She is an inspiration in my life. Most importantly is that we see eye to eye and walk hand in hand, side by side in our faith.

To Bryan, Stephen, Christer, Katie and Rachael and all the grandkids with whom I look forward to hiking.

Acknowledgments

Gᴏᴅ's Hᴏʟʏ Sᴘɪʀɪᴛ, who has led and guided me through this entire process. He is my best friend.

The numerous "old-school" Bible teachers I was blessed to hear in the formative years of my faith.

My very talented editor, who took a manuscript and made a book out of it. In the process, smoothing out bumps to provide you the reader with a great read.

ABOUT THE AUTHOR

CHRISTER WAS BORN and reared by Swedish immigrants who settled in the Swedish district in the inner city of Chicago. His parents were both born-again believers in Jesus Christ.

After being reared in a Christian home, Christer received Bachelor's Degrees in Social Sciences for Secondary Education and Mechanical Engineering. His engineering career began as a test engineer in the space program, which led into a long career as an aircraft structural design engineer.

Christer is married and has five grown children and grandchildren. He lives in the country and loves the outdoors, hiking, gardening and cooking. However, his primary passion is his relationship with his Lord and Savior, with whom he has walked for over 45 years.

The main intent of this book is to walk believers through the core elements of our faith, through weaving a story with a dialogue explaining the elements of our faith as recorded in Scripture. His main desire is to see people come into relationship with the Lord, and he prays that this book will help many do so!

TABLE OF CONTENTS

EXPERIENCING A "GOD THING"

THE CROWD STOOD still. Pressed to the edge of the curb, Sam stood beside his sister Kate. His daughters, Chloe and Sophie, stood to his other side. Chloe, his youngest, was pressed against her dad's side. Sophie, the farthest away from him, was the first to see the light change and started to step off the curb. Chloe also began to step off the curb. In mid-step, a big arm came down in front of Sophie, like a border-crossing gate, the arm stopped her advance as she bumped into the obstacle. "SHWOOSH!" Every person on the curb felt the draft of the car speeding by. The car may or may not have increased speed to catch the last fleeting microseconds of a yellow light. No matter, the driver's gamble failed to pay off. Everyone in the crowd heard the "click" of the red-light traffic enforcement camera.

Sam had seen everything, and Sophie was out of his reach. Sam was not as much frozen in horror as unable to react fast enough. The wall of people on the curb also saw what had happened—what had almost happened. A collective inhale/exhale exploded from their midst: no tragedy today. The arm was gone, the street was clear and the wall of people surged off the crosswalk.

In that moment of frozen shock, Sam saw the stranger who had saved his daughter's life. Their eyes connected. The stranger responded with a quick warm smile and slight nod. Their connection was brief, only seconds. The next second found the crowd held back to wait for the changing of the traffic light.

Safely across the street with all his girls, Sam stopped to look around.

The stranger who acted by instinct was nowhere to be seen. The whole surreal incident still had Sam's heart tied in a knot that seemed halfway up his throat.

Intent on changing the mood, Kate took each girl by the hand. "Sam, my place is at the far end of this block. We're going to skip the rest of the way. You'll have to skip, run or walk really fast to keep up with us!" Laughing, Sophie and Cloe were completely caught up in the moment.

Sam watched them take off skipping down the city sidewalk with their aunt Kate. "We'll see you at the doorway," Kate called over her shoulder.

Quick thinking, Sis. There's nothing like skipping to put a smile on a kid's face. Sam called, "Girls, hang onto your Aunt Kate."

But seeing an open stretch of sidewalk, the girls dropped Kate's hands and skipped ahead. The entrance to Kate's apartment building was at the far end of the block. Sam knew Kate would keep them linked together like a chain until they arrived. With nothing more than open sidewalk from here to there, he watched them skip ahead. At the end of the block, he saw them stop, turn to look, wave and then duck into Kate's building with their aunt not far behind.

～

The door opened on the first ring. "Jack!" Stan greeted. "I'm glad you could make it."

Smiling warmly, Jack replied, "The directions were too good; you left me with no excuses." Stan was known as the best freehand sketcher in the office—a skill Jack himself wanted to improve. "I made a copy of your artwork to carry with me, so I could keep and frame the original."

"Whatever you do, just don't post it online." Stan looked seriously at Jack and then melted into a hearty laugh. "My apartment is already over maximum capacity, and I don't want the building manager to blame me for an overflow crowd on the roof."

After a year of working together, Jack was familiar with Stan's sense of humor. "Hey, man, I'm extra-glad you fit me in. I promise no online postings."

"If you're only in D.C. for one Independence Day, you have to see the fireworks over the monuments. It's not a law, but it should be. Food is on the breakfast bar, and drinks are in the cooler on the deck. My wife made some infused fruity iced green tea. You'll find it in the glass five-gallon tap jar."

"The one I see that's full of floating fruit?"

"It's her summertime specialty—iced green tea with slices of juicy fruits. The fruit gives it a rich mellow flavor." Stan picked up a red cup and handed it to Jack.

Jack accepted the cup and filled it with the summertime specialty.

Leaning over the railing, Jack looked down. "I can't believe the lemmings down there. You'd think a big game just let out."

Stan looked over the railing. "...or about to start. Those are the last-minute folks flowing toward the National Mall for the big show. The fireworks are launched from the Lincoln Memorial Reflecting Pool. From the rooftop, the fireworks display will appear above and just to the right of the Washington Memorial."

"You said this was a rooftop party?"

"Yes, it is, and since this is the tallest building between here and the Washington Memorial, it's a prime spot for the show. You may recognize some local celebrities up there."

"When do the fireworks start?"

Stan glanced at his watch. "In about twenty-five minutes, so it's about time to head to the party upstairs." Stan looked around the room to see that some of his party veterans had already left to claim choice viewing along the south side of the roof. "It's your choice: stairs or elevator."

"How many flights?"

"We're five floors from the top, so it's around ten or twelve flights."

"I'll take the elevator."

"That's your call. But you may have to wait for a while for an elevator. I'll save you a spot at the railing."

"Tell your wife this tea is delicious," Jack said as he stepped back into the apartment to refill his cup. Stopping at the bar, he wrapped some chips and celery sticks in a napkin, left the apartment and headed for the elevators.

Jack kicked himself for not having thought far enough ahead when accepting Stan's invite. *Fireworks are fun; physical limitations are not.* Still recovering from last year's cardiac episode, Jack did not feel like he had it in him to walk up so many stairs. The ER trip last year was the follow-up to the big one three years earlier. The first event had felt like a severe muscle cramp deep in his chest—a real showstopper. The ambulance ride was intense. The EMT had been honest about his slim chances of survival. To look death and eternity directly in the eye was sobering.

As the ambulance arrived at the ER, a cardiac team was already waiting. The time from the ambulance transference to the operating room was barely two minutes. In another minute or so, Jack felt immense physical relief as the cardiac catheter balloon expanded and cleared the blockage. The relief was so overwhelming that the stent installation went unnoticed. Lying flat on his back, Jack felt like the weight of the world had lifted.

He later learned that his right coronary artery had been completely blocked. Last year, he had recognized the same level of deep lingering internal strain that had preceded "the big one." This time, with the blockage only at ninety percent, his heart did not undergo the severe bruising of his first cardiac event with a one-hundred percent blockage. Thankfully, this second event had been caught in time before any more damage occurred. Since then, recovery was constantly on his mind.

Four years of feeling damaged had driven Jack to keep to himself. For the first two years, he did not even share with his wife how he often wondered whether or not he would make it home from work on any given day. Thank God, those days had passed. Today, the walk from Union Station to Stan's apartment building was an epic triumph. But that long walk had been enough. *I'm feeling too spent to do anything more. I've made my appearance. It would be nice to fade out, go home and lie on the sofa,* Jack thought as he walked over to the elevator and pushed the "up" button. Sipping his tea as he waited by the elevator, he watched the entire party file out of Stan's flat. Nodding to him as they walked past him, they headed for the door below the exit sign to the stairwell. *Ten flights…I might as well try to climb Mount Everest. Please, Lord, send an elevator with space for me.*

Ding, the elevator door opened, and he had just enough room to squeeze in. Standing between two seniors, he looked down at them. The look he received was easy to read. *What's your problem, big guy? You look fit. Are you too lazy to take the stairs like everyone else your age?* Looking around, he realized he was by far the youngest person on the elevator. He felt like half the eyes in the elevator were on him and were saying the same thing. Thankfully, the next time the door opened he saw a rooftop full of fireworks viewers.

The rooftop deck, which had been designed for these gatherings, was the full footprint of the building. Tonight, the decking was filled beyond capacity. Grateful for the elevator ride, Jack stepped out onto the roof. He saw Stan and his party to the left. Apparently, someone had scouted earlier and had secured a spot for optimal viewing. The people he had seen at the party were congregated at the southern edge of the roof's west end.

Jack began walking toward Stan's group. To his right, he saw someone heading toward him. *Isn't that the guy from the curb—the one who looked at me after the car drove by?'*

Sam walked up to Jack. "Hey, excuse me, but did I see you on the street earlier?"

"Yes. Are you the guy with the girl on the curb?"

"Actually, girls—plural."

"Sorry if I was too forward. Instinct just seemed to kick in."

"No, no, that's okay. You literally reached out and prevented a tragedy. All I can say is thank you, thank you, and thank you again. It happened so fast. I should have had the girls on each side of me. I know they can be impetuous."

"I had three of my own. At that age especially, one of them was always on the edge of being out of reach. You know how Dad instinct is, once primed, it never really goes away. I was not going to let a tragedy happen in front of me if there was anything I could do about it. Honestly, I didn't even think, I just did what I would have done with one of my own."

"And a very good thing you did."

"Everyone is safe; that's all that matters. Are you a tourist in D.C.? Jack asked.

"My sister lives here, but we're visiting from out of town."

"Let me guess: Pacific Northwest."

"Why do you say that?" Sam asked.

"The girls have a cutting-edge trendy look to their clothes, and neither looked both ways before stepping off the curb. Even at that age, Easterners have it ingrained in them to look both ways whenever stepping onto a street. Their clothes say *urban*. I lived in Seattle once, and I remember the fashion as cutting edge."

"Nice to meet you, Sherlock Holmes," Sam said as he extended his hand. "Thank you again. And yes, we are from the Pacific Northwest."

Firm handshake…that's always a good sign. Jack thought as he took Sam's hand, matching the grip. "The name is Jack."

"I'm Sam. My sister has a flat in this building. She said we had to come see the fireworks from the roof." Sam turned and waved. Kate had been watching them from their spot on the southern wall.

Seeing Sam wave, Jack turned her way. Kate smiled and waved back. The girls were too busy looking over the edge at all the action on the street below.

"One of my co-workers has a condo in here too. He invited me to his annual rooftop fireworks-viewing party. I have to say I am impressed." Turning southwest, he noted, "This must be one of the tallest apartment buildings in the area. It should give an unobstructed view of the show stamped with the upper part of the Washington Monument. The fireworks should be D.C. picture–perfect."

"That's my plan. I brought my SLR camera and tripod. I like to play with shutter speeds. The tripod keeps the background details crisp while the fireworks make the photo. It'll be good to have some pictures to remind the girls of the trip." Sam added, "I believe it's a father's mission to pack their kids' heads with positive memories."

Jack looked at the girls. "They look to be at that age when the long-term memories start to stick."

Sam smiled. "That's why we're here."

"Hopefully, your redhead will remember to look both ways before stepping off a curb!"

"I don't think she'll forget today's almost tragedy. I know I won't."

Jack added. "Life is like that; sometimes there is an unseen hand."

"Unseen hand? Your reaching out to block my Sophie?"

"More of a 'God thing.' I was just His instrument. God had me there and then. He just used my arm."

With a big grim, Sam added, "And I'm sure glad you were and did!"

"There are no coincidences," Jack said, paused and then added, "Have you ever felt that there was more to things than you thought at first?" He could see Sam bite on that thought. Before either could say another word, *BOOM* interrupted their conversation. The air shook. All the voices on the roof went silent. All heads turned south toward the Washington Monument. Everyone silently followed the first streak of light arcing over the Washington Monument.

"Yes, I have. Well, that's my cue. The girls love fireworks, and my sister Kate has really been building up this event. Nothing is quite like sharing stuff like this with your kids."

"All the things done with kids are the best things in life." Jack raised his palm in greeting. "Enjoy."

"Got that right! I'll look for you after the show." Sam smiled as he turned and headed back to the girls.

HIKE 1
The Hike to
SALVATION

PROLOGUE

Jack's intent for subletting a second-floor apartment was to force himself to exercise. Four months had passed since he had moved in. At first, climbing the stairs had been brutal. The first couple of weeks demanded a mid-flight rest before climbing the full flight. He remembered the early weekend days of not even leaving the apartment for dread of climbing those stairs. In time, the daily routine of climbing those stairs built stamina. By the holidays, the steps were actually starting to feel like a stretching exercise. Somewhere after the holidays, Jack caught himself taking two steps at a time. For the first time since before the heart attack taking two steps at a time had been the norm. Jack was beginning to feel normal again.

Confidence gained on the stairs led Jack to take walks for exercise. The walks were now getting longer and more varied. He found it easier to scope out inner-city walks and trails. Weekend walks along the Snohomish River in Everett and out onto Spenser Island were leisurely, flat and solitary. The Seattle and Edmonds waterfronts confirmed that walks for a reasonable distance would not be an issue. Those walks also created an excuse to self-reward by eating in one of the great restaurants to be found within easy walking distance of the waterfront. So far, Jack found all the walks easily done with his trademark Chuckies.

The mile-long Picnic Point Trail was the nearest woodland trail to the apartment and came with a four-hundred feet descent down to Puget Sound. A holistic splash of reality, the trail began paved and turned into fine-cut gravel as it descended suddenly along the northern side of the gulch that would open to the Picnic Point beach. After about two hundred yards, the beauty of the tall fir trees, ferns and moss was overtaken by the realization that what goes down must come up!

Walking back up to the parking lot seemed like an endless staircase without landings. Absolutely out of breath, Jack collapsed on a bench right below the parking lot. While regaining his breath, Jack reflected on the failed hike. *This trail will have to be conquered—if only to experience that secluded beach. I'm going to need more training, so for now, it will just have to go onto the list of easy-to-access local hikes. One day this trail will be good for mountain-climbing prep. Someday, I'll be back and do this hike to catch the sunset after a long day at work.* Breathing deep, Jack closed his eyes. *Walking in the woods is like a drug.* The moist freshness of the air filled his lungs. The fresh memory of walking among the tall trees and ferns that bordered the trail rested on the insides of his eyelids. *This is what I miss about this place.* Jack opened his eyes and looked down the trail curling into the woods. *Enough of city walks. I can do that anywhere. Sauntering through a Pacific Northwest rainforest is something that can only be done in the Pacific Northwest.*

Returning to the apartment, the stairs felt like nothing. *I may not be ready for Picnic Point, but I can do some climbing. There must be something easier around here. It's time to break out the boots.*

Japanese Gulch was a four-mile trail with half of Picnic Point's elevation gain. The trail climbed up from the waterfront to a plateau where nature met industry. The gulch's name came from the earliest Japanese settlers in the area. Seeing how a community had once dotted the hillside was easily visualized. Now the gulch was a park, and other than park signage with Plexiglas-encased photos, no physical traces of the area's history were to be seen anywhere. Nature had reclaimed the gulch, and the trail was as rugged as anywhere in Puget Sound. The ascent was irregular and reasonable for training. Whenever Jack felt winded, the trail leveled out. Climbing over roots and rocks demanded more ankle support than his Chuckies would have provided. *But his boots? What had happened? Did the boots shrink or his feet grow?* At the summit of the hike, Jack felt triumphant as he sat on a big rock and removed his boots to massage his feet. *At least this time I'm parked at the bottom,* he humorously thought to himself. Putting his boots back on, he knew his feet had not swollen. And they were not as sore as they had been. The foot massage had been a good idea. *Next Saturday will be boot-shopping day.*

Parking under the building was easy. The endless flights of stairs became annoying as he walked up one landing and flight to another landing and more. The stairs continued. *The parking and store access must be a filter, limiting only the fittest to shop here,* he decided. Emerging from the parking decks, Jack entered a broader flight of stairs, only to turn and find another. He walked over to the far end of the oversized landing. *What have I gotten myself into?*

With a firm grip, Jack grabbed the railing. *I shouldn't have had such a big breakfast.* Looking over the railing, far below the treetops he saw what looked like a garden. Between the trees something moved fast, following what looked like a path below the canopy. He spotted a mountain biker. *A mountain-bike test course! How cool! I wish I could have done that when I bought my last bike.* Watching the biker rip around the course provided a valid excuse for lingering at the railing. Breathing evenly and not feeling any strain, he let go of the rail and turned. *Heigh Ho! Heigh Ho! Up more stairs I go!*

Feeling slightly winded, he finished the last flights and entered the store. Facing another flight of stairs, he looked left, then right, then up. *I can't believe it!* Jack sighed. *Of course, the designers would put the boot department at the highest point.* A year ago, all of these steps would have been a deal breaker. Elevators were a legal requirement in any business establishment with more than a second story. Here they were artfully hidden by an architect's design. What did it matter? In a store like this, unless you were pushing a stroller, using an elevator questioned whether or not you were fit enough to be on the premises. The multitude of steps had been a strain, but they felt more like exercise. *It is a good day for new boots,* Jack thought as he finished the climb, glad to have re-membered to pace his breathing. *At least, it's all downhill from here.*

Hiking with the old boots the previous weekend had been a mas-sive disappointment. Smart enough to listen to his feet, the decision had been made. Throughout the week, Jack had shopped hiking boots on the Internet and had anticipated coming to this outfitter who was once located in the loft of the original grungy warehouse where he had bought his first pair of mountaineering boots. This outfitter had grown past its early grunge days and had expanded upscale to grow with the recreation equipment market. They still had the best selection in town…or in any town for that matter. This flagship location took pride in providing the broadest selection of anything the chain carried.

Jack walked the wall of boots at the back of the shoe department. *Looks like I came to the right place. Where to start?*

Holding a mid-range priced boot upside down, Jack studied the sole pattern. In the corner of his eye, he saw someone stepping directly toward him. Following his eyes, Jack began to turn.

"Jack the hero hikes?" Sam greeted him in a neighborly way, stop-ping a couple of arms lengths short of Jack. *I'm fairly sure his name is Jack. It's been a while, but sounds right. If I'm wrong, he'll correct me…*

As Jack turned, a smile lit his face. *Ah, the guy from the fireworks last summer.* "Hi, how are you doing? Great memory…I'm impressed." Jack turned to extend his right hand.

"Sam," Sam volunteered as he stepped forward and reached out to meet Jack's grip. "Nice to see you again."

"Good to see you too."

"I was down below with my girls. We were bike shopping. I thought I saw you pass by. When I saw you head up the stairs, I had to run up and say hi. By the way, 'Thanks again,' for what you did last summer."

"No problem—all in a day's work," Jack replied with a smile, paused and asked, "If I remember right, you're local to here?"

"Seattle, native." The words proudly rolled off of Sam's tongue. He cocked his head to the side. "Aren't you from the other Washington? Vacationing?" Sam looked at the boot in Jack's hand.

"Home is in the Carolinas. When we met last year, I was working on a project in Baltimore. This year, I'm working a project here in the Pacific Northwest. It should last through the summer. I like to consider what I do as a working vacation. Work my tail off when I'm on the clock, and I don't squander a minute when I'm off the clock. Wherever I find myself, I like to explore whatever a place has to offer."

"Cool beans! I get it. Working to vacation on location."

"Sure beats moaning about not being home. Attitudes steer and determine the quality of our journeys. I miss being home, so I temper it with doing cool stuff wherever I am. Then I get home when I can."

Sam looked at the boot Jack was holding. "Are you considering some hiking?"

"I remember Puget Sound having some great trails. I lived here twenty years ago, and I was thinking of hiking some old familiar trails and some new ones."

"Time for new boots?" Sam asked.

"I just retired my old boots. I don't see anything remotely like them."

"You won't; trail footwear has evolved, but you have come to the right place for the best of what's available." Sam scanned the shoe department.

Jack looked around too. "I don't see any salespeople."

Sam looked at Jack. "As it happens, I do a lot of hiking and upgraded my boots last year. Anything a fellow hiker can share?"

"It's been a long time since I've shopped for or even thought much about new boots. Any words of wisdom for me?"

"Listen to your feet." With a quizzical look, Sam looked down at Jack's Chuckies.

"Insoles. The secret to wearing these is to add high quality insoles. With the right soles, you can go all day. The funny thing is that the uppers feel like slippers." Jack laughed.

"Yeah, a nurse friend said the same thing. She prefers Chuckies and spends her working days on her feet."

"Chuckies are great for pavement in town. Last weekend I did some trail hiking in my old boots, and my feet protested, saying it was time to retire the old boots. I listened. I value happy feet."

Sam chuckled. "Sounds to me like you are in tune with your feet! You should have no problem getting something they'll approve of and be happy with."

"My first pair of real hiking boots were mountaineering boots like those." Jack pointed toward the bigger boots on the far end of the display wall. "At a full gait, they walked themselves. Otherwise, they were way too heavy and clunky. With all the new designs and tech, I should be able to find something lighter that walks as well. I'll completely pass on the hiking shoes. I know I need ankle support. I'm shopping for trail wear—not office wear."

"I hear you; there's a big difference. A lot of people just want to look the part—even if the only hiking they do is between the copier and coffee pot." Sam looked at Jack in a mock serious tone. "Of course, they may also be good for city walking…if you don't have Chuckies."

It's nice to see this guy has a quick wit. Jack smiled. "I'm fine with my Chuckies."

Sam chose a boot from a display shelf right below eye level. "You may know this, but if not, you'll find it a useful tidbit." He held the toe with one hand and the ankle of the boot with the other. "The sole is key to ankle support." Sam twisted the boot, and it rolled between his hands like the ribbon in a bow. "You don't want that to happen on the trail. One bad misstep and the fun part of your hike is over."

Sam handed the boot to Jack, who held it the same way and gave it a similar twist. "No kidding. It's painful just thinking of my foot going one way while the ankle goes another."

Sam replied, "A bad step on a loose rock, a root or slick moss and apply 200 pounds of pressure. Things could literally go sideways."

"That would be a show stopper." Jack fully flexed the boot one more time. "You could say these boots are form over function."

He listens and learns. Sam could tell Jack's light bulb was switching on.

"So, the sole is the backbone of the boot. I hadn't thought of that before." Jack had that look of someone who had just learned something new. "Then a stiffer sole would keep the boot from twisting and thus keeping your ankle from twisting?"

"Quick study, eh?" Sam smiled as he thought, *This guy seems sharp. He may be fun to hike with and talk with out on a trail.*

"I guess you could say that the soles are not for traction alone."

"Stability and traction. One bad twist or slide could trash a whole season." Sam took back the boot and returned it to its display. He then picked up another boot displayed next to the one he had just returned to the shelf. Holding it in the same grip, he twisted it using the same torque as with the previous boot. "This one is better," Sam said as he handed it to Jack.

Jack took the boot, gripped and twisted. "This one barely twists. I see your point. This boot would provide much more support, and it's as light as that flexible one."

"The firmer the sole, the better the support and more secure the footing."

Jack twisted again. Then he held the boot and looked at it. "But this one is just too ugly."

"Yeah, that it is." Sam chuckled.

"Thanks for the sole torque lesson." *I should have thought of that. Thanks, God, for providing this guy with the knowledge to explain something so fundamental.*

"Thank the salesman who helped me pick out my last pair of boots. The guy was a natural teacher. I kid you not; if you get the same guy, he'll change the way you lace-up."

"Well, that would be interesting," Jack quipped. "I have been successfully lacing and tying my boots for quite a while."

"Joke now; be surprised later."

"Okay, I'll be open-minded," Jack said as he returned the ugly boot to its display. *Between functionality and looks, I should be able to narrow down the selection fairly easily.*

"Don't forget to use the big rock." Sam pointed at a simulated mountaintop in the middle of the shoe department. "Every boot feels different walking downhill. Stand on the steepest part and compare the traction. You will be surprised." Sam smiled.

"Thanks for the primer."

"So where were you planning to hike? The Lake Washington Arboretum or the Pacific Crest Trail?"

"I was thinking of progressing through the season to progress from the one up to the other."

"Hiking is a favorite pastime of mine. Over the winter, I've let myself get out of shape. I know of no better conditioning than by doing it." Sam casually looked over the boots in the various displays. "Were you planning on trying out your new boots anytime soon?"

Jack was caught off guard. "Actually I was, but I hadn't decided which to do first—the Lake Washington Arboretum or Discovery Park. I was planning to check the GPS to find which one was easier to access from here. I was a regular at both way back. They will each probably be my next hikes."

"I have actually been thinking about doing the arboretum this weekend or next. I am free this afternoon."

"We should catch some early spring colors," Jack commented

"That was my thinking. Let's do the arboretum. I've got my boots in the VW. How 'bout two o'clock?"

Jack was pleased. *A new friend in the making?* "Where should we meet?"

"Parking is best in the North Lot. I'll be somewhere in there. Enough people come and go that finding a parking spot may demand patience but should not present a problem. Look for my VW; it's a classic. You won't miss it."

Jack pulled out his phone and checked the displayed time. "Sounds like plenty of time. We're on."

"See you at two." Sam turned and returned to his girls in the bicycle department. He had plenty of time to get them to their grandparents' house for the handoff with their mother. Then he could easily get to the arboretum by two.

Jack prayed, *Thanks, Holy Spirit. Interesting that You have us meet again like this. I can feel Your unseen hand working here. I know You are watching out for me, and it appears You are watching out for both of us. Please help me be in sync with Your leading. I dedicate this day to You. Thanks also for caring enough to see to it that I could make an educated choice for my new boots.*

He picked up one of the better-looking mid-range boots and gave it a twist. *Nice resistance.* Then he felt inside and smiled as he pulled out a removable insole. *Even better... improvable.*

What Is a "God Thing"?

THROUGH A HANDFUL of turns, the GPS had taken Jack to I-5 and immediately tracked him to the right and onto the 520. The change of roads and sudden descent into the picturesque Montlake Cut happened fast. Jack caught his exit right before committing to crossing the floating toll bridge. *First things first. Then straight for the arboretum.* At the end of the ramp, Jack turned left. Crossing the 520, he headed north toward University Village. Jack found a pharmacy with easy parking.

There will not be any hiking without upgrading these insoles. Jack had compared shoes and insoles enough in the past. It was easy; he simply grabbed the best pair designed for performance. On the way to the counter, he added some cold waters and a bag of nuts.

The northern approach to the Arboretum was the friendliest. Cross a couple of bridges, hang a left, cruise through a couple of residential blocks, and Jack entered the arboretum and began looking for a spot to park. Where the parking area bent like a boomerang sat a sixties vintage VW microbus. *Sam wasn't kidding! I couldn't miss that anywhere,* Jack thought as he pulled into an open parking spot across the access aisle from Sam's microbus. Sam seemed to be occupied with something at the door on the far side of the microbus. Jack nosed in to the parking spot.

Jack climbed out of the cab of his truck and did some preliminary stretches as he stepped around the bed to the tailgate and dropped the gate. When Sam heard the sound, he turned to see Jack setting his gear on the tailgate. Sam smiled and waved. Jack returned the wave with one of his own.

So Jack drives the kind of vehicle that can get into back country trails. I see some mud around the wheels. That's a good sign, Sam observed.

With an agile pivot, Jack sat on the tailgate, his legs dangling like a little kid. On his left were the new boots; on the right were the new insoles. Jack was unlacing his Chuckies when Sam sauntered over. "Glad to see you made it."

"How could I pass up what promises to be a walk in the park with good company? Besides, I have to try out these new boots."

"It's a beautiful day for a hike."

"Yes, it surely is a beautiful day to be out," Jack replied.

"The arboretum has about six miles of trails." Sam commented.

"I remember the arboretum being full of crisscrossing and parallel trails. I figure we could be walking fresh ground while we would not be much farther than a mile or two from our vehicles."

"Unless we go as far as Madison—where we'd have passed through the park. Sounds like you've given the trail some thought…"

I like to know what I get myself getting into, Jack thought. Vehicle proximity had been an unspoken safety blanket for years. "I remember the arboretum from twenty-something years ago. Now I'll see how good my memory is."

Sam picked up one of Jack's new boots and gave it a sole torque. "Good resistance." *He listened.* "Within the first mile, your feet will let you know how they really feel about the boots."

"My old pair didn't wait that long." Jack laughed.

Sam looked at the footgear on the tailgate. "What's with the insoles? You just bought new boots."

Jack popped the removable insoles out of each of the boots and handed them to Sam "Take these." Jack pulled out his pocketknife to open the package containing the new insoles. Removing them from the packaging, he handed the new set to Sam. "Compare those with these." Sam examined the insole the boot came with and compared it with the upgrade. "I see a significant difference in the heel and arch. I like the gel spots too. I'd never really given much thought to upgrading the inside of my boots. I simply wear thick socks."

"Thick socks will help. These do more," Jack asserted as he fitted the left upgrade to his new boot. "To me, it's about where my feet land. The rest is padding."

"I prefer products that allow for improvement. My old pair of boots didn't. These boots came with exchangeable insoles. I knew I could do better than the one that came in the box."

That gel pocket is in just the right spot. Sam thought of a tender spot under the ball of his foot as he handed the insoles back to Jack *This guy thinks stuff through. Today may prove to be interesting.*

Jack took a breath. "Over the past few years, I've become foot conscious. About ten years ago, certain types of thick-soled shoes became cripplingly painful to wear. The ball of my foot would feel like I was walking on rough gravel with broken bones. At the same time, my toes went numb. I tried different fixes. What worked for me was to discard all my fancy engineered shoes and dial back my footwear to the types of thin-soled shoes I wore when I was younger. The pain in the ball of my foot and the numbness in my toes went away. Then I added topnotch insoles. My feet are much happier, and those foot problems have not returned."

"Now these boots will get the same treatment?"

"It's a formula that's working. I like my Chuckies more now than I did as a kid. If this goes well, I'll be saying the same for these boots too." Jack slipped in the right upgrade and fitted it to his new boot. "When I was a kid, my grandfather encouraged me to always keep thinking. 'Don't be afraid to think things through before and when you do them' was one of his favorite phrases. He also said I should take care of my feet because that is how we get around. I heard it enough times to have absorbed the concept. Now I take care of my feet since they are how we get around." Jack smiled.

Sam nodded. "Weren't the easiest lessons to learn the ones that came with a solid reason why?"

"Simple words, yet common sense when I think about it. My grandfather's words of advice have kept me walking happily through the years." Jack grinned.

Jack jumped off the gate, raised his leg, and firmly tapped the boot's heel on the tailgate, nesting his heel securely in the boot. In seconds, he finished with a double knot and repeated the process with the other boot. He folded up the gate and threw his Chuckies into the cab. He checked the interior, making sure he was leaving nothing that a smash and grabber would find enticing. Satisfied that things looked boring inside he grabbed his pack. Together the two men headed to Sam's VW. Midway across the access aisle, Jack turned to see his lights blink when he clicked the locks.

Sam commented, "I've been thinking of having my cousin add one of those to my VW."

"Your cousin?"

"Yeah, he has a VW shop and loves working on the classics. His wife moans that her greatest competition is any classic VW coming through their door in need of attention."

Jack choked on the mint he had stealthily slipped into his mouth. "I hope she can handle it. Classic cars turn a guy's head faster than any bikini," Jack said after he had swallowed.

"Ain't that the truth! Lucky for him, his wife has a great sense of humor and knows he'll return to her every night—even though he may be dreaming of a Karmann Ghia."

"Rag Top…"

"Four-speed…"

"Smooth corners…"

"Nice to know you appreciate a classic ride!"

The map posted at the trailhead showed more trails than Jack remembered. He took out his cell phone and snapped a photo of the map.

Sam went into tour-guide mode. "The first incarnation of the arboretum was a log skid and timber mill. Later, Azalea Way became a quarter-mile racetrack for horses. Now it's the arboretum's main promenade."

"In Seattle's early days, nearly every ravine that met water was a log skid, and you would have found at least one timber mill near the bottom. Even the term 'skid row' came from Seattle. I did not know that about the race track."

"Then let's start up Azalea Way." Sam pointed to the trailhead to the right. "From early spring through late fall, this place is never at a lack for color."

They headed up the trail. The path began single file. Ahead, a clearing could be seen.

"Back in D.C. last summer, I looked for you after the fireworks. I wanted to introduce my sister to the guy who saved her niece's life."

"Sorry to have missed her. Saying hi would have been nice. I fell into the crowd exiting the roof and flowing down the stairs. Before I knew it, I was outside, trekking back to Union Station."

"That's totally understandable. I looked, but we chose to stay up on the roof until the crowds died down. I figure everybody else had farther to go to get home. We only had to go down a few flights of stairs to get to Kate's place."

"It was going to be a late evening, and I had to be at work the next day."

"We were on vacation, so we took out time," Sam replied casually.

The path opened to the promenade that was known as Azalea Way. For the first bit, they walked quietly, looking at the flora. Jack was consciously gauging the feel of his boots, and Sam was composing his thoughts.

Sam cleared his throat to speak. "You said something last summer that stuck in my mind. I've thought about it more than a few times. This morning while preparing breakfast, it came to mind. Later on, after I had left you at the outfitter store, it came back again."

As Jack listened to what Sam said, he wondered, *what could I have said? Holy Spirit, what did You cause me to say that would remain with Sam?* "Hmmm…we didn't say that much. What stuck?"

"You referred to an 'unseen hand' and 'God thing' in reference to the incident on the curb. I don't know why, but that phrase 'God thing' just stuck with me."

"When one person wants to communicate something to another person, it starts with the one person getting the other person's attention." Jack let his words hang and then continued, "It's the same with God. Do you think God may have been trying to get your attention?"

"Hmm…" Sam paused and then continued, "In the last few months, a number of things have happened that have caused me to pause and take notice. Afterward, I found myself reflecting on what happened. When I reflect, my mind connects it to being a God thing."

Sam looked at Jack and could see he was following what he had been saying. Satisfied, Sam continued. "A couple of weeks ago, I had an appointment downtown. The appointment had been scheduled for months earlier. I had made it for the last available time slot. The appointment required a short in-person meeting to prove who I was. I knew their door closed early, shortly after my appointed time. I had given myself plenty of travel time, but unexpected traffic delayed me.

As I pulled up to the building, I saw an open metered parking spot in front of the main entry. Finding a choice spot like that is like winning the lottery, especially when enough time was left on the meter to cover the appointment. Even the elevator I stepped on was a non-stop to that floor. I arrived for my appointment one minute early. If I had used the parking lot under the building or any other parking or had a bad elevator experience, I would have been late and forced to reschedule.

When returning home, I reflected on my good fortune and found myself thinking, *It was a God thing—no way could any of that have been better coordinated.* Sam drew a deep breath and continued. "Another time, I kept having things delaying me from leaving my home in the morning. I spilled my coffee and dropped my breakfast. The delays were almost comical. When I finally got on the road, I saw a terrible accident had taken place at the first major intersection, which appeared to have happened about the time I would normally have passed through there. I still remember looking at the wrecked cars and the ambulances. Were those delays a God thing? Did the delays have an unseen purpose? After the almost accident, I really started noticing more of these kinds of incidents happening."

Jack responded, "It sounds like God is trying to get your attention. Sometimes God will be 'in your face' direct, and sometimes He's subtle. There really is something to that phrase that 'God moves in mysterious ways.'"

"Mysterious?" Sam stated, paused, then asked, "Do you mean *hidden, secret,* or *not obvious to our understanding?*"[1]

"Understandable, but not always obvious," Jack replied.

Sam thought, *Jack seems like a practical guy. He may provide a perspective I had not considered. I'll go with this.* Sam replied, "If there is something I don't understand but could understand, I'd be open to your opinion."

Jack prayed, *Holy Spirit, give me wisdom and the right answers to what Sam is looking for.*

Sam continued. "The events are not logical, and I cannot see them being repeatable. Each incident that seems to happen is so random and unique that I notice. The one thread that ties them all together is that they could be considered God things." Sam took a breath. "We serendipitously met last summer. At that time you said something. We randomly meet up today. Now we're hiking and talking about God things. I do not believe in coincidences, so I would not pull that card."

"I don't believe in coincidences either. To me, it sounds like you may very well have been experiencing God things." Jack smiled. "Maybe the thought had to be reintroduced in different ways to gel and catch your attention?"

"Hmmm…" Sam let his spoken thought linger. "That's what I'm talking about."

"Sam, how did you feel about God before?" Jack asked.

WHAT IS A CULTURAL CHRISTIAN?

"**B**EFORE WHAT?" SAM questioned.

"Before today, before last summer? Before the God things got your attention." Jack could tell that Sam was digging, but that was okay. Sam was looking for answers.

"Honestly, I didn't give God much thought. When I was a kid, my family went to church. I hung with the church kids until I met my first girlfriend, who later became my wife, and now my ex-wife. My girls attend a Christian elementary school on the north end. I guess it's *God, baseball and apple pie.*" Sam chuckled.

"It's actually *baseball, hot dogs, apple pie and Chevrolet,*" Jack responded with a grin. "That ad was part of the soundtrack for my best teen summer." Jack smiled as his memory flooded with flashes of memories, including the first summer of driving, the first Chevy, the first girlfriend, faces.

"Yeah, it all goes together; it's what we all grew up with." Sam's words brought Jack back to the trail.

"Having a Christian culture is one thing; that's the macro. The micro is the person. When being a Christian is part of the culture, like what you drive or eat, that's being a cultural Christian. Many people like to think of themselves as Christians—not because they know God, but because it's part of their cultural identity." Jack smiled and added. "Is that why you put your girls in a Christian school?"

"Yeah, I guess that would be part of it. Mostly, it was the school's academics. Their school ranks as one of the highest on the north end for academics. I felt high academics was best for them, and a little religion doesn't hurt…to teach kids that they should not lie, cheat or steal because if they do, they run the risk of angering God." Sam grinned. "A little fear of God doesn't sound like such a bad idea."

"It's a start."

"Besides, it's one of the few areas my ex-wife and I could agree on. For now, I simply pay and try not to rock the boat."

"Count your blessings and your kids' blessings," Jack added with a smile. "What about you? It sounds like you quit church."

"I guess I transitioned? I married my high school sweetheart. We met about the time I got my driver's license. That was also about the time my parents divorced. I just phased out of the church stuff and into her. She did not care for church, so we left it behind. Church was then. Looking back, I guess going to church had been a good cultural indoctrination. I was hoping for at least that much for my girls. I remember the church stuff, but that was then—like looking back at middle school." Sam continued, "The God stuff. I didn't get the God part. It's all so vague."

Jack looked at Sam. "Mind if I ask if you have met the Creator of the universe? Have you heard of being *saved?*"

"Now, that's what I'm talking about. A year ago, I would have laughed, and our conversation and our walk together would have ended. But now I get this feeling[2]—a feeling as if there is something I should know that I want to know, but don't. I know it sounds illogical but not silly."

"Illogical because of science and culture and all of that?" Jack asked.

"I guess so. Sometimes I feel like I've been force-fed one side of an argument, and the puzzle seems incomplete. I want a better picture. I can think for myself. After all, they did teach critical thinking when I was in school." Sam chuckled.

"Everybody has his own opinions. My gut tells me to get the bottom of what is true, you have to test and question everything. If something is real and true, it will stand examination.[3] Fakes and falsehoods collapse when put to testing," Jack spoke confidently. "Real Christians are free thinkers who go to *the source* for truth."[4]

WHAT IS TRUTH?

SAM REPLIED, "ISN'T truth relative? Isn't everything relative?"
Jack replied, "When my kids were little, they got caught in a lie. I took them aside privately, and we talked. I told him there were two reasons not to lie. The first is that recovering from a mistake or a problem is always easier when you tell the truth instead of lying. It is hard to trust someone who has been proven deceptive, especially someone who lies to cover up his or her own wrongdoing. People prefer to deal with honest people. The other reason is that God is made of truth,[5] and Satan is void of truth.[6] If you want to know God, truth is where you need to be looking and if you want to know truth, God is where you need to be looking."

"God is made of truth?"

"Yep! God is truth,"[4] Jack replied. "Jesus said He is the truth."[4]

"It's been a while since I did church. Isn't church and God like a yin and yang of each other?"

Jack drew a long breath and began to explain. "Church and God are unique of each other. God is the Creator of the Universe.[7] God is man's Creator.[8] Church can be many things; but God is only one thing. If you have church, you may miss God. If you have God, church will happen.[9] It's about pursuing God. Ideally church becomes a gathering of like-minded people who are also pursuing God. That's why church is often referred to as God's house."

"Ideally?" Sam quipped. "What about reality?"

Jack responded, "God prefers to deal with individuals. Individuals gathering together to pursue God corporately would be the ideal church. On the other hand, too many churches have forgotten God and have pursued other causes. Gradually, these churches devolved into social clubs, which is why so many have withered away and closed their doors."

"That would describe the church I grew up in, and walking away wasn't too hard. Years later, it closed its doors and has reopened as a brewery."

"Social clubs come and go, and so do breweries."

Unable to hold back a chuckle, Sam stopped and looked at Jack. "Sounds like a management issue to me."

Jack replied, "Projects fail when management loses its vision."[10]

"I didn't miss church any more than I missed middle school when I moved on to high school."

"God and church may overlap, but they are very different and should not be confused."

"Church stuff does not ring my bell. But I want to know more about God."

Following Azalea Way, they passed through the grove of ornamental fruit trees at peak bloom. Jack asked, "Have you ever seen the D.C. cherry trees in spring?"

"Only in pictures," Sam replied in that light distant way someone does when responding to a question while deeply in thought."

"When I was working in D.C., my favorite escape was to ride my bike. One of my favorite routes was entering the monument district by way of the old C&O Canal towpath. The trail follows the Potomac River, then loops the monuments, the mall and the tidal basin. The second week in April, the tidal basin is covered with pink snow—much like the patch below that cherry tree." Jack pointed to his left at a double blossom cherry tree in peak bloom surrounded by a skirt of pink petals.

"I once split a round of seasoned cherry. The grain parted to reveal a deep rich Merlot-colored vein in the wood. The red was rich, bright, very noticeable, and it crossed more than a few of the grains. It looked like the wood had been bleeding. I felt like I was opening an Easter egg."

"Were there any more like that?"

"None that I found. I remember splitting that round down to kindling. That was the only spot I found in that or any other piece of wood from that tree."

"The stain sounds as engineered as that parking spot. Only God would know[11] when you would need that parking spot or where your axe would part the grains."

"You called it an Easter egg?" Jack asked.

"My oldest had her first Easter egg hunt the following morning. Family came over, and I remember showing the naturally red-stained grains in the wood. The piece was unique and too pretty to throw into the fire."

Jack said, "It sounds like a God thing to get your attention. What does Easter really stand for and your *wooden* Easter egg? Yeah, I see a connection."

"That happened years ago. Except for when I split firewood, I haven't thought about that piece of wood since. I do see the connection. If I were to concede that God is trying to get my attention, how would I know?"

"There is a test.[2] When it comes to spiritual matters, you either get that there is something to it, or you think it's all foolishness."

"Jack, if I thought we were talking foolishness, we wouldn't be talking. Any kind of talk about God used to be an annoying noise to me. All I'd hear was static, and I quickly tuned out of the conversation. Today's signal is surprisingly clear—like dialing an old radio tuner, Sam felt the signal emerging through the static.

"It sounds like God's Holy Spirit is adjusting your frequency band to the spiritual and fine tuning your reception for His signal. It gets that way when the Holy Spirit awakens us."

"Yep, the signal-to-noise ratio appears to be improving."

Jack took Sam's confirmed interest as the sign to go deeper. "God's Word says that the carnal or unspiritual mind is hostile to God,[12] but the Spirit-enlightened mind has an interest in God and the things of God.[13] The time comes when God calls to each of us. That happens when His Spirit draws us.[2] How do you know when God is calling you? Does the gospel of Jesus Christ sound like something you want to know more about?"

"Sure, why not?" Sam felt at peace with the course of their conversation. He thought to himself, *I'm game; let's see where this goes.*

Sam continued. "Many of those God words sound familiar, but their meanings are muddy. I would not feel comfortable saying that I know what most of those words actually mean."

"Would you like to break down some classic terms and concepts?"

"Like the legend on a map?" Sam replied.

"More like deconstructing the basic elements," Jack continued. "It could save us from misconceptions and make sure we're speaking the same language."

What Is the Gospel of Jesus?

SAM REPLIED, "POINT taken. A good place to start. Okay, you mentioned the gospel of Jesus Christ. What does that mean?"

Jack replied, "Gospel means 'good news.' The gospel of Jesus Christ is 'His good news.' The good news of Jesus Christ is God's salvation."

What Is Salvation?

SAM ANSWERED, "OKAY, the gospel of Jesus Christ is *salvation*— a big, ambiguous word that sounds distant and is one of those words that I was referring to. What does salvation actually mean?"

"Salvation literally is life versus death. *Salvation* specifically means 'deliverance from the molestation of enemies.'[14] Salvation also means 'victory, rescue, safety,'[15] 'personal welfare, saving' [16] and 'deliverance.'"[17]

Sam commented. "That didn't sound vague or ambiguous. I can only recall having heard the word *salvation* being used in vague religious context. Your definition makes salvation sound like something you would think everyone would want."

WHO IS SATAN?

"SALVATION IS 'THE deliverance from our Enemy.' Satan is the Enemy.[18] Satan lies[6] above and deceives[19] with the goal of misdirecting people away from God. Satan blinds the minds of unbelievers to the gospel and confuses people as to who God really is.[20] People seek, and Satan blocks[21] or he simply points people in the wrong direction. In the end, Satan's intent is to block people from knowing who God is."

"So, Satan is God's antithesis?" Sam asked.

"Not even close."

WHO IS GOD?

JACK EXTENDED HIS right hand with the palm side up. "God is unique,[22] omnipotent,[23, 24] eternal[25]; He created everything."[26, 27, 28] With each attribute, he raised his open palm higher.

Jack then extended his left hand. "Satan is a created being."[29] He lowered his left hand. "Satan, by his very nature, is a liar."[6] He turned his left-hand palm side down. "Satan is so much lesser than God."

"Satan even duped himself into believing that he could usurp God.[30] But, in the end, Satan will be brought down.[31] The book has already been written.[32] In the end, Satan is broken, defeated, and will be exiled to hell for an eternity of torment, with no reprieve."[33]

Sam took in every word. "That sounds like deliverance on the macro scale."

"The biggest! It's a promise from God. When we accept God's salvation, He will watch over us forever.[34] His salvation comes with promises. God says in His Word, the Bible, that He will never leave us or forsake us.[35, 36] God promises us that if we resist the Devil, the Devil will flee from us.[37] When the Devil attacks, God is faithful and will not permit our testing to go beyond what we are capable.[38] Salvation comes with a kit of spiritual tools and armor.[39] In this life, salvation is deliverance from the molestation of the Enemy. Satan is the Enemy. In heaven, there will be no Satan.[19, 33] Therefore, God's salvation washes away our sins and is the eternal deliverance from the molestation of the Enemy."

"Salvation means that God protects us?" Sam asked.

"On the micro scale—here, today, God protects and preserves us individually. God's salvation also has provision for our personal welfare."[40]

"I could use some salvation."

"When you discover what God's salvation really is, you question why you didn't know about it earlier," Jack replied.

Azalea Way had been lined with blooming trees. As the promenade began to narrow and veer to the right, there were noticeably less blooms. Ahead to the left, an opening came into view. The opening revealed a trailhead with steps that led up the hillside into a grove of deciduous trees. "Let's follow that trail." Sam looked over to Jack for concurrence, then led them toward the opening. Jack followed a few steps behind. A few steps up the trail, they were swallowed by foliage.

Partway up the hillside, Sam stopped and turned to look down at Jack below. "So if God is so almighty and greater than Satan, why does He tolerate Satan?"

Jack looked up at Sam. "Think of it like a test for everyone. God gives us free will.[41] Then we have to make up our own minds and choose between God and Satan."[42]

"Then Satan would be the sleazy politician who will say anything for a vote…" Sam commented. "At some point you are confronted with the red pill and the blue pill?" Sam continued as he followed the trail uphill.

"Good analogy: the red wakes you up to the reality of God and the spiritual world, and the blue lulls you back to sleep."

"I'll take the red pill; I prefer to be awake." Sam offered as he stepped up and onto the primary trail.

"God wants us awake, and Satan wants us sleepwalking," Jack said as he took the step up to join Sam on the wider trail.

Jack stopped to take a deep breath and pulled out his cell phone to check the map and buy a minute or two to gauge his heart. *Not feeling winded and any cardio strain. Not really feeling much of anything. I think I'll be good for the whole trail.* One tap on the black mirror and the map appeared. "I see where we are." Jack pointed to crossing lines on the smart-phone screen.

"We're about halfway through the arboretum." Sam pointed to where one trail bridged two others. "The rest of the arboretum trails are mostly like this." He looked ahead along the wider woodland path they were now standing on.

Jack pocketed his phone. He felt good about today's hike. *Good on all fronts.*

Able to comfortably walk side by side, they continued south on the wider trail. Jack said, "God has a plan."[43]

"What's God's plan?"

"There is a short answer and the story."

"The short answer is that God wants to rescue us from Satan. We have the opportunity to live on this earth. During our lifetime, we get to choose. Do we want a healthy, eternal, loving relationship with God or eternal damnation with Satan? We live with our choice for eternity without any chance of reprieve."

"No travel, relocation packages, shades of gray, suburbs?" Sam asked.

"It's the ultimate binary switch! The story is actually God wanting to restore relationship with man—the relationship with God that man had originally been designed for."[44]

Jack continued. "Satan cheats. He is the deceiver. When he lies, he speaks his native language.[6] above all, Satan's deception is to confuse people about God's salvation, who God is or even if God is. If Satan can accomplish any of those objectives, then he has scored another soul. It's just a game for Satan. He knows he has already lost.[45, 46] He continues to pretend to be the usurper and plays to score as many souls as he can.

Thankfully, God offers a rescue program! The Gospel of Jesus is God's plan of salvation to rescue people and return them to a healthy relationship with God."[47]

"So, what is the story?" Sam asked.

"God created this world[28]; it was a perfect place [48] with people pure in thought and actions. God created people in His likeness.[8] He created them with a free will.[41, 42] Adam and Eve knew God; they walked and talked with God.[49] Then Satan came as a serpent and tempted Eve[50] to challenge God by eating the fruit that God had warned them 'not to eat or even touch, because doing so would bring death.'[51] Eve doubted what God had said and allowed herself to be tempted.[52] Then Adam joined Eve[53, 54] and together they fouled their relationship with God.[49] Through their act of disobedience, sin, death and entropy entered into the world.[55] Ever since, it's been a wrestling match between God and Satan with people as the ultimate prize. God wants people to reconnect with Him. Satan simply wants people not to connect with God. Reaching out to man, God gave numerous laws as a path for people to follow with the intent of restoring their relationship with God.[56, 57] These laws were a foreshadowing of God sending His own Son Jesus to be the ultimate sacrifice and the atonement for our sins.[58, 50] Jesus was the only One who could do it. He is our only way of salvation.[4] The first part of God's plan is returning to relationship with God.[60] The rest is living God's plan of salvation as He had originally designed it to be."[61]

Sam said, "Death, entropy and sin—an interesting combo. *Entropy* is "degeneration from order to disorder with the loss of energy." In scientific terms, it is death. Sin is another one of those words that I find to be ambiguous. Obviously, sin is bad, but what is sin? Where does sin fit in? What exactly are sins?"

What Are God's Laws?

Jack replied, "Sins are violations of God's law that have the effect of creating a divide that separates man from God."[62]

"Breaking laws does cause problems and ignorance of the law is never an acceptable excuse," Sam continued. "Relationships are like that too. If you have wrong intentions, your actions can cause cracks in the relationship."

"Too true. God gave us His law that we might become conscious of our sin."[63]

"Then what are God's laws?" Sam asked.

"Think of God's laws as guidelines to keep us safe. When your girls were little, you told them not to play near traffic, right? I feel certain they thought you were terrible for denying them their desire to play between the cars."

"Oh, I remember those years too well." Sam shook his head and laughed. "The twos were the worst! Eventually they learned to obey, and we all survived."

"Two year olds are simply pushing their envelope. They are only armed with a two-year-old's level of understanding. Understanding grows with maturity. Eventually, they grow thankful that you cared enough to establish the boundaries you did—when you did."

"Respect for their father was good wisdom for the girls then," Sam said as he stopped in the middle of the trail, stood extra straight and grinned enormously." Still is now," Sam added and broke into a laugh.

"More than you'd imagine," Jack replied, not loudly enough for Sam to hear. *It's always healthy to hear a guy connect with his fathering.*

They continued on the trail. Jack took a deep breath and resumed, "'God the Father,'[64] also set up guidelines and boundaries.[65] Some are obvious, and some are not immediately seen. As our understanding grows, our response evolves from 'why?' to 'thanks!' Mysteriously,[1] God's boundaries reveal wisdom. God's laws are not fickle[66] and never burdensome. [67] They are perfect and cause the open-minded to become wise.[68] Respect for the Lord is the beginning of wisdom and understanding."[69]

"That's a mouthful. But I can easily think of my parents' house rules. They seemed so burdensome then. Now I think they were too lenient." Sam chuckled.

THE TEN COMMANDMENTS: SIX ARE INTERPERSONAL

JACK ASKED, "Do you remember the Ten Commandments?"

"Other than do not kill or steal, I cannot recall any of the other commandments. They are another of those *religious* things. Overall, I would have to say that I am more familiar with the term than the content."

"It's the foundation for what comes later. The Ten Commandments were the first written law given by God to man. They were literally written by God's own finger and given to man[70]—twice."[71]

"Twice, eh?" Sam chimed in. "God must sure have wanted to make sure that His message got through."

"Six are directed toward our interpersonal relationships and the other four focus on our relationship with God. The first of the people-related commandments comes with a promise. We should honor our father and mother that we may live long."[72]

"Yeah, but my parents were difficult. I was glad to move out of their house at the first practical opportunity," Sam commented.

"Our parents are or were just like you and me—only one generation removed. A helix reaching through time, cycling on the same issues over time. Meanwhile we do the kid thing, then the parent thing, and if we're lucky, the grandparent thing."

"The perspective sure changes when you become the parent," Sam conceded.

"Some people have great parents, and some people have terrible parents. It doesn't matter. We get the hand we were dealt. We are simply told by God to honor the parents we have. If we do, we will be blessed."[72]

"What does honor entail?"

"To *honor* is 'to be respectful in word and action.' Throw in an attitude of esteem for their position."

"That sounds reasonable."

"My parents lived a full life. They passed in their early nineties, each with different degrees of senility. I saw them shrink from the proud and mighty giants they had been to humble, helpless individuals. When they became challenged by the most basic of tasks, I interpreted the commandment to say that I should do what I could to make sure they were properly cared for and living in dignity. On particularly bad days, reminding myself it's what God commanded me to do took the edge off."

"I'm sorry you had to see your parents decline like that."

"Yes, I'm sorry that I had to experience that," Jack reflected as they walked, then said, "God really does give strength to do the right thing."[73]

"I can see how that commandment makes sense. The basic family unit is the cornerstone of civilized society."

"God designed it that way. A commandment may sound burdensome—until you look at it from different sides."

"The next two should be pure common sense: don't kill[74] or steal."[75]

"*Kill* is pretty broad. What about war?"

Jack replied, "The Hebrew word inscribed on that stone tablet translates as 'premeditated murder or assassination.'"[76]

"Yeah, I believe premeditated murder is a death sentence in most courts. Doesn't everybody just naturally hate thieves? Those two belong together in the prohibition bin." Sam assented.

"When Jesus spoke of the Devil, he referred to the Devil as a thief, who only comes to steal and kill and destroy."[77]

Sam asked. "So, if you murder and steal, then you are about the Devil's work?"

"That would be a direct translation," Jack replied.

"Jack, so far the commandments sound like the building blocks of a civilized society."

"Take care of your family, and don't steal other's people's stuff or murder people. So far, do they sound taxing to you?" Jack asked.

"They sound as reasonable as lanes in traffic."

"The next people commandment is not to commit adultery."[78]

"Okay, I knew that a curve was coming. These are modern times; everybody sleeps with everybody. If the relationship is consensual, why not?"

"What does adultery do to a marriage?" Jack asked. He paused and then answered his own question. "Adultery kills the relationship, destroys the home and steals what the home should have been.[77] Especially is this true if there are kids involved."

"My ex-wife is a nurse. We had a sweet little family of four—the two of us and our two little girls. A couple of years ago, when she switched employment at hospitals, she made new workplace friends. Somewhere in there, she started acting a little different, and the next thing I knew, she wanted me to move out. I was completely blindsided when she insisted on a legal separation. Before I could respond, she had the court ordering me out of my own home. Shortly afterward, one of those new co-workers moved in. Assembling those puzzle pieces didn't take too much effort."

"What did the court say?" Jack asked.

"The judge said that I needed to be understanding of her sexuality. The judge followed that by ruling on the amount of money I would be required to give her. I tried to express concern for the safety of my little girls, but the judge would hear none of my concerns. He only cared about how much money he could transfer from me to her."

"Ouch!" Jack could feel Sam's pain.

"I get the point of that commandment. The adultery killed our marriage and destroyed the home and family we had worked so hard to build. Her infidelity robbed our daughters of their home and the family they rightfully should have had."[77]

"I'm sorry to hear the Devil had a 'steal-kill-and-destroy' party in your home."[77]

"Yep, me too," Sam commented absentmindedly, which did a poor job of covering up the lingering hurt.

They both walked in silence, each briefly reflecting on former spouses. Each was ready to move on with any other topic.

Jack coughed to clear his throat. "The next commandment goes from actions to thoughts. You should not desire your neighbor's wife, house or belongings."[79]

Sam's thoughts drifted to his older daughter's homeroom teacher, Mrs. Fischer. *Wow! She was perfect!* Without thinking, he spoke. "I can see how desiring a married woman could lead to thoughts of adultery."

"Don't let your thoughts get out of hand. The way we think is who we are."[80]

Sam's thoughts hit the brakes hard! *I like her, but I do not want her. Besides, Mrs. Fischer is married. That's not the kind of guy I want to be or the kind of stuff I want to do.* Sam shivered in a physical display of clearing his thoughts. "Could you repeat what you just said?"

"Sure. The way we think is who we are."[80] Jack repeated.

"Sounds like a battle for the mind. Curb the interest for the neighbor's wife, house or stuff before it becomes a craving. Things are always easier said than done."

Jack agreed. "Our thoughts follow the same pattern development as the way deer trails are made. The first deer steps on some foliage and breaks some branches. The next deer breaks more branches and tramples more foliage. Eventually their trail becomes a highway. We cannot control what thoughts pop into our minds. We can control where we permit our thoughts to dwell. Where we allow our thoughts to dwell becomes their comfortable space for seeding future thoughts."[80, 81]

Sam commented. "It surely sounds obvious when you put it that way. Where we choose to park our thoughts in turn seeds our future thoughts."

"What about stuff you want or feel like you really need?" Sam added.

Jack said. "Our brains have two primary thought centers. The first is the limbic system where we have our basic survival instincts and the flight-and-fight response. At about seven years old, the limbic system should be fully developed.[82] The Bible refers to the limbic system as your heart,[83] the seat of deep passions, emotions and love. The limbic is also the battleground where we struggle with addictions. The heart can drive uncontrollable passion and desire.[84] The prefrontal cortex, which is the reasoning part of your brain, should be fully developed by the mid-twenties.[82] The Bible refers to the prefrontal cortex as your mind.[85] If your heart is the gas pedal, then your mind is the brake pedal. When your heart says, 'Let's go for it,' your mind weighs the pros and cons."[82]

"Yeah, sanity is lost when passion consumes." Sam was instantly reminded of misspoken words and bad decisions made in the heat of passion.

"Is that when the heart pirates the wheel and the mind is exiled to the back seat?" Sam chose humor to chase away those haunting memories.

"It happens," Jack replied. "The limbic is strong and stronger in some than in others. It's one reason why bad ideas tied with emotions can spiral out of control. It's how passions or the fight-and-flight response or cravings for an addiction can overrule reason."

"A little self-control goes a long way."

"It sure does," Jack agreed. "The last of the people-related commandments tells us not to lie."[86]

"You said earlier that Satan was the father of lies."[6]

"And lying is the Devil's native language,"[6] Jack firmly stated.

"The commandments sound like reasonable boundaries," Sam commented.

"Jesus rephrased the commandments into only two. He told us first to love the Lord our God with all our heart, soul, mind and strength. Then he told us to love our neighbor as we love our own selves."[87]

"That makes God's rules proactive," Sam noted in a thoughtful tone. Jack sensed the light bulb brightening.

Sam continued, "I have a rule of my own that I like to live by." He paused for a dramatic effect. "What you give out is what you usually get back."

Jack looked at Sam. "Okay, go on."

"If you treat people with kindness and respect, you usually are treated the same way in return. If you treat people rudely, then more often than not, people are rude right back at you."

Jack kept walking, silently reflecting on past interactions rapidly running through his mind.

"That's actually quite true, and God gives us the guidelines to keep us on the right footing. Too much of life can get like walking on an edge. With people and events, how should we approach the known and how should we approach the unknown? God's rules literally are the guidelines that keep us a straight path, blessing us[88] and keeping us from falling off the precipice."

Maintaining his gait, Sam brushed aside a wispy branch that extended into the trail space.

"When the people commandments are violated, it really is a crime."

WHAT IS SIN?

Jack said, "Well, the act of violating God's laws is referred to as sin."[89]

"I was going to ask about that. I know sin is bad. Everybody knows that. What exactly is a sin?" Sam asked.

"Sin starts with temptation. People are tempted when they are enticed by their own physical, intellectual or ego-driven desire(s). If the desire for the enticement is allowed to flourish, it builds its own desire for fulfillment. When the desire for fulfillment has conceived, it grows to give birth to sin. When sin is full-grown, it leads to death.[90] Or put another way, the hunter uses a seductive bait which the prey will intensely desire. The bait is designed to lure the prey out of the safety of its own self-restraint. If the prey surrenders to the desire, it is then lured out of its safe place. When the prey bites the bait, it is hooked, trapped and soon dead."

"I've done some fly fishing. Each type of fish has its own preferred fly. If you choose the right fly, the fish are helpless to resist. You will come home with fish. If you use the wrong flies, the fish will not show any interest."

"Like any hunter intent on being successful, Satan studies his prey to know what we want and where to maximize our weaknesses.[18] That becomes the bait he uses to tempt us."

"Satan sees us as prey?" Sam asked.

"Yes!" Jack stated, paused, and then continued. "As the hunter, he baits us with something we want badly enough to allow ourselves to be lured out of our safe space. I like to refer to the bait as candy—something sweet that satisfies the desires or as a carrot to chase like a donkey chasing a carrot tied to a stick suspended in front of the animal."

Sam stopped and shrugged his pack off his shoulder, setting it on the ground. "When you said *carrot*, I remembered a red-headed girl-friend and the bandanna of hers that became a self-appropriated souvenir." Crouching over the pack, Sam fished out a baggie from the main pocket. The baggie was square and stuffed to appear like a pillow. In the baggie were three neatly folded bandanas: one red, another blue and the third a faded green."

"Let me guess, the green one? You know that's either a bit weird or very sentimental."

"Back then, all the bandanas I had ever seen were either red or blue. Then here is this colorful girl with colorful bandanas. I still like the bandanna, but I haven't given her any thought since. I have not seen her since college and would not know how to return it to her. Besides, these days I have lots of bandanas, and that is just another one."

"So which was it—carrot or candy?" Jack asked.

"Definitely candy. It was a comfortable memory. Now I don't know…" Sam slowed his words as he looked at the green bandanna he held.

"I thought you said your ex-wife was your high school sweetheart?"

"We had a hiccup while we attended different universities."

"Life does have its adventures. Look, you have a souvenir of at least a couple of forgotten sins: coveting and stealing. You're guilty," Jack kidded Sam.

"I'm human," Sam admitted.

"We all are very human. In the big picture, those are little stones in the wall. Spiritually, our sins build a wall that eventually hides God from us."[62]

Sam replaced the baggie in his pack's main pocket and stuffed the green bandanna into his back pocket. They continued walking down the trail.

Holy Spirit, where do You want this to go? Jack prayed earnestly.

"I actually have thought of getting rid of this one." Sam pulled out the green bandanna again. "I tied it to a dog I once had. He managed to chew a corner." The tearing was visible. "I see that rough edge, and I think of him. I miss that dog."

"God uses all kinds of stuff to get our attention. The smallest things can get the most emotional mileage."

"Yeah, I'm starting to see," Sam said under his breath. He asked, "There must be a sin scale. Are some more dramatic and some harmless?"

"That's actually a culturally relative question. The answer is that cultures come and go, but God is a rock,[91] He is unchanging,[92] and so are His boundaries.[93] Sin is sin, and sins separate us from God."[62]

"People have struggled with one flavor or another of the same temptations through all of time."[38]

"The same temptations?"

"Satan tempts with what is appealing to the physical senses of our bodies, what entices our imagination or what boosts our egos.[94]

Sam thought it over as they walked. After a few steps, he spoke. "Well, that leaves all fronts open."

"That's why we need God's salvation. Jesus is the atonement for our sins.[59] Jesus is the way, the truth and the life. No one comes to God but by Jesus.[4] There is no alternative method."

"I can't think of anything really bad that I've done. Taking a bandanna or some pens doesn't amount to capital offenses."

"Stated like that, they do not sound like much. The fact is that everybody has sinned,[95] and our sins have separated us from the Father.[62] God has made a place for anyone who has stolen anything, greedy people, drunkards, slanderers, swindlers, the cowardly, the unbelieving, the vile, the murderers, the sexually immoral, those who practice magic arts, idolaters and all liars.[96, 97] Satan will be there[33] because this place was made for Satan and his followers."

"Those are strong words. It also sounds like we're really screwed."

"Without God and Jesus, we are," Jack replied.

"But these days most of the things you listed are culturally acceptable."

"They were also culturally acceptable in first century Rome too. Paul had a gift for opening up God's truth to anyone who would listen. His letters made Christianity easy to comprehend. His letters, which were directed to different groups of Christians, targeted issues they were confronting. Then Paul clarified God's perspective on the issue. The first-century Christians were the radicals of their day. They abstained from sexual immorality because they understood it put their mortal souls in peril."

"Yeah, but sexual immorality? What's that? We're living in the twenty-first century."

"People have struggled with the same sins through all of time.[98] The only things that change are fashion and tech. We are just as thoroughly soaked in the culture of our times as Paul was in his. The sexual culture of the Romans is well-documented. Paul had studied under Gamaliel, the greatest teacher of the law in that era.[99] Paul became the bridge between Old Testament Judaism and the New Testament church. When Paul wrote to the church in Corinth, his audience was composed of brand-new Christians, who had grown up in the sexual culture of first-century Rome. These new Christians were struggling with their own sexual culture. In his letter, Paul said that other sins were external actions done to others or toward God Himself, but sexual sins[100] are committed against the body.[101] Paul took the matter so seriously that he implored believers to flee from sexual sin."

Sam's mental rolodex paged through the women with whom he had slept since the divorce. "It's interesting that you say that sexual sins are sins against our own bodies. Since the divorce, I can remember being with different women. Everything was consensual and fun. Later, I often felt dirty and sometimes even nasty."

"I'm glad you retained your conscience. When people intentionally go ahead and continue doing something they know is wrong, they either deny or justify. Either way, their conscience dulls."

"I felt justified with what I did when I did it. If she did, then why couldn't I too? Looking back, the justification I used then does not make me feel any more justified now."

"The sexual revolution teaches us to disrespect our bodies. The current slang for genitalia is junk. Do you remember when we had respect for our 'family jewels'?"

"Jewels to junk. The words tell the story."

"What has the sexual revolution given us? An epidemic of broken families, tens of millions of abortions and a rampant epidemic of STDs. "Ugh!" Sam shuddered at the overwhelming possibility of catching STDs, and the idea of people killing babies for profit made him nauseous. "Sex can be awesome. Why is it followed by so much bad stuff?"

Jack had the answer for Sam's dilemma. "God designed intimacy to be an exclusive relationship between a husband and his wife. The bonus is for it to be enriching in the right context. On the other hand, sex out of context[102] becomes an illustration for the price of sin. A moment of pleasure can potentially return a painful souvenir and or the murder of an innocent life."[93]

"When you put it that way..." Sam's words caught in his throat.

Jack replied, "That's sin.[89] It steals, kills and destroys.[77] For what? For pursuing a desire for something that's forbidden? For allowing that pursuit to build its own desire for fulfillment? Even if the fulfillment of that forbidden desire leads to sin and death?"[90]

Sam thought on the questions. "It seems all of the sins you listed really do have long-term detrimental effects to the sinner."

"The road to ruin, which is charted in this life and realized in the next, can be slow or quick. The wages of sin is death, but the gift of God is eternal life.[103] There is a heaven,[104, 105] and there is a hell."[97] In one is eternal life[106]; in the other is eternal death."[97]

Sam looked for an escape. "Do you really think so? What's to say we just don't expire, go into the ground and that's the end of it?"

WHY IS JESUS THE ONLY WAY TO GOD'S SALVATION?

"OUR PHYSICAL BODIES are temporal.[107] It's your spirits[108] that live on."[109, 103]

"Like reincarnation?"

Jack replied, "No, we are only get one life on this earth.[110] Reincarnation is a doctrine of Hinduism and Buddhism. One is polytheistic and the other atheistic. By definition, they leave it up to the follower to work out his or her own salvation."

"Isn't that the way it is? We have to figure it out ourselves?"

"To a degree. It's why God has given us free will.[42] We choose. There are lots of choices, but there is only one way. That one way is through Jesus.[4] Salvation is a gift from God. There is nothing you could do to earn it.[111] But it's up to each of us to weigh and decide. God's Word says: It is appointed for men to die once then after that, the judgment.[110] Then it goes on to say that whoever hears my word and chooses to believe and accept Him who sent me will have eternal life and will not be judged but will have crossed over from death to life."[112]

Sam stopped in the middle of the trail and looked straight up. "All these years I've thought of myself as a carbon-based life form. Now I discover I'm a spirit being?"[114, 109]

Jack looked up to see where Sam was looking. "Consider yourself a spirit trapped inside a carbon-based life form,[113] and your spirit has an eternal future."[114, 109]

"I've always had difficulty swallowing what we see is all there is. That there is nothing beyond this. It all seems like a recipe that gets passed on but with a key ingredient missing." Sam resumed hiking.

Jack kept step with Sam. "Now you have the key ingredient. We live on.[106] The question we face is eternal life in heaven with God or eternal death in hell with Satan. That is the fork in the road."

Turning a bend in the trail, the cut stone gazebo appeared before them. The Lookout gazebo sat on the junction of a number of trails. The gazebo was designed to be a sheltered place for wanderers to rest with a panoramic view. Jack entered first. Sam stepped in and walked up to the northern opening. The valley below was draped in a mosaic carpet of flowering fruit trees. At the bottom of the valley, they could see where they had been walking on Azalea Way earlier.

"Sure is a beautiful day to be out here. I'm enjoying talking about this God stuff with you," Sam mentioned as he shrugged out of his pack.

"We're not done talking, are we?" Jack asked.

"Oh, no, our hike is only somewhere near the middle. This is only break time." Sam pulled out his water bottle. "I haven't heard any moaning. How are the new boots treating you?"

"The boots? I guess I haven't even thought of them since we started."

"Then they must be a good fit. Do you want to head back or go all the way to the end of the arboretum? Madison Street boasts a couple of good places to grab a bite."

"Well, my feet say, 'Let's do the whole hike.'" Jack drained his water bottle. "Besides, I could use another water bottle." Jack caved in the sides of his empty bottle. The flattened recyclable bottle slipped easily into the mesh side pocket of his pack.

"If I remember correctly…there's a convenience store on the corner of Madison Street and Lake Washington Boulevard." Sam snacked on a baggie of granola.

Using the gazebo's structure as a launching point, Jack went through a series of deep stretches.

With his thirst quenched, Sam returned the bottle to its pocket. "You should do that *before* you hike."

"I forgot. I was starting to feel a little tight."

"Your body will tell you when you've been spending too much time behind a desk." Sam sealed the baggie and returned it to the side pocket of his backpack.

"Ain't that the truth!" Jack laughed lightly. "It's always good to listen to your body."

"Listen or have a full conversation? Next time you'll feel better longer if you stretch before."

"Okay, *Doc*."

From the corner of his eye, he noticed people coming up one of the converging trails. Three small children bolted up the trail toward the gazebo. A couple was right on their heels. The woman yelled, "Kids, slow down. Be careful!" The man, who was obviously savoring every step and moment, wore a big controlled smile that said, "so what if my kids run wild? This is my day off. Nobody is raining on my parade."

"We've had our time in the shade. Time for a handoff." Sam nodded to Jack, as he hoisted his pack onto his shoulder.

Jack had acted before Sam even said anything. They made for the path heading due south. From behind, they could hear light steps scramble up the long stone staircase leading to the gazebo. The sound of their steps echoing from the gazebo announced that the new residents had claimed territory. Before the older voices could be heard joining the younger voices, all the voices faded to the sound of the fresh gravel crushing under each step.

MEETING THE CREATOR OF LIFE, THE UNIVERSE AND EVERYTHING

KICKING A PINE CONE off the trail, Sam commented, "You said something earlier about meeting the Creator of the universe."

"At some time in his or her life, everyone will arrive at a fork in the road. Which path will he or she take? To follow Jesus or not to follow Jesus."

Jack continued, "At the decision point of that fork stands the Creator of life, the universe and everything. One path shines God's light into us.[115] The other path hardens your heart."[116]

"Choose life,"[42] Sam quietly spoke to himself.

The trail crested. "Let's stop for the view." Jack felt a little winded after the sudden climb.

Sam let down his pack and arched his back. "Okay, I'll be honest, I've sinned."

"I have too. We're all sinners, and God knows that. God gave us a way to clean the slate—Jesus."[117]

JESUS, OUR ROAD TO SALVATION

"*God so loved the world that he gave his one and only Son, that whoever believes in him shall not perish but have eternal life.*[106] Jesus is God incarnate.[118] He came to the earth as a man to live as a man and to be tempted as a man. He offered Himself to be sacrificed as the atonement for our sins.[58] Jesus then rose from the dead on the third day to prove He was greater than death itself.[119] All you have to do is declare Jesus is Lord and believe in your heart that Jesus is the Son of God and that God raised Him from the dead, and you will be saved.[120] God does not want anyone to perish. He wants everyone to come to repentance[121] and be reconciled with Him."[122]

"Why did Jesus have to die?" Sam asked.

"In the Hebrew law of the Old Testament, God prescribed animal blood sacrifices for men to atone for their souls.[123] Some sins can only be cleansed by blood.[124] The shedding of blood illustrated the gravity of the price to be paid for atonement. The problem was that these sacrifices were only a covering for sins.[125] So, the offerings had to be done regularly.[126]

"Then why bother if it only became an exercise repeated over and over?"

"Maintenance." Jack let the word hang. "There were two reasons for the sacrifices. God wanted man to acknowledge his sin. The process brought man face to face with the importance of his need to atone for his sin, and that atonement had a price. The process became a regular participatory reminder[126] of their personal need for atonement. The other reason was that the sacrifices served as a foreshadowing of the future ultimate sacrifice[127]—the one great sacrifice that would render all future animal blood sacrifices obsolete.[128]

"So Jesus became the ultimate sacrifice?" Sam asked.

"The system was set up to be a foreshadowing of Jesus. The law demanded the best to be sacrificed to God.[129] Jesus was the perfect lamb without any inherited defect or physical injury.[130] Being without defect meant that He was born without the original sin that the rest of us all inherited from Adam and Eve's original sin in the garden of Eden."

"The virgin birth?"

"Yes.[131, 132] Jesus was born without sin and then lived a life without sin.[133, 134] He had nothing for which to make atonement. Being without sin[135] He chose[136] to pay the price of our sin[137] by allowing Himself to be crucified.[138] Being without sin made Him the perfect sacrifice to make atonement for our sins once and for all. All we have to do is accept."[120]

The trail narrowed and dropped onto a sidewalk that was more of a wide curb to the boulevard. "That was a sudden end to a trail." Jack looked across the road. "I see that ball field over there. What a sweet spot to play ball!"

"We've reached the end of the Arboretum. See those buildings past the field?" Sam pointed past the ball field. "Madison Street is right up ahead."

"We've already gotten to Madison? I forgot we were in the middle of the city."

"It's easy to do in there."

"I feel like chocolate. I usually carry some in my pack, but I didn't plan ahead."

"Chocolate sounds like a good idea, and there are plenty of businesses on Madison where we can get some. We'll burn off those calories off doing the return leg."

Repentance

Armed with chocolate and ice-cold bottles of water, they crossed Madison and followed Lake Washington Boulevard back into the Arboretum.

"I like that medieval-style stone cottage. It matches all the other stonework in the arboretum.

"Probably the same workmen made this," Sam said, looking at the cottage.

"I'm guessing it could have been designed and built for an onsite caretaker?"

"It probably was," Sam agreed.

"It's always fun to discover gems on a hike. This place must have been inspirational for the caretaker's artistic side."

"Anyone who works in here experiences art."

Shortly past the cottage, the road forked. The right was blocked, forcing all vehicle traffic to the left.

"Let's go up the road past that Jersey barrier." Sam pointed to the barrier barring vehicles from using the road.

"Isn't this the old Arboretum road?" Jack asked questioningly. "I remember it being open for traffic back when I lived here. I used this scenic shortcut when driving in this part of town."

"Too many people taking the scenic route is probably the reason why the city planners closed the road. For years, it's just a very wide path for walking. I'm surprised the city hasn't ripped out the pavement and planted something."

"That's likely planned for a future budget."

"Unless they keep it for show and tell with visiting dignitaries." Sam laughed.

"Well, it's obviously not for the rest of us." Jack laughed with Sam.

The road led up, cresting a hill, and then turned west into the park. Unnoticed, the sound of the boulevard's traffic had faded completely. The two men walked past the Pacific pavilion on a graveled trail that wove into the woods.

"You said God wants everyone to come to repentance?"[139]

"Yes, Sam, God does not want anyone to perish but for everyone to come to repentance."[121]

"Repent is another one of those religious words that I do not have a feel for what it means."

"The original Bible was written in Greek and Hebrew. I have an app to trace words in the Bible back to their original Hebrew and Greek. Understanding the words that the authors used clarifies the message they intended."

"Is that what you did when I asked you about salvation?"

"Yeah, I'd actually looked salvation up a couple of days ago, so it was still fresh in my memory. The process may sound a bit pedantic, but it does keep me from straying from the author's intent or getting caught up in modern linguistic gymnastics." Jack stopped and pulled out his phone. "My preferred Bible app has a concordance." In a few finger strokes, the app had already done a comprehensive search for the word *repent*.

"Check this out." Jack held his phone for Sam to see. "The Greek word for *repent* literally means 'to think differently. To change one's mind for the better.'"[140]

Sam added, "It also says 'amend for one's past sins.'"[140] Sam repeated under his breath. "Think differently."

"The Hebrew words for *repent* mean 'to be sorry and have compassion, to turn back, be restored and repair.'"[141, 142]

Sam commented. "That's a mouthful of concepts, Jack, but they all head in the same direction."

Jack slipped the phone back into his cargo pocket and started walking.

"So, for all the times I've heard the word *repent*, 'turning around' is what it really means?"

"Sam, repentance is not simply an action. Repentance is a process—a process that touches your heart, causing you to act and think differently."

"Act and think differently?" Sam questioned under his breath.

"Repenting starts with awakening to a personal sin, as well as to the impact that sin is having on your own life and on the lives of others. The sin disturbs you to the point you find the sin abhorrent and want to rid yourself of its presence in your life. Repenting begins when you awaken and decide to stop doing the personal sin. That process is called being repentant. Following through by not doing the personal sin is called living in repentance."

"I see the process—awaken, decide and follow through," Sam quickly responded. "The one who repents makes the choice to repent."

"Repenting is more like awakening with a disgust to something you did or are doing, acknowledging what it is and taking responsibility for it. The loathing drives you to stop, disassociate yourself from the sin and then follow through by not returning to it.[143] True repentance touches the heart, which is our seat of deep emotions. The heart is also where strength is mustered to follow through with the commitment to change."

"Well, if your sin disgusts you, it will be easier to turn from," Sam commented.

Sam reconstructed what Jack had been saying. "So, with your mind you understand something you are doing is wrong and why it is wrong. In your gut, you are horrified. You find yourself driven to take action to end the wrong and do what it takes to follow through with ending and distancing yourself from the wrong." He paused to check Jack's response.

Jack smiled. "The mind can reason or justify anything. In the heart is where character changes are realized, and new habits are developed."

"Making the connection that the workings of the heart and mind are what we know as the limbic system and prefrontal cortex is a key puzzle piece."

"That's the physical side. Repentance is a real physical action with a spiritual side. Repentance is your sin being exposed to you and seeing your sin for what it is, what it is doing to you and what it's doing to your relationship with God. This insight creates a sorrow in you.[144] That sorrow drives you to repentance. You acknowledge what you have done, ask God for forgiveness and make a conscious decision not to continue doing the sin. God wants us to turn from our wicked ways, and He promises to reward us with healing."[145]

Jack could see Sam was chewing on this concept. They walked in silence for a little while.

"What if you feel the grief and understand why what you have done is wrong, but you refuse to repent?"

"When you feel the conviction of your sin and refuse to repent, it causes your heart to harden.[116] Hardening your heart silences the conviction, making the sin easier to commit. Sin takes over and controls your life, making it harder to repent. A hardened heart eventually brings trouble[146] and God's judgment.[116] The actual Hebrew word used to describe sin as *evil* is *ra*,[147] which is most commonly translated as 'evil or wicked.' *Ra* is also translated as 'giving pain or unhappiness' or simply that a situation goes from bad to worse."

"From bad to worse, eh?" Sam cleared his throat with a cough and said, "Repentance sounds like the case of a kid caught stealing. The good parent explains to the kid what he did, why stealing is bad and the repercussions of stealing. When the kid's understanding gels, he will grieve for what he did and why it was wrong. To avoid future repercussions and the taking the experience as a lesson learned, the smart kid resolves not to steal in the future. When the kid is tempted in the future, he intentionally refrains from stealing. Soon enough the temptation to steal fades."

Hearing Sam's interpretation, Jack added, "And if the kid chooses not to repent and continues stealing, he may get away with it for a time. Eventually he will find himself paying for his crimes. Prisons are full of people who at some early point were confronted and refused to repent. Hell is populated by people who refused to repent, choosing for the rest of their days to continue pursuing their sinful ways."

"Wow! That really highlights why a parent needs to be involved in a kid's life."

"Good parenting with results," Jack concluded as he prayerfully thought, *Thank You, Holy Spirit. Only You can bring enlightenment to Sam's mind.*[148]

"Yeah, this God stuff does kind of sound like parenting, doesn't it?" Sam kidded Jack.

"The kind of parenting we all wish we'd had. It's not a coincidence that God is referred to as the Father."

"I've never thought of God and Jesus in a personal relationship context before. God does seem to fit the parent role."

"God knows us better than we know ourselves. He wants for us what is good for us."[149]

"So, it would just be smart to encourage the relationship?" Sam asked.

Jack nodded. "If we confess our sins, He is faithful and just and will forgive us our sins[150, 151, 152] and remember them no more. Then Jesus said he would be faithful to help us,[153] and not let us be tempted beyond what we can endure."[38]

Jack continued, "When you believe and live in repentance, you clear the air between yourself and God. Having the air clear between you and God is critical to developing a relationship with God. Part of God's salvation is walking with God and building a relationship with Him that will grow on through eternity."

"Earlier, you mentioned all those sins. I haven't done them all, but I can claim a few—if only in my thoughts."

"As a person reasons in his or her heart, so is that person.[80] All actions start as thoughts, which makes you only an action from fulfilling your thoughts."[90]

"Too true. Learning to control your passions is part of the art of being an adult."

Jack responded, "Self-control is also a sign of a Christian's spiritual maturity. Still, we have all sinned and fallen short of the glory of God."[95]

"I'm not going to argue that."

WHO IS THE HISTORICAL JESUS?

"**Y**OU AND ME both. Lucky for us, Jesus paid the price for our sins.[135] While we were still sinners, Christ died for us.[154] Jesus died for our sins, was buried and rose on the third day, and afterward was seen by over 500 people.[155] Jesus said He was the way, the truth and the life, none gets to the Father other than through Him.[4]

"Is there an actual historical record other than what the Bible says?" Sam asked.

"Yes, there is a secular historical record written by Josephus who was a Roman historian.[156]

"But he's a historian. When did he live?"

"Josephus was the son of a Jewish priest, born a couple of years after Jesus' crucifixion. A well-educated man, Josephus had served as an envoy from Jerusalem to Nero's court before the Jewish-Roman War. He then fought in the war, was captured and made a slave. As a slave, he was tasked with documenting the history of the Jews for the Romans. He rose in stature to become a Roman citizen and Caesar's designated Jewish historian for the Romans.

"Keep going," Sam encouraged.

"Josephus grew up in Jerusalem during the early development of Christianity. He walked among people who had seen Jesus, heard Jesus and, in some cases, personally interacted with Jesus. The crucifixion of Jesus was public record. It was common knowledge that Jesus died by crucifixion on a cross, was buried and rose from the dead on the third day after His crucifixion. After the crucifixion, at least five hundred people saw Jesus.[155] Josephus certainly knew some of them and heard their stories firsthand. His secular writings support the historicity of Jesus.[156]

"So Jesus was a real person and not just some mythical character from antiquity?" Sam asked.

"Yes, Jesus was a real person, well known in Judea. He was crucified, buried and days later came back to life, and there were plenty of witnesses."[155]

Sam said. "Wow! So there really was a Jesus."

Jack thought he could hear the echo of a coin hitting the bottom of a deep well.

WHAT DOES IT MEAN TO BE SAVED?

"IF JESUS IS real, and what you are saying is true, then how do I get in on this?"

"Jesus says that He stands at the door of our heart knocking. If we listen to hear His voice and open the door, He will come into our heart.[157] To have Jesus living in our hearts is what it means to be born again.[158, 159]

Sam stopped in the trail and looked directly at Jack. "How do I invite Him in?"

"If you declare with your mouth, 'Jesus is Lord,' and believe in your heart that God raised Him from the dead, you will be saved because it's with our hearts that we believe, and our mouth is how we profess our faith and are saved.[120]

"How do I know?"

WHEN IS IT HOPE? WHEN IS IT FAITH?

"WE'RE SAVED THROUGH faith—not by anything else that we do by ourselves."[111]

"*Faith* is another of those words loosely thrown around. What exactly is faith?" Sam asked.

"Faith is the confidence of things hoped for, the assurance of what is not seen."[160]

"Aren't faith and hope just different words for the same thing?"

"Hope is anchored in the domain of the mind. It's a mind thing—an attitude of expectancy concerning the future."[161]

"Isn't faith the same?" Sam asked.

"Faith is a confidence of something real and definite. It's in your gut, your core, your heart, and you just know it—even if you have yet to see or experience it." Jack paused. Tomorrow's sun will rise, but will it? From what we know about the solar system and a lifetime of dawns, we expect the sun to rise tomorrow morning, but we haven't see it do so yet. That's faith."

Sam replied with his own metaphor to assure Jack he understood. "Hope is the worker who works hard and hopes to get a raise or better job within his present place of employment. Faith is the worker who gets training to improve his skillset. Faith is driven by the confidence that an enhanced skillset will lead to better paying jobs."

"Very good." Jack raised an eyebrow, nodded and continued. "Hope is nice and has its place; it keeps us going. Faith is a substance, a confidence, something real and definite within us that we possess in the here and now. It's a heart issue not in your chest, but in your gut. Faith produces something within us that is so real that it can be described by the word *substance*."[162]

"How do I get faith?"

"Faith comes from hearing the message, and the message is heard through the word about Christ.[163] The more you learn, the more your faith grows."

Sam replied, "Through life, it seems like the deeper I dig and the more I get to know people and about things, the more disappointed I get."

WHAT IS THE BIBLE?

"WELL, SAM, PEOPLE are always a wild card. But God's Word is the rock that does not change.[164] There are no false fronts with God; He is truth.[4, 165] The deeper you dig, the better it gets." Jack let his pause hang in the air. "The Bible doesn't do any false advertising; it is pure truth."

"Isn't the Bible complicated?"

"The Bible is not a 'book.' The Bible is a collection of 66 books written by over 30 authors. By faith we believe God inspired the Bible.[166] We also believe that God has preserved the integrity of the Bible. The Bible was compiled topically. However, when the story is read chronologically from start to finish, the flow is smooth and consistent. The Book becomes the gripping story of God and man, from before time, through all of man's time on earth and on into eternity."

Sam stopped in the trail and took a long breath. "I guess you either think this is real or foolishness, right?"[167]

Jack looked at Sam. "That's the test."[2]

The trail wove through the forest and came around a bend. Rhododendron trees towered over the trail. Jack stopped and looked straight up. "Some of these rhododendrons must be over 40 feet tall; those blooms are the size of my forearm. The plaque says this particular species is from the Himalayas. I'd love to see the Himalayan foothills carpeted with these."

"Whenever their spring is." Sam laughed.

"God is such an artist."[168] The more you saturate yourself in nature with an open mind, the more you see God in it."

"Maybe that's part of why I've had such a hunger for being out in the wild," Sam reflectively commented.

"Holy, holy, holy, is the Lord God Almighty, the whole earth is full of Your glory."[169] Jack paused before adding, "That's what they say continually in front of God's throne in heaven."

The trail continued to follow the upper outline of the small valley, crossing other minor trails. Each quickly disappeared into the woods.

"When it comes to the Bible, people can get so opinionated."

"That's a people thing—not to be confused with the Bible itself," Jack replied.

"In the end, faith is believing that God meant what He said in His Word. When we see God's Word as our wellspring, opinionated people just sound like noisy water birds, flapping and chattering."

They walked silently for a few minutes. Sam stopped at a bend on the trail where there was a window-like view into the valley.

"I can't remember talking to anyone so easily about God stuff. To my gut, this conversation meshes like synchronized gears. I'm actually finding myself a little bit upset. I feel like I should have known this a long time ago."

"Well, Sam, when you consider the gospel of Jesus, nothing is challenging or complex to understand. It is quite direct and simple—simple enough for children to understand.[170]

"A dose of truth can be a paradigm changer." Jack looked at Sam. "It sounds like the Creator of the universe is drawing you to Him."[2]

"I can say that my mindset is not what it was when we started our hike. I thought this kind of stuff was foolishness. Now not so much. To think that I can go to heaven, avoid hell and purge sin from my life while getting to personally know the actual Creator of the universe sounds like something I want."

"God says He forgets our sins.[171] God also said He would never leave us or forsake us."[36] That's a solid promise toward relationship building. Any relationship takes two parties. God gives His guarantee that He will stand up to His side of the relationship."

"So you are telling me that when I call on God, He will be there and that I can talk with Him about whatever?" Sam asked. "Through personal struggles and triumphs, He will be there to listen to me and He will care?"

"Working through things together is how you build relationship. Yes, God listens and cares about every area of your life and is wanting to help."[172]

"But, Jack, for all we've been saying, I feel God is distant from me."

"God is *omnipotent*.[173] God is also *omniscient*. He is here, there, everywhere. He is all-knowing.[11] He knows everything that's going on in our lives, and He cares.[174] His understanding has no limit.[175] If you acknowledge who Jesus is and invite Him into your heart,[157] He will help you conquer your sins and overcome struggles. In the process, you grow a relationship together that starts here in this world and runs through life eternal."[176]

The trail passing the gazebo wound through the woods. To the right were steps that headed steeply uphill. Passing the first step, Jack looked up and saw a bench. He stopped, and as he turned in that direction, said, "Sam, let's go this way."

The trail went up some steps to an opening some ten to twelve feet above the trail they had just been walking on. The opening, which provided a box seat view of the valley, was just wide enough for a bench with some clearance to pass. The trail could be seen heading out the other way. Turning, they saw the valley known as Azalea Way. As far as they could see, the valley was lined with blooming cherry and plum trees. The park designers foresaw that people would enjoy semi-private recesses away from curious passersby, yet as open to the view as stadium seating at a Huskies' game.

"Mind if we take a break?" Jack asked as he turned to take a seat.

"Perfect timing…and you even found us some stadium seating with a view." Sam had already taken out his water bottle as he settled onto the other end of the bench.

THE SINNER'S PRAYER

J ACK PULLED OUT his wallet. From the back sleeve, he drew out a laminated card that fit in perfectly with the others.

"I thought the wording on this was perfect."

"Wording?"

"It's called 'the sinner's prayer.' Remember how I keep saying that when it comes to God, it's all about relationship?"

"Yeah…" A curious questioning tone filled Sam's voice.

"Consider the sinner's prayer as a formal introduction to say you understand and are sincere. Nothing is magical about the words; it's all about what they mean. Let's walk through it."

"Sure, if I have any objections, I won't hold back."

Jack acknowledged and looked back at the card. "Let me read it first; then we can say it together."

"That's fair," Sam replied. Jack was learning how Sam liked to take things at his own pace.

Jack began, "Dear God in heaven, I come to You in the name of Jesus. I acknowledge to You that I am a sinner, and I am sorry for my sins and the life that I have lived: I need Your forgiveness."

"I'm not going to list my crimes."

"You can do that privately with God later," Jack responded with a smile. "That is between you and God; you have your own direct line. Let's continue." Jack took a breath and resumed. "I believe that Your only begotten Son, Jesus Christ, shed His precious blood on the cross at Calvary and died for my sins. I understand my sins are an impediment to our having a relationship. I ask Your forgiveness for my sins, and I am willing to turn away from my sin."

"What does *begotten* mean?"

"To *beget* is 'to sire or produce'—like a parent having children."

"Okay, that's the virgin birth, right?"

"Yes. God conceived Jesus in Mary by the Holy Spirit."[132] Jack could see Sam was mulling over this answer.

"If God is the Creator of everything, then He could do that?"

"Yes, He is, and yes, He did." Jack parsed the phrase, looking at Sam with a wide warm smile. "God said in His Holy Word in Romans 10:9 that if we confess the Lord our God and believe in our hearts that God raised Jesus from the dead, we shall be saved."[120]

"Because it's with our hearts that we believe, and with our mouth that we profess our faith. That's how we get saved?" Sam cautiously replied.

"Consider that the key to unlock the door is a moment that you can point to. Living in repentance and becoming a disciple of Jesus is the follow through."

"So good so far." Sam felt comfortable that he understood.

Jack read the card. "Right now, I confess Jesus as the Lord of my soul; with my heart, I believe that Jesus is the Son of God and that God raised Jesus from the dead. This very moment I accept Jesus Christ as my own personal Savior and according to His Word. Thank You, Jesus, for Your unlimited grace which has saved me from my sins. I thank You, Jesus, that Your grace never leads to license, but it always leads to repentance. Therefore, Lord Jesus, transform my life so that I may bring glory and honor to You alone and not to myself. Thank You, Jesus, for dying for me and giving me eternal life. Right now, I confess Jesus as the Lord of my soul. Jesus, I choose to follow You.[177] AMEN."

Jack took a breath and looked at Sam. "What do you think?"

"My heart says yes, and my mind agrees." Sam felt like he was at the end of a diving board ready to jump and confident the pool was deep enough. "Let's do it."

Looking back at the card, Jack added, "This is God's will."

"God's will? What's God's will?"

"In the macro, God's will is that all people should be saved and come to a knowledge of the truth.[178] In the micro, God also has plans to prosper us and keep us from harm and give us hope and a future."[61]

"I know where my life has been going. In some places I have to admit that I've seen not good stuff go from bad to worse. I could use God's salvation[14] in my life. Yes, I'm all in."

Jack held the card. "Follow me and repeat what I say." Reading and pausing at every sentence and mid-sentence break, Jack read, and Sam followed.

Dear God in heaven, I come to You in the name of Jesus. I acknowledge to You that I am a sinner, and I am sorry for my sins and the life that I have lived; I need Your forgiveness.

I believe that Your only begotten Son, Jesus Christ, shed His precious blood on the cross at Calvary and died for my sins, and I am now willing to turn from my sin.

You said in Your Holy Word in Romans 10:9 that if we confess the Lord our God and believe in our hearts that God raised Jesus from the dead, we shall be saved.

Right now, I confess Jesus as the Lord of my soul. With my heart, I believe that God raised Jesus from the dead. This very moment I accept Jesus Christ as my own personal Savior, and according to His Word, right now I am saved.

Thank You, Jesus, for Your unlimited grace which has saved me from my sins. I thank You, Jesus, that Your grace never leads to license, but it always leads to repentance. Therefore, Lord Jesus transform my life so that I may bring glory and honor to You alone and not to myself.

Thank You, Jesus, for dying for me and giving me eternal life. Amen.

"Amen," Sam finished and felt his eyes well-up. Opening his pack, he dug out the bandanna packet. Selecting the red one, he dabbed his eyes.

"The Bible says that anyone who belongs to Christ has become a new person.[179] Are you feeling a little something?" Jack asked.

"Yeah, I can't explain it, but it *feels* right. More like an 'I know' than an 'I feel.' I know Christ came into my heart. I know this was the right decision to make. I have peace about this decision," Sam said dabbing a tear.

"Welcome to the family! God said He will be our Father, and we will be His sons and daughters."[180]

"So that's where the Christian brothers and sisters thing comes from?"

Jack replied, "Yes, and God's Word says that in Jesus Christ, you are a child of God through faith." [181] This is what it means to be born again.[182] I get choked up when I think of what God and Jesus have done for me.[154]

For a few minutes they sat on the bench staring at the beautiful landscape.

Sam broke the quiet. "Okay, Doc, what's the script?"

"Build your relationship with God by communicating with Him. Get to know God by reading His Word[166] and talking with God by praying to Him.[183] Honestly pursue God, and you will find He's been pursuing you even longer."[111]

"That sounds like a challenge with a reward." Jack and Sam both stood, stretched and exited the alcove. In a few steps, they were back on the main ridge trail.

STARTER SCRIPTURE: THE GOSPEL OF JOHN

"SAM, I PROMISE you that walking with Christ is a well with no bottom. The best place to start is the gospel of John. Each of the four gospels tells the same story from a different perspective. The gospel of John focuses on the divinity of Christ. He was there with Jesus and wrote a firsthand account of what he saw.[184] Reading John will give you a solid feeling for who Jesus is and how He feels about you."

"Okay, John it is. What should I read next?"

"When you've finished reading John, read it again. You'll see things you missed the first time. Luke's gospel and the book of Acts[185] are two parts of a continuous narrative that take you from the birth of Jesus through the life of Paul. They were both written by Luke, who was a Greek physician.[186] Luke documents in a non-Jewish perspective what he saw and what he heard from eyewitnesses. His writing spans from the birth of Jesus through the life of Paul. Luke and Acts are the historical books of the New Testament. Afterward, read through Paul's letters to the churches."

"What about the Old Testament?"

"I'd recommend reading the New Testament first. The Old Testament leads up to Jesus. The New Testament is Jesus, and He is the One who opens God's salvation to all people, regardless of ethnicity, gender or status."[187]

"Oh, so that's why they are 'Old' and 'New'?"

"You could say that. The Old Testament is actually what is referred to as the Scriptures of Jesus' time."

"Fascinating!"

HOW TO PRAY

"BUT FOR NOW, save the OT for later. Jack continued, "You should talk with God too. You prayed just now, and that's a start. You can pray or talk to God anytime. In fact, Paul said to pray continually."[183]

"Literally?"

"He meant that we should be in a continual attitude of prayer. Think of it like God walking with you. What would you talk about? Praying also gets you to thinking about God's perspective."

"What do I say? You had a card. Are there other prayers?"

"Sam, praying to God should be freeform. He wants us to speak from our hearts—not just repeat the same lines over and over.[188] That said, prayer should have some structure."

"How should I pray?" Sam asked.

"Jesus' disciples asked the same question.[189] Jesus answered with an example. Have you heard of the Lord's Prayer?"

"I've heard of it, but I don't know it."

"Jesus gave us the Lord's prayer so we would have a pattern to follow." Jack took a deep breath and from memory recited the Lord's Prayer. *"Our Father who is in heaven, holy is your name, your kingdom come, your will be done, on earth as it is in heaven. Give us today our daily bread. Forgive us our debts as we also have forgiven our debtors. Lead us not into temptation, but rescue us from the evil one.*[190] In Jesus' name. Amen."

Jack paused and waited. He could tell Sam was digesting what he had just heard.

"So, you start by addressing God—like opening a letter? You acknowledge who He is and that He is the source of our daily sustenance?"

"You are addressing God, the Creator of life, the universe and everything. Let God know you are talking to Him and that you understand who He is as much as our mortal minds are able. He is your source; be thankful.[191] Be as elaborate as you want. It doesn't take long before you realize all good things come from God,[40] and He loves a thankful heart."[192]

"But the forgiveness part...I thought we covered that in the prayer we said. You know, the one that was on that card."

"When we asked God to forgive us our sins and invited Jesus to come into our hearts, our sins were forgiven. Yes, that was the prayer we prayed. Consider that your benchmark, which means that you have a clean slate with God. Whatever happens after that, Jesus specifically told us to forgive others of sins against us, which releases God to forgive us of our sins against Him. He said, if we don't, He won't."[193]

Sam dramatically breathed deeply before sheepishly admitting, "There are a few people who have done me wrong, and I get all perturbed when I think of them. I see what you mean: the thought of them robs me of my tranquility. I've tried to 'let go,' but whenever I think of them and what they did, the disquiet returns."

"Well, Sam, you now have the cure. Forgive them of what they did. Your forgiving them goes way beyond just 'letting go.' Forgiving is like taking a bath. It makes God happy and He in turn forgives you of your sin.[193]

"I'll think about that."

"Do more than just think about it. Do some forgiving of them—at least between you and God. Throw the load onto God.[194] God forgave you, Sam. You forgive them. You'll feel lighter."

"Okay, I'll try."

"Sometimes forgiving others can be a real challenge. Talk it out with God. Ask for His help. He will help if you ask in prayer and believe."[195]

"In your prayers, make sure to ask God to protect you from Satan's temptations, and He will.[196] His promise to us is that when we are tempted, He will provide a way of escape from the temptation."[38]

Sam nodded as Jack continued, "Jesus said that whatever we ask in His name with the intent that the Father may be glorified, He will do it.[197]

"Then freeform after that?" Sam asked to confirm his understanding.

"Yes. Think of it like a conversation. Make sure you hit those points and let God know that you are thankful for what He has done. All good things come from God.[40] Sam, thank Him for life. You now have eternal life. I'm sure it won't take much to come up with an endless list of things to thank God for. Today I thank God for blessing me with these feet and for the stroll they have taken me on in this beautiful place. I thank Him for my eyes and the things I have seen and your becoming my brother in Christ."[198]

"I think I may discover that I've taken a lot of stuff for granted. I've never given thought to being thankful for basic things like being able to see and walk. Yeah, I'm very thankful for my feet and my eyes."

"Well, don't tell me; tell God! Say it."

"Thank You, God, for my feet and eyes."

"And how was that?"

"This may sound corny, but I really am thankful for them, and I feel like He heard me."

"He did.[199] The other part of praying is to freeform."

"Freeform?"

"Tell God about your day. If there are any ups, downs or whatever, tell Him about it. God listens, and God cares. Don't forget, He is the Creator of everything, so always be respectful. Then pray that you will get to know Him better. Something is incredibly powerful about spoken words.[200] Where our thoughts are more like seeds, spoken words make things happen."

Jack could see the visitors' center coming into view, and he knew their vehicles were not far beyond. "I've really enjoyed our hike together."

"So have I." Sam knew this hike was coming to a close. 'That's okay. A lot for one day...but my appetite is still whetted for more God stuff. My schedule is work and planning around court dictates. Let me see how my calendar looks. How 'bout a tentative plan for another hike in two or four weeks. We'll see how the weather goes."

"What about Discovery Park? I remember that loop." Jack felt confident with his cardio. This was the longest hike he had done in years. Having done so well hiking across and back through the arboretum was encouraging—encouraging enough to commit to a bigger, more strenuous hike.

"Only if we do the lighthouse too."

"Deal!" Passing the visitors' center, Jack saw his truck and Sam's VW. "This has been a good stroll, and my feet are happy."

"I was going to ask. I figure we did about three miles—not quite a hike status, but more than a reasonable test for new boots. Your feet should know if they like the boots."

"Both feet agree; the boots are keepers."

"I like what I found today too," Sam added with a warm smile.

"Sam, would you like to get together for coffee sometime this week?"

"Honestly, I am so busy between work and the kids that I don't have time for myself. If I can, I'll text you. I really liked today and look forward to next time."

"Then let's plan on that hike. Rain or shine?"

"Unless it's hard rain."

"We'll play it by ear. Outside of work, my schedule is loose. It may be easier for me to match your schedule."

"What's your number, and I'll text you when my schedule firms up," Sam said as he took out his cell phone.

After exchanging numbers, Jack dropped his truck gate and sat on it. The boots unlaced themselves and slipped right off. Closing his eyes, he massaged his toes. Blocking out the world around him, Jack seized the moment to pray. *Heavenly Father, thank You for today. Thank You for my new friend and brother. Thank You that we could talk about You. Thank You for loving me so much. Please take care of Sam; he sounds genuine. You know his heart. If it's Your will that he and I go hiking again, let it happen. When we are hiking, give me the wisdom of what to say and when to say it.*

Slipping on his Chuckies, Jack watched Sam's VW pull out. Sam turned to Jack and waved with a warm smile. Jack returned the wave. *God bless and keep you my brother. See you next time.*

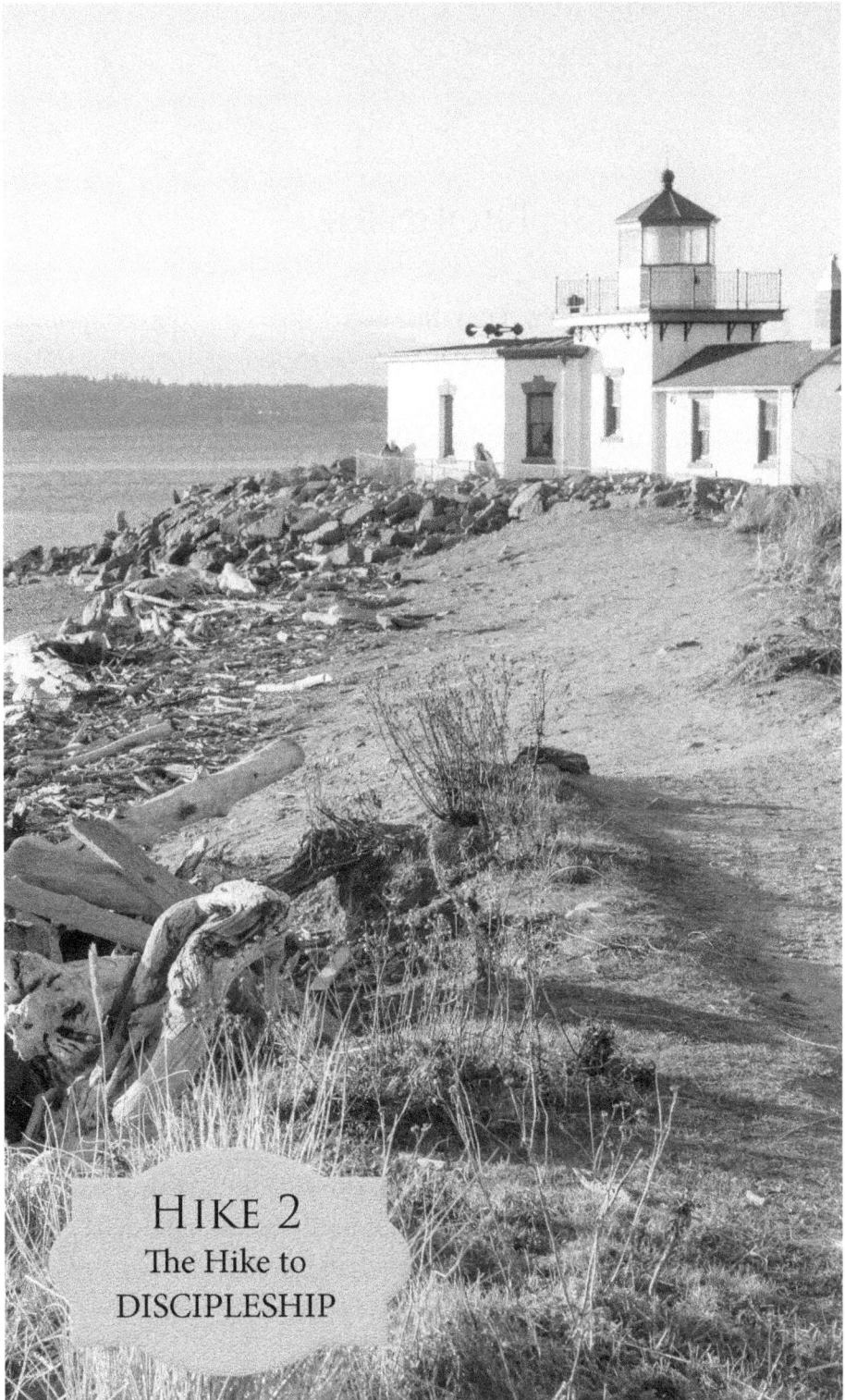

HIKE 2
The Hike to
DISCIPLESHIP

PROLOGUE

DONE CORRECTLY, LEAVING home to work on assignment could be considered a working vacation with long days full of work and touristing on the off days. On previous assignments, Marie had joined him, and the two had enjoyed exploring new places. This time, she had decided not to join him as her declining elderly parents needed her more than she needed to be spending her weekdays hanging out in a minimalist apartment in a strange city, all the while fretting over their care.

When on assignment, Jack's daily routine was a long day of work with nightly video chats. Working ten- to twelve-hour days could seem like trudging through a valley of deep snow. Since, there was no work available near home, this was their compromise. Every day, Jack missed Marie. Their private time consisted of video chats of an hour or more that were the hilltops and highlight of each day. The chats were not the same as being together in person but enough to stay close as they touched each other's hearts. Their monthly routine was built around a weekend rendezvous. The roundtrip home was the highlight of the month. The cycle repeated itself over and over again through the course of an assignment.

The current client had work that needed to be done and was willing to pay a fair wage to get it done. The simple guideline was that the base rate had to be enough to pay all the bills, afford lodging, living expenses and regular travel home. Overtime could only be thought of as gravy. If overtime was required to break even, then the contract was a risk. At the end of the assignment, something had to be left over to show for the time spent apart—at least enough to be a cushion until the next assignment came along.

The next weekend's flights were already booked. This Saturday would be the light at the end of this week's tunnel. Jack looked forward to this day to disengage, get out into nature and refresh. The past two weekends had been rainy but not enough to hinder some local short hiking—perfect for breaking in the new boots. With or without Sam, rain or shine, Jack had planned on a longer hike before the rendezvous weekend.

Since the Arboretum hike, Jack thought daily of Sam and how he was doing with his spiritual awakening. *Did he follow up with You, Lord?* Midway through the first week, Jack texted him. When he received no response, he wondered if he had the right number. That week the client had deadlines to meet, which made his workdays longer than usual. Coordinating a time to meet after work would have been a challenge. The second week, Jack's thoughts turned to wondering if he would ever hear back from Sam. *Okay, God, it's in Your hands. I like Sam, and it would be nice to hear how he's doing.* Sam passed through Jack's daily prayers. He had no doubt that when they had talked and prayed together that something had connected with Sam.

The gospel is so much like seed. The apostle Paul put it best when he said that he had planted the seed. Apollos, an early church elder, watered that seed, but God was the One who made the seed grow.[201] Jesus had said that the seed is one thing, but the ground it lands on or in, is another thing altogether. Some ground is fertile, but some ground is rocky or infertile. Sometimes the seed flourishes; sometimes it dies for lack of water or sprouts to be choked by weeds.[202] Jack had shared the gospel with people in times past and had seen them come to Christ and experience being born again. He had also seen people fall away when they later caved to disbelief or sinful desires. *I don't want to see that happen to Sam!* Like a new baby, new believers are so vulnerable. When Jack thought of Sam, he found himself praying. *God, I believe that the seed of Your Word was planted in fertile soil within Sam's heart. I pray that it will be watered by You either directly or indirectly, and I pray that Your will be done, growing a thriving new life in You.*

It was almost the end of the third week since their arboretum hike. Thursday had been another twelve-hour workday. One step at a time, one step after another, Jack climbed up to his flat. Halfway up the flight of stairs, he heard a *ping*. Once on the landing for his apartment, he pulled out his phone to see the same number Jack earlier used to text Sam. The text read: "2 p.m. Saturday, south lot, Discovery Park." Before opening the door to enter his flat, Jack quickly checked his weather app: 65° and clear skies. "See you there," Jack texted in reply. He slipped the phone back into his pocket, inserted his key into the lock and paused to look up at the evening sky.

Thanks, God. Please bless our time together. Thanks too for giving us good hiking weather.

~

Pulling into the south lot, Jack saw Sam sitting in the open side door of his VW Microbus. Sam was midway through the process of swapping street shoes for hiking boots. Conveniently, one of the only available parking spots was right next to Sam's microbus. Jack saw the opening, swung the truck around and aligned it to back up into the open spot. With one boot on and the other foot wearing only a sock, Sam theatrically grabbed the second boot, and as obviously and comically as he could, he lifted both legs way up. Jack laughed when he saw Sam's antics in his back-up camera. He rolled down his truck window and in a loud clear voice called to Sam, "I haven't flattened anyone's feet," and after a dramatic pause, he added, "...yet!"

"I'm not taking any chances," Sam replied. "I came to hike—not waddle."

"Me too." Jack proceeded to nest his truck perfectly in the parking spot.

After taking a drink of his coffee, Jack rolled up the window. Looking into his side mirror, he saw that Sam had set his feet back down and was putting on the other boot. *Looks like he's in good spirits.* Jack shut down and exited the cab. Stepping over to Sam's open door, he extended his hand. "Glad to see you again. Looks like we've got a good day for a stroll."

"Yes, we do." Sam stood up, extending his right hand to meet Jack's. "I'm glad we could get out again." Sam turned to the open side entrance and grabbed his laces. Lifting his leg, with a single thud, he snugged his heel in the boot. He paused to gauge the fit, then pulled to tighten the laces and began to thread the hooked eyelets. "This is as good as spring weather gets around here."

"I would say about perfect." Jack stepped around the side of the truck and dropped the gate. Sitting on the tailgate and letting his feet hang always made him feel like a kid—a frame of mind that always went well with an afternoon outdoors. Sitting on the tailgate, he began unlacing his Chuckies.

Another thud told Jack that Sam had nested his other heel in the second boot. From his perch, Jack heard Sam call out to him. "What was the final verdict on those new boots?"

"They're keepers. When we did the arboretum, I had happy feet that evening and the next day. The last couple of weekends, I did some short hikes. No complaints."

"Where did you go?

"Spencer Island and Saint Edward. It rained on and off the whole time, so I did just enough to stretch my legs and confirm the boots."

"I'm glad the boots are working out for you. Today's hike will be longer. The full loop is three miles with an added bonus loop that would take up to the beaches and lighthouse," Sam said as he stood up and did some torso twists and side stretches. Walking around to the front of his VW, he leaned to balance himself against the "A-pillar" just above the headlamp. Then he proceeded through a series of calf and thigh stretches.

Jack jumped off the tailgate and grabbed the ends of his laces. He raised his extended leg above the tailgate and dropped the boot to nest his heel. Pulling to tighten the laces, he turned to see Sam stretching. "Thanks for the reminder."

"No problem. Today will probably be longer than your last two weekends."

"I'm hoping so," Jack said as he double knotted the boot.

Having changed into his boots, Jack went through a series of stretches using the truck's bed to launch from. Sam grabbed his pack and locked up his VW. "I'm glad to see that you are doing your stretches before we hike," Sam teased Jack.

"Someone recently reminded me that I'd last longer if I did," Jack casually replied, as he lifted and closed the tailgate. Stepping around to the driver's side door, he looked in the windows to assure there was nothing to entice a smash and grabber. Opening the door, he threw his Chuckies on the driver's side floor and picked up his coffee. Turning to Sam, he saluted with his coffee cup; Sam returned his smile and nodded. Jack tilted the cup to his mouth and drained it. Returning the empty cup to the cupholder in the console, he reached over to the passenger seat, grabbed his pack, pulled it out, stood and closed the door.

"We can pick up the loop at that sign," Sam pointed to a group of people standing in front of a signboard near the southwest corner of the parking lot.

Walking down the sidewalk toward the sign, Jack turned and gave a click to lock the doors.

"I've got to get one of those clickers," Sam commented when he saw the truck's lights flash.

"Like the back-up camera, I didn't know how handy they were until I got a vehicle that had them."

At the signboard, Jack stopped where the other people had stood. With his phone, he took a picture of the trail map that was mounted behind a sheet of plexiglass. "Nothing like having a map in your pocket."

"I saw you snap that 'instant map' at the Arboretum. I may copy that idea when I do unfamiliar hikes."

"Invention is the mother of necessity." Jack smiled and slipped the phone into the side pocket of his pack.

"On your right," Sam stated in a very clear voice, and Jack glanced to his right to see a skateboarder rapidly emerging from around a bend in the paved walkway.

They both took a step closer to the signboard as a skateboarder blew past them. "I wasn't expecting that. How much of this is paved?"

"There are plenty of hidden and forgotten streets that I'm certain the boarders know all about. Other than this stretch, they are not part of the loop trail. Fort Lawton was originally built around 1900 to hold big guns for protecting Seattle's harbor and the entry to Lower Puget Sound. In World War II, over a million soldiers passed through here on their way to fight in the Pacific. It was also a major traffic point during the Korean and Vietnam wars. In the 1970s the land was given to the city of Seattle to be a park. Most of the buildings were removed but plenty of vintage sidewalks and streets still remain." Sam pointed up the paved path. "Just over that rise, this path meets the road you would have been on had you not turned right inside the gate. Past the road, the trails are all too rustic for the boarders."

True to Sam's prediction, a hundred yards up the paved path, the woods abruptly stopped where the path met a curb. Across the street spread a large flat field. Looking up the street, Jack saw the road bend and wrap to define the perimeter of the parade ground. Past the parade ground, the road continued up the slope and led to a group of important-looking, old style yellow-and-white clapboard buildings. On the other side of the street, the land dropped to acres of level land dressed in tall grass. Before them, two divergent trails cut across the field toward either end of the distant bluff, both heading into a beautiful vista of Puget Sound and the Olympics.

Sam took the lead and chose the trail that led toward the southern end of the bluff. Crossing the field, the waist-high grasses danced to the soft breeze blowing in from the Sound. The waving grass reminded Jack of kayaking on the Chesapeake. One deep breath after another, Jack waded through the waves and kept his focus on the snow-capped peaks above the Sound. Sam was relaxed and happy to have the afternoon to do what he wanted to do—hike and talk more about this God stuff.

Exhaling one long deep breath after another, Jack felt the week's tension losing its grip on him. He felt his senses awaken. Vistas were a favorite eye candy. "It's so clear today, I think I can see for a hundred miles."

"Maybe not that far, but we can clearly see all the crisp snowy peaks of the Olympics. I always think the Cascades and Olympics look their best when they are dressed in white and set against a deep blue sky." Sam passionately loved the mountains surrounding his hometown.

"I'm glad we're out hiking again. We've been blessed with perfect weather twice."

"Don't tell anyone. Us locals want everyone elsewhere to think it's always rainy and miserable here." Sam laughed.

Sam continued, "For me, I need this stuff. Between work and every allowable minute with the girls, I sometimes feel like I'm drowning."

The Sabbath Was Made for Us

"Our bodies and our minds need to take a break, periodically disengage and do something different. It's just healthy for us. When God made the world, He did so in six days. Then He took the seventh day off to rest.[203] He wants us to follow His lead."

"Disengage, yeah. That's why I'm here." Sam nodded as he replied.

"Me too. God made us and knows we'll burnout without chill time. One of the best sermons I ever heard was about personally practicing a 'Sabbath rest.' The preacher said whatever we do for a living, we should do something different for a day or two a week to mentally and physically disengage. The person who does physical labor for a living should disengage by not doing physical labor on the seventh. If you do intellectual labor for a living, then do something physical on the seventh and so on. Our bodies were designed to 'mix it up.' We need that down time to recoup. God gave us a pattern:[203] work six days and then disengage by doing something completely different on the seventh. His example to us was resting."

"Creating everything must have been hard work," Sam replied. "I get paid to spend my workdays in a cubicle, mostly staring at a screen. Being out on days like this is like a reset for me. When I work straight through a weekend, I always feel spent the following week, and my body screams for me to do something different," Sam said as he drew in the cool breeze.

"It's just how we were made. We have to disengage to renew and refresh ourselves."

"Well, I've been working every day since our hike in the Arboretum. I briefly saw the girls last weekend, but they ended up spending most of the weekend with my parents. Getting out today and doing this has been the light at the end of my tunnel," Sam added with a laugh.

Oh, boy! This guy really is that busy, Jack thought to himself. "Then I'm extra glad we got out today."

"Me too. By the way, I saw that you had texted. I'm sorry that I didn't respond sooner. My days have been overflowing into my evenings. My free time evaporated, so I didn't want to commit to anything. For hiking, I wanted to wait until I felt confident that the weather would be acceptable. You seem pretty hot to hike, so I felt confident that we would be out on the trail again. Besides, I liked our last hike and was looking forward to more."

Jack replied, "We're good. I'm glad we both got out today. When I didn't hear back, I figured that you were busy. I remember when I went through my divorce that work was my escape. The work I do can be mentally consuming. I used it to get my mind off of stuff and focused onto something other than what I was going through. Work became my distraction for survival."

"Yeah, I can understand that. It's too easy to lose the healthy balance between work and living. Practicing a personal 'Sabbath rest' sounds like a healthy prescription for balance."

"Jesus said the Sabbath rest was made for us.[204] It just makes us healthier, feel better and be fresher when returning to the rest of the week."

"I like Jesus' thinking," Sam commented.

"Me too," Jack replied. "I had three kids of my own. After the divorce, I had to do the kid visitation dance. The court intentionally made everybody's roles difficult." Jack paused and laughed to himself. "I'm not sure if the worst part was dancing around irregular schedules for demanding projects or dancing around the rigidity of my legalistic ex-wife. It took a while for me, but eventually the Sabbath-rest principle sunk in. Now I feel better balanced. On your earlier note, you are right, I am that hot to hike. This is my spring training."

"Ambitious plans for the season?" Sam had thought that it would be nice to have a hiking buddy. Weekend without the girls became too easy to think about how things should have been. *Yeah, I would prefer to be hiking than hanging out around home mulling.*

"I lived here in my 20s and 30s, I want to redo some of the hikes I did back then. My season-end goal is Mt. Rainier's Skyline Loop for the autumn leaves."

"Fall foliage on the mountain and looking out over the valleys?"

"That's my intent," Jack replied.

"Sounds like you are planning one Kodak moment after another."

At the southern bluff, their trail merged with the loop trail which arced around the southern perimeter of the parade grounds. To Jack's surprise, the loop trail near the bluff was sandy. The sand was as dry and loose as any sandy beach beyond the water's edge. "We must be a hundred yards above the beach below. I forgot these bluffs were made of compressed sand."

Sam replied, "From below, the bluffs look like stone, but they are only compacted sand. Compacted sand can fool people into thinking it is rock. Foolish builders may even think it's solid enough to build on. Then a powerful storm or a series of storms blowing through can compromise the foundation."

Jack responded, "Jesus said something like that, and he quoted:

Everyone who hears my words and puts them into practice is like a wise man who built his house on the rock. When the rain comes and the streams rise and the winds blew and beat against that house, it does not fall, because its foundation is on the rock. But everyone who hears my words and does not put them into practice is like a foolish man who built his house on sand. Then when rain came down, the streams rose, and the winds blew and beat against that house, and it fell with a great crash." [205]

"So that's where that principle came from!" Sam was surprised to find one biblical precept after another steeped with practical common sense.

"Jesus had a very practical perspective. He was a carpenter.[206] In today's language, we would probably call Him a builder or a craftsman or maybe even an engineer. He understood how things were physically made and from what they were constructed."

A few steps up along the loop trail from the point where the trails joined stood a large leafy tree perched on the edge of the bluff, stubbornly clinging to a patch of grass. Stepping over to stand under the tree, Jack took out his phone, turned to Sam and smiled. "It's Kodak-moment time."

The vista was a majestic view of Puget Sound and the entire Olympic Range from the Strait of Juan de Fuca to the low rolling hills south of the mountains. Beyond the sandy edge, the treetops made a green carpet leading to the blue water. The scene layered from green to blue to the dark distant shore topped with jagged white peaks and blue again. Looking like children's toys in a big bathtub, large container ships and pleasure boats lay scattered before them on the blue Sound. The water below them was calm enough to show wakes from the faster moving boats.

Sam stood with Jack looking out over the water. "Yeah, this is today's Kodak moment."

"Sure is," Jack agreed, snapping photos with his phone. "By the way, did you know that this is the most popular camera in the world?"

Sam pulled out his phone to join the picture taking and save a memory of the day. "I'd believe it, but it's not like we have much choice." Together they both laughed at the obvious.

Jack had fun framing pictures and making a video of the full panorama. "I like to send my wife pics and let her know where I am and what I'm seeing."

"You haven't said much about her."

"I miss her very much. I'll be going home to see her next weekend."

"She's not with you?"

"She's back home caring for her parents. They were diagnosed with Alzheimer's and now reside in memory care at a facility near our home. When things began to decline, they came to her. I guess by instinct. She has been watching over them since. Even though their care has exceeded her skillset, she continues to make it her mission to assure they are well cared for.[72] We've noticed that the caregivers seem to be a little extra attentive when they see that their wards have family members who make the effort to visit."

Sam looked at the ground. "My grandmother passed of Alzheimer's couple of years ago. She went from repeating herself to forgetting how to walk and eventually forgetting how to breathe. It's a sickness that seems to be the hard on the caregivers."

"Mercifully for the person with the Alzheimer's, they are relatively oblivious. Their decline is just tough on everyone else," Jack added.

"Yeah, it was."

"Do you remember the Ten Commandments we discussed the last time?" Jack asked.

"Wasn't one of them to honor your parents?"[72] Sam asked.

"My wife is living that commandment."

"It sounds like your wife is a good woman."

Jack smiled. "She is the best woman I've ever known. It's a good life when we are together. She loves nature and hiking, which is a pleasure we share. Since she's not here, I take lots of photos so we can share. I always wish I were with her doing stuff together. Sharing videos is a way we share. Then just about every evening we video chat. So, we're not too far apart." Jack slipped his phone back into his pack.

"Probably closer than a lot of couples that live under the same roof..." Sam noted, remembering how he and his wife had drifted apart.

"Alas, the work is happening here and not there. Whatever, it's income, and that's the grease that keeps the wheels turning and pays the bills." Jack tried to make light of his situation.

They left the tree and began walking south along the sandy trail. At first, they walked in silence. Jack thought of his wife, and Sam thought about his grandmother's last days, remembering how he had hovered over her even though she did not recognize him. A caregiver had once told him that his grandmother had asked about him, calling him "that nice young man."

Sam finally broke the silence. "On the last hike, we talked about God's Ten Commandments, but, as I remember, we only talked about some of them."

"Yes, they fall into two groups: the ones that pertain to our relationship with other people and the ones that pertain to our relationship with God. Honoring your parents[72] is actually the first of the people ones."

"Jack, let's see if I remember the people ones: honor your parents, don't kill, lie or steal. Don't cheat on your spouse and don't even think of pining for your neighbor's wife or stuff. They were too common sense to forget. During the week, I found them returning to me. It dawned on me that they were the building blocks of a civilized society."

Sam continued, "Preserving family is as core to civilized society as it gets. Our parents took care of us then we take care of them. Spouses watch out for each other and together raise the next generation. The individual lusting for other people's belongings just leads to dishonesty, theft and killing.[77]

Jack followed his line of thinking. On a micro scale, wanting other people's belongings leads to resentment and decay, rotting our very substance.[207, 208] On the macro scale, wanting other people's possessions leads to war.[209] God wants us to edify each other, live in peace [210] and be thankful."

"It doesn't take much effort to see that God's guidelines for interpersonal relationships are good for all people, and violations naturally lead to bad stuff."

"That's without even considering the sin factor," Jack replied.

THE TEN COMMANDMENTS:
FOUR ARE BETWEEN US AND GOD

"WHAT ABOUT THE God commandments?" Sam asked. "I'm glad you asked. All of the commandments are equally as important. Jesus even condenses them to two that cover all the original ten and more."

"Okay then, what are the other God commandments?" Sam asked again, kicking aside a stick as they waded through the soft sand along the top of the bluff.

"The God commandments are actually the first four of the ten commandments. God sees our relationship with Him to be our most important relationship. The first commandment is that we should not follow any other gods other than the one true God."[212]

"It sounds like God does not like to share the spotlight?"

"God is exclusive.[213] He is only one true God, no other.[214] Satan just wants to deceive and distract us."[6] Jack gathered his thoughts. "There is only one true God.[215] He is omnipotent, all-powerful, the Creator of life, the universe and everything. The only path to God is through His Son, Jesus.[4, 216] Using deceit, many other gods try their hardest to be usurpers of the one true God." [217]

"One God and many other gods? Jack, can you clarify what you mean for me?"

"To avoid confusion, let's start by identifying the one true God with a big 'G' and all other gods with little 'g's. The last time we hiked, we talked about big 'G'—the one true God."

"Yeah, the big 'G'—Creator of life, the universe and everything. While we are out, I want us to talk more about God—the big 'G' God."

"Okay, let's." Jack was glad to hear confirmation of Sam's continued interest in God.

"By the way, I didn't get a Bible, but I did listen to the book of John on audio through my phone."

"When I heard how busy you had been, I wasn't sure if I should ask. I'm glad you are taking a step in the right direction."

"Oh, don't worry. I want to follow up. After listening, I can see why I would want my own hard copy," Sam replied.

"The more you read, the more you will want to make notes and highlight passages. A hard copy is better for that than a digital copy."

"Yeah, your notes are still there when the power goes out," Sam snickered.

"Or the Internet is down." Jack joined Sam's snicker.

"Tech is convenient, but not the be-all and end-all. You're not selling me on anything new. The printed copy is just better for some things. Besides, I like to hold a book in my hands when I read."

Jack said, "Okay, back to the small 'g' gods. In Hebrew, a *god* is defined as 'a ruler, a judge or a divine one.' [218] Someone or something that you have allowed to have power over you or has usurped power over you is a *god*.

"Going through my divorce, I felt like a victim. Without regard to evidence and arguments, the judges made judgments as if they were following some scripted agenda. Every ruling disregarded evidence or reality. They sounded as if they had all came out of a political correctness playbook. I learned that law and justice are completely unique concepts. One judge even said my problem was that I was a big guy and that because I was a big guy, I must have done something wrong. He followed that judgment by pronouncing a wrongful verdict and an unjust sentence. After the hearing, when the judge stepped up from the bench to exit the courtroom, I saw that he could not have been more than five feet tall. I felt like I was being made to pay for his poor self-image. At my lowest point, I went to see a therapist. The courts made a series of insanely crippling unjust rulings that made me feel absolutely helpless and abused. The therapist I spoke with said something to me that helped my perspective. *'There are things you can control and things that you cannot control. However, you are always in control of how you respond to the things that happen to you.'* Those words did not help me with the bad rulings, but they did help me rein in the insanity of the injustice."

Jack felt Sam's pain. "It's always difficult having to deal with people who think they are better than others, especially if they have some real power and an agenda. Abuse is abuse however you look at it. Your therapist was wise with her practical words for coping. You could say that those judges you faced were acting like gods."

"More like the fickle gods from Mount Olympus who thought humans were their playthings—tools for their purposes." Sam shook his head in that not-knowing-whether-to-laugh-or-cry kind of way.

"In ancient times, people who had not heard of the one true God, worshipped a variety of gods. People who do not know the one true God or do not want to know God fall prey to Satan's lies.[219] Today, Hinduism is the last major religion based on a pantheistic spectrum of gods."

"I can see a parallel between the Hindu animal deities and the Greek and Roman gods." Sam interjected.

"The pantheistic religions are all more similar than dissimilar. Often the same gods are identified by different names. However, there is only one true God,[214] and He is a jealous God.[220] He will not bear any rival.[212] He orders us not to make any images in the form of anything with the purpose of worshiping it. He promises to punish those who do for generations. On the other hand, He promises to reward the people who do keep His commandments for generations.[221]

Sam commented, "I remember reading about a former President who bragged about keeping an idol of the Hindu monkey god in his pocket. When he was left office, the country was in chaos and more divided than when he had assumed office. The President who followed him did the opposite. He had all kinds of pagan idols purged from the White House."

"National leaders speak for their nations, and their nations are either blessed or cursed by their actions. The Old Testament contains plenty of stories of both good and bad rulers. Some followed the one true God, and others followed false gods complete with idols and such. A barometer of the spiritual state of a people is that God gives the people the rulers they deserve."[222]

"Well, I don't have any idols in my home."

"Religious idols are easy to identify. Other things can become idols to people. What you love is where your thoughts want to gravitate. Allowing your thoughts to gravitate there and dwell there excessively can lead to worship. What you worship becomes your god."

"I love to hike. For me, hiking is more of an escape and part of my identity."

"Would you be crushed if you could not hike?" Jack asked.

"I'd be very sad, but I'd survive."

"Then it's probably not an idol to you."

Sam remembered a former co-worker. "I worked with a nice guy who had a particular 1960s muscle car that he loved. I think he loved that car more than anything or anybody else in his life. I heard more obscure details about that car than I did of every other part of his life combined. During the two years we worked together I do not know if I ever even heard his kids' names enough times to be able to repeat them. But I can still give stats on the car's block size and transmission. When it had 'old-car problems,' he would go into a severe funk. His real world went on hold until his Cougar was running again. He had other cars he used for commuting, but his reality revolved around that muscle car."

"From what you're describing," Jack said, "it sounds like the Cougar may have become an idol to him. I grew up with a guy who was that way with a Corvette he owned before he married. A few kids later, his wife forced him to sell the Corvette, and he went into a terminal funk. It wasn't long before she lost him. We all knew he loved her, but he loved the Corvette more."

"I love my VW, but if I lost it, I'd be sad for the loss. Then I would just get another vehicle. The microbus would just get filed away as a nifty memory, and I'd move on to the next neat vehicle. Things are things; that's that. I'd classify those guys' relationships with their cars as over-valuing their cars."

"Overvaluing things or even overvaluing people can lead to making idols of them," Jack replied.

With the approaching tree line, the vista dwindled to gone. The loose sandy trail firmed to dusty sandstone as they entered the tree line.

"Sam, think of God as insisting on a monogamous relationship with us. He refuses to share our worship with any usurper, and He does not want us to have reminders of other gods to distract us."[221]

"That's primary relationship stuff. My ex-wife was very socially ac-tive, but when it came to our marital relationship, I always felt that we both circled our wagons. I insisted on monogamy and honored her by being monogamous. I even discarded trinkets from other relation-ships…well, everything except that bandanna. I should probably chuck that too…" Sam felt a wave of sadness. "I wish she had felt the same."

"I could not agree more with the parallel. We should be as jealous of our marital relationship as God wants us to be monotheistic and not even have representations of competition." Jack thought, *Sam seems to have good instincts. God must have been working on him longer than he even realizes.*

Walking under the canopy, they came to a signpost with two ar-rows. One confirmed that they were indeed on the loop trail. The other-directed hikers downward to the West Point Lighthouse.

Sam pointed to the stairs below the sign. "That one will take us to the lighthouse."

"That was the plan; let's do it," Jack replied.

In a few steps, they had descended below the fork in the trail.

"The third commandment is not to misuse God's name. God will not consider anyone innocent who misuses His name."[223]

"I have always felt uncomfortable and sometimes even cringed when I heard someone say 'God' or 'Jesus' within a string of profanity," Sam said. "I know it's so very common to hear, but that's always sounded wrong to me."

Jack asked, "Have you ever heard people use Dali Lama, Mohammed, Confucius or Buddha in a string of profanity?"

"Nope, not the Pope, Mother Theresa or any other major religious figure—just God and Jesus." Sam answered in a flat serious tone. "I never understood why hearing profanity bothered me so much. Hearing the name of God and Jesus used that way felt so wrong."

"It goes to show there is just something about the name of God.[224] It's our path to salvation, and Satan does not want us to understand that vital truth."

"But names are just names, aren't they?"

"How would you feel if people used your name in a string of profanity?" Jack asked.

"I once had a supervisor who did that. I hated it," Sam replied.

"What did you do?"

"I quit—but only after I had brought it up to our manager. The manager said he valued the guy's technical skills enough to tolerate his terrible people skills. Not long after I quit working there, the company was bought by another company, and neither of them found themselves working there. The company made an excellent product that should have dominated the industry, but the company itself no longer even exists. Now that product is an orphan. I don't know if the customers who bought their product can even find aftermarket parts?"

"I would not have put up with that kind of abuse either. God may seem silent, but He does not tolerate the misuse of His name. He wrote that commandment with His own finger."[70]

"I will watch my tongue," Sam commented.

The trail narrowed, and Sam slipped behind Jack. While they walked, Sam prayed quietly under his breath. *God and Jesus, I'm really sorry for when I've said Your name when I've sworn in anger or in a string of profanity. Thanks for letting me know why it felt harsher than other swear words. I'm sorry, really sorry. You've been so good to me. Please forgive me, and I will try not to do it again. Can You help me not to do it again?'*

Jack had not heard Sam's prayer. But in his spirit, he felt prompted to share something he remembered that Jesus had said. "It's always a good idea for us to watch what we say. Jesus said that the things that go into a person's mouth, go into the stomach, then pass through to exit the body. On the other hand, what comes out of a person's mouth speaks of the condition of the heart and is what can defile the person. It's good to be mindful that a soothing tongue is a tree of life, but a perverse tongue crushes the spirit."[226]

"Oh, boy! Ain't that the truth!" Sam was flooded with flashes of memories of horrible things he had said to people over the years. He had often wished he could unsay many of these comments, but once those words had been released, they always seemed to hang there, unable to be unsaid. Like a boiling pot, those words perked to the surface. They held bad memories for what had been said and for the fallout some of his words had precipitated.

The rustic stairs descended downward in a repeating pattern. Steps, where it was too steep and graveled trail where the slope was too gradual for steps.

Since the last set of steps, the graveled trail had settled into a gradual descent. Descending in silence, Jack could tell Sam was thinking hard about something. *I hope he's okay.*

Jack gauged their descent to be about halfway down from the plateau to the shore. Ahead, he could see a trail spur leading to a deck jutting out into the canopy. *What a great place for a treehouse!*

Sam knew the balcony, though rarely stopped there on downhill treks. "Let's take a break. That balcony has benches, and I could use a drink of water."

The deck was made for lounging. The hillside hand railings were benches. Sam and Jack stepped onto the deck, unshouldered their packs and set them both down near the corner where the two bench railings met. Sam sat first and pulled out his water bottle. Jack took out his water and stepped over to the hand railing on the side of the deck with the view. Through the trees, they both looked out at the blue water of the sound.

Sam broke the silence. "I was not expecting that."

"Expecting what?" Jack asked in return.

Sam pulled another deep draw of his water bottle. "What we were just talking about—the power of words. I remembered times of being hurt by someone and verbally retaliating. The words felt so justified and righteous. Looking back, I didn't understand that I could be so cruel. At the time, I did not care because of how badly I was hurting. Now the memories are awful, and I feel ashamed." Sam paused and took another sip. "Looking back is like being a third person observing the exchanges. I saw myself saying things that cut like daggers. The words that came from my pain cut the other person even worse. Some words cut so deeply that the other person was stunned and could not even reply. At the time, I thought of myself as being defensive, acting in a self-preservation protection mode. Now I reel at the deep pain my words caused. I wish I could take back those words. That would be like trying to retrieve confetti spilled in a windstorm. As soon as those words were released, it was already too late to unsay them."

Jack turned to Sam. "That's called Holy-Spirit conviction. Other than feeling conviction, how do you feel about it?"

"I feel like I need to find them, apologize and ask for their forgiveness. I have no idea where to find most of them, and if I did, they would probably never ever want to see or hear from me again." Sam choked up. "I've always chalked it off as collateral damage. I don't think I can do that anymore."

Jack could tell the Holy Spirit was convicting Sam. "You're right. If you feel like you should ask forgiveness, then you should."

"Yeah, but how?" Jack asked. "Unless they find me, I won't be able to find them."

"You have a helper. The Holy Spirit brought this to your mind. He can also help you resolve this."[227]

"How? It seems a lot easier to just bury it and let it be forgotten." Sam felt perplexed.

"How has that tactic worked so far?" Jack asked.

"It's like green peppers on pizza. They taste good the first time. Then for the rest of the day, I belch and taste them over and over and over. It's not long before wishing I'd not had any in the first place."

"Do you know how molten metal is purified?" Jack asked.

"Yeah, I worked the kiln when I took my high school's foundry class. The metal was heated, then a chemical agent called *flux* was added. The flux collects on the surface and draws the impurities to itself. Then the flux with the impurities is scooped off the top of the molten metal. We called that stuff *slag*. We would repeat the process until the surface of the molten metal would reflect like a mirror. Only then was the metal ready to be poured into a mold. Without fluxing, the castings were always trash. When the metal was pure, the castings were as good as the molds they were poured into."

"The Holy Spirit has thrown some flux into your metal. It's your job to scoop off the slag."[228]

"How do I do that?"

"The Holy Spirit is our advocate.[227] The flux you are feeling is His bringing this to your attention so He can help you to clean off the slag. You could say He's decided it's time for you to do some housecleaning."

"How?"

"When you prayed the sinner's prayer, God forgave you of your sins; you became a new creature,[179] and that became your spiritual benchmark. Now the Holy Spirit is letting you know that you are growing and have some cleanup to do."

"Why?" Sam moaned. "I'm forgiven; isn't that enough?"

"Maybe God wants to help you to clear up your conscience.[229] Maybe God is working on that other person, and you asking him for forgiveness will help him on his road to God.[201] Think of this housecleaning as spiritual growing pains."

"Growing pains?" Sam looked at Jack. "Ouch!" he said with his mouth while his eyes asked *how?*

"No pain, no gain. Talk to God about it. Start with forgiving those people for whatever it was that hurt you enough for you to have felt the need to retaliate.[230] God said He will forgive us when we forgive others who have wronged us.[193] Then tell Him how you feel and ask how to make it right."

Sam chewed on the slag.

Jack looked around. *This is going to get real private, real fast.* He was glad nobody else was within earshot.

"There is a time and place for confession. Confess what you did and ask forgiveness for the verbal darts you threw. Tell Him you don't know how to find these people whose forgiveness you are seeking. Ask Him to be their proxy."

"I really don't want to repeat some of the words I have remorse over." Sam felt horrified and ashamed to recall some of the painful words he had once hurled at others.

"Confession and forgiveness is between you and God. There are no intermediaries, priests or whatever. You have a direct line with God. God is omnipotent. He knows your heart." [231, 11]

"Yeah, He does know my heart, doesn't He?" Sam replied.

Jack sat on the bench that connected to the bench where Sam was sitting.

Sam stared out at the water. "I don't know what to say."

"Wanting to do all he could to help his friend, Jack asked, "We can pray together."

"I'd like that. I'm normally good with words, or at least I like to think that I am. Right now, I'm feeling somewhat tongue-tied."

"We'll just follow the prayer pattern: acknowledge who God is, thank Him for what He has done and then make your request. When you've made your petition, follow it by thanking Him for answering your prayer and seal the prayer with Jesus' name."[197]

"Go ahead. Let's do it like we did before. You say, and I'll repeat." Sam trusted Jack to not make the prayer weird.

"I'll keep it general. Later when you talk with God, you can get into the nitty-gritty."

"Thanks," Sam smiled slightly and nodded to let Jack know it was okay to go ahead.

Jack took a deep breath and began. "Dear Heavenly Father, Creator of all things. Thank You for sending Your Son Jesus to be the atonement for my sins. Thank You for raising Him from the dead and bringing Him back to heaven so that Your Holy Spirit could come down and be my comforter and guide. Thank You for revealing to me my sins, so that I can ask forgiveness for them. I ask forgiveness for the sins I have committed against You. I ask forgiveness for the sins I have committed against others. At times I have said vile and hurtful words. I wish I had never said them, and I ask forgiveness for saying them—all of them. I wish to tell the persons individually. But since they are not here and You are, I ask You, God, to stand proxy for those against whom I have sinned. I ask Your forgiveness for what I have said and done. If You want me to speak to them personally, then I ask that You set up a meeting. Then please help me with the words I will need when I speak with them. I also ask that Your Holy Spirit helps me guard my speech so that I can avoid saying hurtful things in the future.[232] Thank You for life, for breath and for Your forgiveness. In Jesus' name, Amen."

At each of Jack's pauses, Sam repeated the prayer. As he did, he felt better. When he said "Amen," he felt as if a load had been lifted from his shoulders.

Jack looked at Sam. "Are you okay?"

"More than okay. I feel lighter. While we were praying, one of the people I have hurt came to my mind. I didn't realize I had blocked her and the related ugliness out of my mind. I know I hurt her, and I know where I can find her. But I also know that she does not want to talk to me, and…uh, I can't blame her."

"If the Holy Spirit truly brought this person to your mind, then she may be open to at least hearing an apology. You may want to pray that the Holy Spirit gives you an opening so she does not think you are coming to give her more."

"I'll pray for that opening, but I find myself interacting with her irregularly. I just buried the ugliest of what had happened and those horrible words we had exchanged. Now I'm tasting green peppers again."

Jack looked at Sam, and Sam could see the question in his eyes.

"When things fell apart, my ex-wife and I fought very hard. I had been blindsided and hurting terribly by what she did. I thought I was justified in saying what I said, but my words were just hurtful and spoken in anger. It's a bitter pill, but I'm going to have to tell her that I am sorry for all that I said. I even thought I'd rather just sweep it under the carpet. I guess real housekeeping cleans both the carpet and cleans out what's hidden beneath it."

"That is does. Sounds to me like God has touched your heart and has given you an assignment."

"I don't think I'll have peace until I do it."

Jack replied. "Then pray for the opening and the awareness not to miss the opportunity when it comes. Smile, the Holy Spirit is doing some housecleaning within you, and you will be better for it."

"I think something happened to me on our Arboretum hike. Three weeks ago, I would never have imagined talking with anyone about any of this stuff. In the past, if there were no immediate negative consequences, then I found justification and denial to be acceptable guilt relievers." Sam said with a childishly guilty look on his face.

Jack looked Sam in the eye. "Denial and justification are the most common tools people use when they don't want to take responsibility for what they've done."

Jack's gaze lightened and with a smile, he added. "I can tell that God has touched you. He will bless you for making things right." The words hung in the air. *Thank You, God, for the work You are doing in Sam's life,* Jack prayed silently.

After the prayer, Jack could sense a return to lightness in Sam's disposition. They sat for a few minutes, enjoying the canopy-shrouded view, sipping their water and sharing a baggie of celery sticks.

A well-to-do looking middle-aged couple came slogging up the trail and stepped onto the balcony. Huffing and puffing, they both appeared to be desperately in need of a rest. Jack nodded at Sam, and they grabbed their packs. As they stood up, the couple looked at them. Jack smiled. "Nice view, eh?" The man smiled with a tired nod, and the woman silently gazed back with a haughty look that said, *Who are you? Why are you talking to us?* Jack and Sam said no more as they exited the deck.

Having exceeded the couple's range of hearing, Sam felt comfortable resuming their discussion. "Now I'm almost afraid to ask, but wasn't there another God-directed commandment?"

"The fourth commandment is to keep the Sabbath holy."[233]

"Weren't we talking about that earlier when we talked about the Sabbath rest?"

"Yes, but that was only the half of it. Physically, we are healthier if we follow the pattern God established at the creation. Work six days and disengage on the seventh. Do something different. Spiritually, our direction is to do the same, but we are also to keep the Sabbath holy."[234]

"Observing a Sabbath sounds practical and healthy. Now you're adding a holy feature?" Jack could hear the question in Sam's tone. "Holy is another of those religious words that I don't quite understand. To me, it just sounds religious and vague."

HOLY

"*Holy* is a rich word which means 'sacred, set apart and dedicated to God.'[235] On the one hand, observing the Sabbath is physically restorative. People and land and mechanical things all need some rest or else they will cease to function properly. Too long of a rest and they could have a challenge resuming their usefulness. On the other hand, the Sabbath is also spiritually healthy. It's a day a week when God wants us to focus on Him, think about who He is and what He has done for us. The fourth commandment dictates that we should have a weekly day set apart and dedicated to Him, and it should be a day of disengagement from our daily routines."

"Go about our daily routine for five or six days, but on the seventh day, disengage and focus on God?" Sam asked.

"Personally, after a week of working in an office, I find it easier to focus on God when I'm out in nature or working in my garden. The disengagement refreshes, and the focusing on God restores."

"People go to church on Sunday; but why not on Saturday? Isn't Saturday the seventh day of the week?"

"Sunday versus the seventh day is a historical matter as well as a calendar problem," Jack replied.

"The sun, moon and seasons are consistent," Sam stated.

"You're right; those are constants, but the calendars have changed over time."

Jack continued, "In ancient times, the most common calendars were based on the lunar cycle. The ancient Hebrew calendar is a lunar calendar. In fact, the moon is so integral to the Hebrew calendar that the same word is used for new moon, month, and first day of the month.[236] This continuity made it easy for anyone who lived anywhere to know what day of the week it was. All they needed was a clear sky so they could determine the current status of the moon. The first day of the month was the new moon. The seventh day was the first quarter. The fourteenth day was the full moon. The twenty-first day was the last quarter and the twenty-eighth day would usually be the next new moon. The pattern was very reliable."

"That would make it easy to determine which day it was. I can see that being useful on a weekly or monthly basis, but that would not work with the seasons, solstices and equinoxes," Sam challenged.

"The Babylonians and Persians were focused on the seasons for growing and solstices for religious high days. They wanted the solstices and equinoxes to be consistent for their long-term planning and record keeping. The Romans developed a variation of the solar calendar which they used for empire business. However, the Romans allowed conquered peoples to continue using whatever system they had prior to their conquest. The original Julian solar calendar had eight days, and each day was assigned a number."

"With different systems, how would anyone know what day it was?"

"That was a problem. Constantine's edict of 321 brought it all together. By decree he forced all of the empire to adopt a revised seven-day Julian solar calendar and enforced it by making Sunday, the first day, the empire's Sabbath. The new week had days that were given names corresponding to Roman and Nordic gods. The Roman elites favored a sun god to whom they dedicated the first day of each week. Constantine's edict decreed that on the sun's days, all government offices and workshops were to be closed for business, and all urban residents were told to rest. For the sake of food production, rural folk were allowed to work on Sundays."[237]

"So…that's why people frown on having to work on Sundays."

"For seventeen hundred years, that has been the Sunday story. The Julian calendar was superseded by the Georgian calendar, which is what we use today. The rest is tradition."

"Sunday is the first day. What about the seventh day being set aside and holy?"[233] Sam asked.

"Tradition. Nearly two millennia of tradition has maintained the sun's day as 'The Lord's Day.' The sun worshipers have faded into history, but the Catholic church followed the emperor's lead. The Protestant churches followed the Catholic church's lead. Along with using pagan god's names for the names of the days of the week, no working on Sundays became a tradition that stuck."

Jack continued, "What matters most is that once a week, there is a day of rest to disengage from our daily routine. God wants us to use that time to focus on Him."

"I can see the physical benefit for burnout prevention in observing a weekly day of rest to recoup. Using that day to think about God stuff doesn't sound like such a bad idea either," Sam commented.

JESUS CONDENSES THE TEN INTO THE TWO GREATEST COMMANDMENTS

"YOU DON'T HAVE to chew very hard on any of the Ten Commandments to see that all of God's commandments have clear and immediate benefits for all of us. Jesus summarized all ten of them when He was asked which was the greatest. His reply drilled them all down to a primary and a secondary: *'You shall love the Lord your God with all your heart, with all your soul, and with all your mind,*'[238] and *'you shall love your neighbor as yourself.'*"[239]

Sam walked along the leveling trail, considering what Jack had just said. "I don't know why people get so bent out of shape over the Ten Commandments. Nothing is burdensome or oppressive[67] about them."

"People who love their sin are almost always in denial of what the sin does to them. A byproduct of sin is that it darkens their hearts.[240] On the other hand, Jesus is light[177] and shines light.[241] Their solution to maintain the darkness is to attack the light,[240] which is God and His commandments. People who love their sin fabricate smokescreens to hide their sin[242] and deny the truth. The truth is that His yoke is easy, and the weight of His burden is light.[243] What people consider burdensome is God's telling us how to best live our lives. He made us, and He knows what is good or not good for us. He wanted to be sure there were no misinterpretations, so He wrote them down with His own finger.[70] The rest of the Bible is God's teaching us how to live and why with lots of illustrations. He made the world. Life just goes better when we play by His rules."

"That's why Jesus came to Earth, lived with us and died for our sins—to fulfill the law,"[59] Sam added.

"Amen," Jack seconded. "Jesus showed us how to live and then became the ultimate atonement for our sins, providing us with the way to get to God."[4]

The trail leveled as it approached the spit of land where the lighthouse stood. Ahead, they could see the forest open where the trail met the road which had descended down the spine of the peninsula from the historical district to the lighthouse at West Point.

Past the road and across the berm, they could see South Beach and headed that way. Crossing the berm, they stepped out onto the beach. To the left the beach continued for a hundred yards before it merged with the foot of the bluff. To the right the beach stopped short of the rocky point where the lighthouse stood. They walked through a field of drift logs scattered on the soft sand before they reached the firmer sand near where the waves lapped the shore.

"The flyer that came with my boots said that they are waterproof," Jack said as he stopped short of the water's edge.

"Mine too. But let's wait to test them fording some freshwater stream up in the mountains as opposed to taking them for a bath in the Sound." Sam laughed.

"Yeah, the first soaking should be with fresh rather than saltwater," Jack agreed.

On the firm narrow strip of semi-wet sand, they walked toward the lighthouse.

Jack continued, "Jesus' summary of the commandments is the core message of the Bible and should be the DNA of believers. It takes us from the old and molds us into new creatures as we learn and grow to know our Creator. Add in some daily sanctifying of our lives by living in repentance.[244] Love God and treat people as you would want them to treat you."[245, 246]

"When I listened to John, I was amazed at the simple directness of Jesus' words. What I heard sounded vaguely familiar, but now it stood out. Some of it even stuck in my head. I got enough that I'm hungry for more."

Jack smiled. "I saturate and bore with most stuff pretty easily, but when it comes to God's Word, I never get bored. I just cannot get enough. I find studying God's Word as limitless as God is omnipotent."[23]

EBIBLES AND HARD COPIES

*T*HIS SEEMS LIKE *a good time to bring up the Bible thing.* Sam took a deep breath and dove in. "While I was shopping for a Bible, I quickly realized that I really do not know where to start. You had recommended that I read the book of John, and I wanted to follow through. I first looked at buying a Bible online but concluded there were too many choices to make a good selection. Then I found Bible apps online. I found audios of different versions of the Bible. I may be a grownup, but it's still nice to be read to. So, I downloaded a Bible app and used it to listen to the book of John. The text was also there so I could follow along."

"I have a couple of Bible apps too. I especially like the search capabilities," Jack interjected. "Faith comes by hearing and instruction through the Word of God.[163] The important thing is spending time in God's Word. Each format has its place. But nothing beats having a physical Bible. Mine has years of notes in the columns, and none of them go away when the power is off."

"I hear you. I keep hard copies of my most important handbooks and manuals." Sam nodded. "We get spoiled with tech, but I still prefer holding a printed book when I read. While I was shopping, I saw so many different Bible versions and different types of Bibles. I thought I'd completely hold off on purchasing anything until we'd talked. Do you have some suggestions?" Sam asked.

"You're right about the number of different types and versions. I should have steered you to one when I suggested that you read John's gospel. If you are interested, we could do a little background on Bibles and discuss the versions. But first, if you don't mind me asking, when did you find the time to listen?"

"At night, just as I'm turning in when my head settles on my pillow and the lights go out for the night. I'll hit the play button and listen as I drift off to sleep. Then too, I often turned the lights back on to recheck the text of what I had just heard. The next night, I would pick up at the last part I could remember. On the notepad I keep by my bed, I made a few notes for looking up later." Sam snickered. "After a few nights like that, I bought a small map light."

Jack nodded. "The very end of the day is a therapeutic time to listen to God's Word. The last input our brains get before we fall asleep steers our nighttime thoughts and even affects the quality of our sleep. Listening to God's Word is the best input your brain can get. Think of it like a spiritual brain balm."

"I was braced to be reprimanded for using John to read me to sleep." Sam didn't hide his surprise at Jack's response.

"Not at all. I've discovered that when I wake and cannot fall back asleep, memorizing Bible verses by rote always puts me in a sound sleep. In the morning, I wake up refreshed and almost always remember the verse or passage on which I was ruminating as I fell asleep. The first Psalm says the person who meditates on God's Word will be blessed."[247]

"I'll have to remember that." Sam made a mental note of this new technique for subduing his insomnia.

"God tells us to listen to His Words and pay attention to what they say because they are life to those who find them and health to their whole body."[248]

"There you go again with the practical stuff," Sam commented. "The nights when I listened to John have given me some of the best sleep I've had in ages. For months, my sleep has been restless. I commonly wake up in the middle of night, and in the morning my body tells me it has not gotten the rest it demands. Each night that I listened to John as I fell asleep, I slept peacefully through the night and woke fresh for the next day."

"I would not directly suggest God's Word as a sleep aid, but it doesn't hurt if you remember what you heard." Jack paused and chuckled. "That's doing better than most people do when they are fully awake."

THE POWER OF DREAMS

"OH, THERE'S MORE. Some mornings when I've awakened, I remember my dreams or specific parts of my dreams."

"God has said He will speak to people through dreams,[249] giving them guidance and at times warnings.[250] Scattered through the Bible are instances where God spoke to people through dreams. God used dreams to speak to the biblical patriarchs Jacob[251] and Joseph.[252] God also used dreams to speak to King Solomon,[253] who was the wisest man who ever lived.[254] God gave Paul [255, 256] instruction through dreams.[257] God told Joseph in a dream that Jesus had been conceived by the Holy Spirit.[258] After Jesus was born, God warned Joseph in a dream to take his family and leave Palestine for Egypt.[259] They were gone before Herod decided to have every male infant in Palestine slaughtered. Joseph's obedience to God's warning saved the life of baby Jesus."

"You're going to tell me that dreams are not just a nighttime diversion or problem solving?"

"Dreams can be that too, but they can be more. There is a substance test for dreams. If a dream sticks in your memory after you wake up, then there may be something to it."[257]

"I've had some dreams that recur or just stick like glue to my memory. Most of them I cannot recall."

"The ones you remember, Sam, are the ones I'm talking about. I keep a pad on my night table and write down what I remember. Then I will ask God if He wants me to glean something from what I remembered."

"I also keep a pad by my bed because I sometimes wake up with thoughts about work or personal stuff. When I do creative work from home, sometimes my best solutions come to me when my mind is morning fresh. You know that time—right before the head gets cluttered with whatever I'm doing that day."

"Our brains never really go completely to sleep," Jack replied.

"I know what you mean. I can't say how many times after watching some late-night movie, I'll wake up having had dreams of war or aliens or even dreaming that I was a character in that movie or dreamed up my own sequel." He chuckled at the thought.

"That's why it's wise for us to be mindful of what our brains consume before we turn in for the night."

"I never made much of a connection between what I dreamed and what my eyes ingested before going to sleep," Sam commented. "I'll be thinking of that in the future."

South Beach narrowed to merge with the jetty beyond the lighthouse. Sam stopped at the first big rock of the jetty and surveyed the rocks. After studying the pile of rocks, he stepped out onto them. Stepping gingerly, he picked his way to the westernmost point. Content with his choice, he gently set down his pack on the rock behind him and took out his water bottle. Standing back up, he turned to where his peripheral vision could only see water to water. "It feels like an island standing out here," he called to Jack.

Jack had watched which rocks Sam chose to step on, followed in his steps, and caught up to him where he stood on the adjacent rock. "Yes, it does. Not many places on the mainland appear like this."

Together they looked out over the water and listened to the lapping of the waves gently drenching the sand and rocks below their feet.

HOW TO SORT THROUGH SO MANY BIBLES

"DO YOU REMEMBER which Bible version you listened to?"

Sam looked out over the water. "I listened to one that sounded like old English. The app always opened to that one. It was the 'king' something... The next one on the menu I listened to was contemporary English. After those, I saw a whole string of alphabet soup."

"It sounds like the app had preset versions ranked by popularity. The most popular Bible in English is the King James or KJV. The next most popular would be the NIV or New International Version."

"Yes, King James, that's it!" Sam snapped his fingers. "When I shopped Bibles online, the KJV and the NIV were the two versions I saw the most. Each one also seemed to have various editions. Some were plain, and some were crammed with special interest commentary. I also saw some other random versions."

"The New Testament was originally written in Greek. The Old Testament was originally written in Hebrew, except for a few passages that were written in Aramaic. In the third century before Christ, the Old Testament Scriptures were all translated into Greek. That version is known as the Septuagint and became the standard Scriptures for the scattered Jewish communities living outside of Israel. The Septuagint contained the Scriptures used by the early church.[260] In the fourth century AD, the Romans used the Greek Old and combined the scattered elements of the New Testament to compile the first complete Bible. These were translated into Latin and were known as the Vulgate.[261] The

Vulgate remained the Catholic standard for over a millennia. Protestant reformers returned to the pre-Vulgate Greek texts to translate the Bible into their own native tongues. Some translations like the King James Version are as old as the Reformation and were translated into the common language of those times. Other translations like the New International Version were translated directly into modern English. Some versions are translated word for word while others are translated thought by thought or concept by concept. Some are merely simplified paraphrases of other more accurate Bibles."

"That would help to explain the many versions." Sam picked up his pack. With the sun at their backs, they both scrambled off the rock jetty and onto the sands of North Beach. On the northern horizon, far beyond the bay, Mount Baker's white peak reflected a perfect snow white in the afternoon sun.

"Paraphrases may make for a casual read, but inherently paraphrases drift from the original author's intent. They are like the kid's game where one kid whispers a phrase to the kid next to him, and he whispers it to another until the phrase is whispered to every kid in a circle. When the phrase has completed the circuit, usually it is not quite what the first whisperer started by saying. Word-for-word translations from the original text tend to be the most consistent with the author's intent. Some may argue that concept to concept may be best. The scholarly solution is to stay as close as possible to the author's original text."

They walked along the firm sand near the water's edge, staying above the murmuring waves gently lapping the beach.

Sam broke the silence. "When police investigate a crime, they look for hard evidence and eyewitnesses' testimony. They may accept less than firsthand information, but that would not be given the weight of what was said by a person who was actually there. The Bible is old. How do you know the originals are good?"

Jack replied, "A third of the New Testament were letters written by Paul. Three of the gospels, the other letters and the book of Revelation, were written by apostles who themselves had walked with Jesus. The fourth gospel and the book of Acts were written by Luke who personally interviewed eyewitnesses. When the New Testament was compiled, one of the criteria used was that only manuscripts which could be traced to the first century would be considered. By the second century, there was general agreement among the early church fathers with respect to the validity of each of the books we now know as the New Testament."

"What about the Old Testament?" Sam asked.

"The Old Testament was written over a period of a little more than a thousand years. By the time of Jesus, the various books were firmly established and simply known as 'the Scriptures.' The various books were penned by many authors from different walks of life. They told a consistent story that was maintained over time by meticulous scholars. Before the Romans sacked Jerusalem and disbursed the Jews, a group of Jewish scholars buried Scriptures in time capsules we now know as the Dead Sea Scrolls. These scrolls were found in the middle of the twentieth century. They testify to the word-for-word accuracy of the same Scriptures we know today."

"With taking so long to write, wouldn't the content be disorganized or confusing?" Sam asked.

"Considering that it was written by so many different people from different walks of life over such a long period of time testifies to a single source of inspiration.[262] What specifically we know of how the New Testament was vetted, along with contemporary archeological finds, testifies to the Bible's inerrancy. They point to the authority of the Bible."[166]

Sam smiled at a memory that flashed back to him. "Oh, Jack, you're going to love this. I briefly dated an archeologist who proudly gushed when she explained the diligence her team would exercise to assure the accuracy of the historical placement of objects retrieved from a site. She detailed the process to 3-D mark of an item's location and depth. Only objects properly recorded were kept for the official record. Anything questionable would be discarded from the official record but not thrown away. The good objects would go into museums. The sloppy objects would become show and tell in classrooms."

"Where did she dig?" Jack asked.

"Her team dug the old port of Caesarea. She said that sometimes early in the morning after a storm, it was not unusual to see fresh erosion to the sandbank above the beach. Sometimes antiquities would wash right out of the eroded sandbanks. She showed me a chipped first-century oil lamp that had appeared that way. Everyone knew what it was and what period it came from. Since it could not be 3-D mapped, there was no way to document it. Her supervisor said she could have it for her school's show and tell. When she was not digging, she was a teacher at a prestigious school. Like her students, I got to hold the lamp in my hands."

Jack was wide-eyed. "You're leaving me speechless. Caesarea served as the capital of Roman-occupied Judea. The city is mentioned in the Bible. In fact, Cornelius[263] and Philip lived there."[264]

"I also held some Roman coins that may have passed through Cornelius' and Philip's hands."

Incredulous, Jack blurted out, "What?!"

"She had a box of vintage Roman coins. She also kept them for show and tell in her classroom."

"What did they look like?" Jack asked.

"The coins, which were well worn, mostly had faces on one side. I assumed the faces were of Caesars. The other side had images of animals or centurions. When I held them, I felt like I was holding history."

"Sounds to me like you had a brush with real archeology!" Jack could tell the experience had impressed Sam.

"When it comes to the professional archeologists, they check, re-check and are rechecked again by peers. They know their profession, love their work and make sure they have the support to assure their conclusions are reliable. I felt confident that I was holding the real articles and not fakes."

"The more people dig to disprove the Bible, the more they discover proof to support the Bible's accuracy."

Jack looked over at the sandbank above the beach. "Wow!" *I would have loved to have seen and held that lamp and those coins.*

Jack resumed his history lesson. "When the Greeks absorbed lands into their empire, they Hellenized the conquered territories. Later under Roman rule, Greek remained the common language of the people in the eastern Roman Empire. Before the Romans compiled the Bible as we know it, all the components were complete in Greek."

"Then Greek would be the linguistic benchmark?" Sam questioned.

"Those who know Greek can go back and read the very same words that Paul, John and other New Testament authors themselves penned two millennia ago. The Old Testament can be checked against both the Hebrew Scriptures and/or the Greek Old Testament. This is all part of the inerrancy of the Bible. The power of the inerrancy of the Bible is that it is open to checking and crosschecking against the original texts."

"Crosschecking is valid for assuring validity. With the originals intact, a good translation is only one step from the original," Sam added.

Jack commented, "The Bible as we know it today was not compiled[261] until after Constantine decriminalized Christianity.[265] Latin was the language of the Romans, and when the fourth-century Christian church leaders set about standardizing Christianity, they brought all the Bible's content into Latin. That became the Bible known as the Vulgate,[261] which initially had the same structure and books we know today. In later versions, the Roman Catholic Church took it upon themselves to add extra material known as the *apocrypha*. Since the Bible was Latin, only people who knew Latin could read it. Greek scholars could not check the validity of the apocrypha.[32] The Protestant Reformers considered the Latin Bible to be corrupt since they considered the origin of the apocrypha to be dubious. To translate the Bible into their own languages, they only accepted verifiable Scriptures."

Sam stopped and looked at Jack. "Was the basis for Europe's religious wars based on people reading their own Bibles in their own native language?"

"People reading their own Bibles in their own language empowered them to question what they had been taught by Rome." Jack smiled and continued. "The ability of someone to read his own personal copy of the Bible became the driving force for universal literacy. Guttenberg's invention of the printing press precipitated the explosion of the Protestant Reformation. Rome set out to restrain the independent free thinking of the Protestants. That effort became the basis for Europe's religious wars. For over three hundred years, empowering people to read their Bibles drove universal access to education. Prior to Darwin and Marx, the Bible was an integral part of public education."

Sam saw the basics of political science at play. "Knowledge is power. People without knowledge have no choice but to accept whatever they are told, making them easy to control. People empowered to study for themselves become people who can think for themselves. If they can communicate, they become the ones who wave a flag that something is wrong. That's why evil dictators commence killing sprees with eliminating the educated populace."

Jack nodded. "The power elite hate it when people can think for themselves. In the spiritual, Satan knows ignorant people are easy prey. God wants us to think for ourselves[166] so we can seek and find Him for His salvation.[266] The Protestant reformers understood this and wanted everyone else to understand this too. The battle cry of the reformers was *Sola Scriptura*."

"*Scripture alone. That's powerful.*"

"For the new 'language-of-the-people' Bibles, the reformers allowed only content that was directly translated from verified original Greek and Hebrew manuscripts. They discarded the Latin apocrypha along with other traditions that the Catholic Church had merged into Christianity. The reformers were driven to get accurately translated Bibles into the hands of the common people. Their goal was empowering all the people to be able to read God's Word for themselves."

"I know that English-speaking North American colonies was originally populated by refugees from the religious wars in Europe," Sam commented.

"Yes, the earliest colonists were Protestant refugees of the religious wars in Europe. The English-speaking refugees carried Geneva Bibles, the first Bible to be fully translated into English. The Geneva Bible was also known for its running commentary of notes in its columns. King James of England considered the Geneva Bible's notes too revolutionary and commissioned his own translation without those notes. The King James Version soon eclipsed the Geneva Bible, and for the next three centuries became the standard Bible of the English-speaking world.

"In the late twentieth century, a New King James Bible was published with a modern language update to King James's sixteenth century vocabulary and grammar. Another translation, the New International Version or the NIV, was also published about the same time. Both translations are accurate to the Greek and Hebrew Scriptures."

"So, the content of the translations is basically the same—just flavored by the time in which they were written?" Sam asked.

"That's about the most general answer," Jack replied.

"With the earlier translations, how do you navigate the thee(s) and thou(s)?" Sam asked. "The King James sounds a bit Shakespearian."

Jack replied, "They are the same vintage. Both Shakespeare and the first Protestant Bibles came from that same explosive publishing environment that followed Guttenberg's invention of the printing press. In the sixteenth century, to say 'you' and 'yours' was the language of the elite upper class and considered highbrow. Saying 'thy' and 'thine' was how the common people spoke, and the common people were the target audience. Don't get hung up on the 'thee(s)' and 'thou(s).' Just think of them as 'you' and 'yours.' The New International and New King James

Versions are modern translations in today's English. Both are perfectly okay if they seem more comfortable to read."

"Which do you prefer?" Sam asked.

"I like the King James. I feel like it has powerful words, and I feel like the NIV gives a smoother easier read. Honestly, I have both. Sometimes I read the one, and sometimes I read the other. When I compare Scripture, it seems like sometimes the one has more punch and is clearer for meaning, while sometimes the other is." Jack held out his hands in a juggling motion. "Six of one and a half dozen of the other."

"I preferred to listen to the NIV because I found it easier to understand," Sam commented.

Jack followed up. "I found the Geneva on my Bible app and have come to enjoy listening to it. Whichever translation you choose is a matter of personal taste. The bottom line is to stay as close as possible to the source code! The King James and NIV are the most common. Each word is translated directly from the original Greek and Hebrew."

"Stay close to the source code. That's an easy key to remember." Sam nodded.

"Exactly. Then there is the concordance, which is excellent to back-check the Greek and Hebrew words to make sure you understand the author's original intent."

"On my app, I saw a number next to a word and when I clicked the number, it revealed the original word and what it means."

"That's the concordance. They make for great study tools. It's also a good idea to have one in hard copy," Jack suggested.

"Now that I understand a little better, I'll be ordering a new Bible when I get home," Sam stated confidently.

"You'll find yourself underlining and highlighting as you read it. Get a hard-copy concordance to match the version."

"I was thinking about that as I was listening to John and later when I used the app to read the actual words. Powerful stuff!"

"A physical Bible will also be nice to take with to church. Then you can follow the minister when he makes references or reads passages," Jack added.

Gentle waves lapped the shore almost to their steps. To their right, above the sand, tall brush laced with berry vines bordered the other side of their passage. Ahead the beach ended where the brush met the water. Above the tide line, people could be seen emerging from a barely noticeable break in the wall. Sam pointed to where the people were appearing. "Do you see those people walking past that sign? They are probably coming down from the North Bluff."

Once Sam had pointed it out, Jack could see a small sign.

The smiling hikers waved at Jack and Sam as they approached. Sam smiled and commented, "Beautiful day for a hike."

"It sure is," the lead hiker replied, and another hiker added, "Have a good one!"

"You too," Jack chimed in.

Walking toward the opening, the sign confirmed that this trail would lead to the North Bluff. Stepping off the beach, they entered the trail. Past the portal, they found themselves plunged into a narrow passageway lined with green walls speckled with tiny pink and white flowers. "Blackberries?"

"In a few weeks, the blackberries, the salmonberries and the raspberries will be good for trail snacking. Every year in late spring, I do this loop with my girls. This is our spot to stop for a quick treat before heading up the hill."

"Just watch for the thorns," Jack added with a snicker.

"Yeah, the thorns do prevent the berry bushes from being overgrazed." Sam joined Jack's snicker.

The dense berry patch reached to the tree line. Under the canopy, the brush thinned, and the trail began to climb. Deep within the canopy, mostly ferns bordered the path. Puget Sound could be seen through the trees. Jack stopped to enjoy the view, soak up the stillness and have a water break.

After a second sip, the silence was broken by loud boisterous people bounding down the trail. Jack and Sam looked up the hillside at the people coming into view. They were heading down the trail toward them. Jack took a last sip and pocketed his bottle in his pack. Sam first, then Jack stepped to the edge of the ferns, making room for the hikers to pass. With nods and open-palmed waves, all passed single file on the narrow trail.

Halfway up the slope, Sam thought, *Jack has sure been quiet since we started this climb.*

The beach to bluff trail crisscrossed the slope, gradually leading them back up to the loop trail. Jack was feeling good about his heart and not feeling any cardio strain. Where the ground leveled after a rise, Jack stopped to soak up the view and to catch his breath. *Okay, God, I think I can. Help keep me paced so I don't push too hard between breaks.*

"At the next switchback, let's stop. I could use some nuts," Jack said to Sam in a breathy voice.

Another stop? It's too soon for another stop. Sam could sense that Jack was making excuses to rest. "I could use some water," Sam played along.

At the bend of the next switchback, Jack saw a bench. He fixated on the bench. Reaching the bench, he sat down, forgot about the nuts and took out his water bottle. Sam sat down next to Jack and leisurely took out his water bottle. A sense of internal panic rose in Jack. *Were all those stairs to the second-floor apartment enough? Had all the conditioning been enough? This part of the hike is really becoming a test.* Uneasiness gripped him. *We must be halfway to the top by now... Oh, please let us be halfway up.* A fear rose that he may have to admit to his heart attacks and explain his personal cardio rehab plan. *Will confession risk me losing my new hiking buddy? Well, we are in the city if things go sideways.*

"There will be some more benches when we meet back up with the loop trail," Sam mentioned as he sipped his water.

"That would be nice," Jack said through deep breaths.

Sam added, "We can do a snack break when we get to the top."

"Uphill climbs get to me." *I just feel like I'm not getting enough oxygen.* Jack took long deep breaths while he fondled the nitroglycerine container attached to his keychain.

"You seemed okay earlier. Are you feeling all right now?" Sam asked.

"Just a bit winded."

"When your wife was pregnant, did you learn the Lamaze breathing technique?" Sam asked.

"Oh, yes. He-he-he-ho-ho-ho." Jack laughed. "Three equal small breaths in and three equal exhales out, then repeat. We joked about it. During the deliveries, it really helped her to focus and stay calm."

Sam looked at Jack. "The technique is also useful to keep from getting winded when you are hiking. Pace your inhaling and exhaling to match your steps. Use three steps to inhale, and the next three to exhale. A third breath per step. I do in-in-in-out-out-out. It will keep a continuous flow of air through your lungs and help you to avoid hyperventilating."

"I don't think I'm about to start hyperventilating on the trail." Jack gave the stink-eye to Sam who just gave a knowingly warm smile in return.

To buy a couple of extra minutes on the bench, Jack retrieved his baggie of raw almonds. "Almonds?" Jack offered the baggie to Sam.

Sam was looking out through the trees. He accepted the baggie. "Thanks."

Watered up and with almonds in hand, they left the bench. They climbed the rest of the rise without a word and without a break. Instinctively keeping an eye on Jack's movements, Sam walked behind Jack up the narrow trail. He could faintly hear Jack's Lamaze breathing. It sounded normal and held to the beat of his steps.

If it weren't for the trail sign, they would not have noticed that they had once again met the loop trail.

When they reached the North Bluff benches, they dropped their packs and pulled out their water bottles.

"I'd forgotten about the Lamaze breathing technique. That was exactly what I needed," Jack said as he turned to Sam.

"It helps me when I'm pushing really hard—especially on steep climbs. After a few of steps, it was obvious that you knew it. You kept a good rhythm."

"I was there for the birth of all three of my kids. I cut the cord of each of them. At first my mind went there. Then I was able to block that out and keep the cadence. I feel much better than I did at our last stop."

"We did a lot of stops," Sam commented in a questioning tone.

"I should come clean." Jack bowed his head and held his water bottle with both hands while looking down at the ground.

"Heart attack?"

"Not today. I know that feeling and do not want to feel it again."

"What feeling?"

"Five years ago, I had a massive coronary. In the ER, the doctors used a balloon catheter to open a main artery and install a stent to ensure it stayed open. A few months before it happened, I had been getting this tight feeling whenever I exerted myself in any way."

"Are you getting that feeling now?"

"No, not at all. I'm much better now than I was then. But two years ago, I was feeling that same feeling. I went to the ER and came home with two more stents—upstream and downstream in the same artery."

"I followed you up the trail. You paced like a champ—not the fastest, but once you got your cadence, you kept it. The way you kept the cadence, I would not have thought the climb was any challenge to you," Sam commented.

Jack said, "Thanks. When I came out here to work my current assignment, I knew it was time to work on my stamina. I started by renting a second-floor apartment. At first the stairs were murder. When they became easy, I took to taking long walks that led me back to trail hiking. After months, I feel like my plan was paying off."

"If you didn't feel any strain and your biggest issue was getting winded, then it sounds like you are not any worse off than if you are just a regular guy who is out of shape."

"Angina is one thing and the way you feel in response to a workout is another," Jack replied.

"For what it's worth, I am a HAM operator. I don't ever go hiking without my fully charged handheld radio." Sam pulled his compact handheld radio from the main pocket of his backpack. "A few years ago, when I hiked with a club, we all got our licenses. We would go out for days and camp together. When we returned to the trail, we would often find ourselves stringing out beyond earshot. The radio was great to keep in contact even when we were out of sight of each other. I rarely see those guys anymore, but my handheld radio has become basic to my regular hiking gear."

Jack continued, "I think I'd like to learn how to do the radio thing. The worse part about going through a heart attack is that it leaves you feeling vulnerable. I always carry my cell phone, but I would like to ramp up my communications capability. I think that would make me feel less vulnerable. Better to have it and not need it than not have it when you need it."

"Jack, if you want to set the pace, that's okay."

Jack turned to look at Sam and smiled. "I have been setting the pace." Both laughed and turned to look out over the Sound.

"You're not the first guy who had a heart attack nor the first one working to recover either. You've been doing great. If we take more breaks than usual, that's okay with me. I'm here for a nice walk in nature—not a fun run," Sam joked.

"Thanks for being understanding." Jack felt humbled and at peace for having been open.

"I haven't lost a hiking partner yet, and I do not intend on doing so. We'll just take it slow. If you feel the need to rest, we can take lots of breaks. If you need more, I can call in the cavalry."

"Thanks, Bro. I know I'm not going to get any better without pushing myself. I've gotten pretty good at knowing when to back off if I've been pushing myself too hard. As for a cavalry call, it's comforting to know it's available. But I'll do my part to keep it at arm's length.

"Deal!" Sam declared as he slipped his handheld radio back into his pack. Rested and ready, they hopped off the bench and returned to the trail.

WATER BAPTISM

"So..." THE WORD seemed to hang suspended in the air. "You said that you listened to John?" Jack intended to redirect their conversation.

"Yeah," Sam had made his point and was also ready to resume discussing God stuff. "I had some things I wanted to ask you about."

"Sure, let's talk," Jack replied.

"As I was listening, one of the first people who caught my attention was John the Baptist.[267] I assume he got his title because he was baptizing people? Later on, Jesus' disciples were also baptizing people.[268] From what I gather, all the people who got baptized came of their own accord to be baptized. It did not appear that infants or babies were brought to the baptizers for baptism."

Where is Sam going? Jack sensed that a twist was coming.

"I find the baptism thing somewhat confusing. The people in the Bible apparently made their own choice to be baptized. When I was a baby, my parents had me baptized. It was their choice, not mine. I don't remember any of it." Sam paused. "Was my baptism valid? Why even get baptized? What is baptism all about? When is it appropriate? Who should be baptized?"

Jack quickly gathered his thoughts. "Oh, I see what you're asking. Let's start with what baptism is."

"Okay, go for it," Sam replied.

"Baptism is one of the only two sacraments prescribed by Jesus. The two sacraments are water baptism[269] and communion.[270] Jesus said that when believers are born again,[182] they should be baptized.[271] Communion should be done as a remembrance.[272]

"Okay, then what is water baptism about?" Sam asked.

"Baptism literally is a ritual cleansing by immersion in water.[273] The Bible has two archetypes for baptism. One archetype was when God parted the Red Sea. This allowed the Israelites to escape their Egyptian pursuers. The other was Noah's family surviving the global flood."

"What's the connection?"

"Let's start with the Red Sea archetype. Jacob, one of the patriarchs of the Old Testament, is also known as Israel.[274] His lineage are the Israelites."

"So that's where Israel came from?" Sam asked.

"This goes back to the very beginning of the nation of Israel. One of Jacob's twelve sons, Joseph, had performed a great service to Pharaoh and Egypt. To reward Joseph, Pharaoh offered the land of Goshen for Joseph's family to inhabit.[275] Goshen was considered the choicest part of Egypt.[276] They liked life in Goshen and ended up living in Egypt for over four hundred years.[277] While they were there, the Israelites prospered and multiplied.[278] Toward the end of that time period, a Pharaoh arose who did not know what Joseph had done to save the land of Egypt. He just feared their numbers, so he enslaved them."[279]

"It sounds like they had overstayed their welcome," Sam commented.

"God had other plans for them. Apparently, He used their enslavement to change their minds about where they were and to give them a good reason to leave. Along came Moses and God used Moses to liberate the Israelites from their enslavement. After a showdown between Moses and Pharaoh, Pharaoh permitted his Israelite slaves to leave Egypt.[280] When the Israelites were about to exit Egypt, Pharaoh abruptly changed his mind.[281] He pursued God's people with his army.[282] At the shores of the Red Sea, Pharaoh and his force caught up with the Israelites. The Israelites discovered that they were trapped between the Egyptian army, the cliffs on either side of them and the sea.[283] God then provided an escape route by sending a wind that parted the waters. To facilitate their crossing, the wind also dried the exposed sea bottom.[284] The waters of the Red Sea stood like walls to form a passageway for the Israelites to cross the sea on dry ground.[285] Pharaoh saw the his former slaves escaping through the opening God had made. He led his whole force into the passageway in pursuit of the Israelites.[286] When all of the Israelites had reached the far shore, the walls of water collapsed to re-form the sea, washing away Pharaoh and his army. Not one pursuer survived."[287]

Jack continued. "When the Israelites found themselves trapped, they called on God who provided a way of escape. God used the waters of the Red Sea to deliver them from their bondage into freedom, vanquishing their enemy in the process."

Sam found himself filled with mixed emotions. "Wow, drowning an entire army intent on reclaiming escaping slaves is both awesome and horrible. What poetic justice!"

"Yes, Sam, God is just."[91]

Jack continued, "God protects those who call on Him.[288] Even for us, He will not allow us to be tempted beyond our capacity. When we are, He will provide us with an avenue of escape."[38]

Sam looked up and murmured, "Thank You, God."

"The other archetype was when God preserved Noah through the great flood. That time, everything on dry land that had breath drowned in the water.[289] Only the occupants within the ark survived."[290]

"God sure can clean house." Sam shuddered at the immensity of considering that every breathing creature that lived on dry land drowned.[289]

"That time, God used the water to wash the whole earth clean."[291]

Jack continued. "In each archetype, God preserved a remnant He passed through the water to take them from their old existence and bring them into a new life."

"Just like God's salvation delivers us from our sin," Sam replied.

"God used water to wash away the wickedness and those who wanted to enslave His people. God is compassionate, merciful and patient,[292] but even God has His limits.[293] While God is known for His justice, the wicked are ensnared by their own deeds."[294]

Wanting to assure Jack that he understood the archetypes, Sam paraphrased what Jack had said. "So, God used water to transition these people from one life to another. In the process He purged the muck in their old lives."

"You could say that in each case, they had been stained by the world they were leaving. In both cases, water was used to wash off the muck of their previous lives."

Jack continued, "In the Old Testament, priests would perform sacrifices to fulfill the law. To ensure their sacrifices would be acceptable to God, before offering sacrifices, the priests needed to make themselves acceptable to God. Part of the process was purifying themselves with a ritual washing.[295] The priest's ritual washing was done at a specific basin located in the temple. The ritual washing was done prior offering sacrifices.[296] In the New Testament, Jesus fulfilled the law[59] by becoming the ultimate sacrifice and atonement for our sin.[297] Baptism then became an outward expression of the inward change driven by acknowledging our sin, repenting and entering into God's salvation. In the way that the Old Testament priests did their ritual washing, water baptism is a sign that our sins have been washed off of us.[298] Our 'old man' has been washed away, and a 'new man' has been resurrected for a new life in Christ."[299]

"What about my baptism when I was a baby?" Sam asked.

"*Christening* or infant baptism is a public act of committing a child to Christ. It's an early tradition that has carried over into most of the mainline Protestant denominations. The basic logic is that that when a baby is baptized, the baby is initiated into the Christian community, inoculated with grace and on the road toward heaven."

"I didn't hear any of that when I listened to John," Sam said.

"It's not there, Sam. The requirements for baptism are illustrated in the New Testament. The candidate for baptism should be a person of good conscience,[291] one who believes and confesses in Jesus Christ,[271, 120] has repented from his sin[152] and is on his way to becoming a disciple of Jesus."[269]

Sam responded, "Babies don't understand any of that stuff. I don't remember and certainly didn't understand any of it. I only know about it from what I was told. I can say that I didn't understand the concept of sin until you explained it to me on our last hike."

Jack replied, "Few nonbelievers of any age understand what sin is or how lethal sins are. Few even comprehend how Satan develops tailormade temptations. His customized seductive bait is designed to lure people out of their own self-restraint. Biting that spiritually toxic bait will get them hooked. Unless rescued, they will find themselves captive."[90]

Sam commented, "That's my point; it takes a reasoning mind to grasp. For me, when that clicked, it felt like the lights were coming on. I remembered a time after my divorce when I dated a pretty gal who coaxed me to watch porn with her. I justified doing what I did because of what my ex had done to me. That gal passed through my life pretty fast and honestly, I felt relieved when she was gone. Deep inside, none of what she lured me to do felt right. I don't miss her or even remember her name, but the porn she got me into stuck like tar. Everything inside of me said it was a road to ruin. Some days, it takes everything I have to stay away from that trash. What she brought into my life made me feel like I had stepped in a fresh pile of dog muck, squishing up between the toes of my bare feet. I would like to forget that any of it ever happened. I don't want to go through that struggle ever again."

Jack shivered. "I remember a kid who always ran barefoot in summer. One day he planted his bare foot in a big fresh pile of fresh dog muck. We were all disgusted! I remember holding the garden hose to help him with the initial rinsing. His whole ordeal was so very gross! Then he went inside for soap and used lots of it." Jack snickered at the memory, then returned to being serious. "Saying that's how porn makes you feel is an appropriate comparison. Making a comparison between porn and dog muck is the Holy Spirit's waking you[2] to the real quality of Satan's bait."

"That's about the quality of it," Sam scoffed. "Squishy, stinky, filthy and toxic."

"God wants to clean the muck off of us and transform us from our 'old man' chewing on the baited hook into becoming a free 'new man.'[244] The process takes us from death to life.[42] To help us overcome our weaknesses, He gives us the Holy Spirit.[300] As a Christian, God promises not to allow any temptation to come at us that cannot be overcome. If a really big temptation comes, He promises to provide a way to escape it.[38]

Sam looked up. *Thank You, God. Thank You, Holy Spirit.*

The trail brought them through the apex of a horseshoe bend. Rounding the gully, a songbird filled the small valley with an unmistakably beautiful twitter. "Jesus said that for every sinner who repents, there is joy in the presence of God's angels."[301]

"That bird sure sounds happy," Sam commented. "I guess hearing angels rejoice would make an even prettier sound."

Jack stopped and listened. "God surely did give nature some sounds that are music in our ears."

When the bird finished its song and flew off, the two friends resumed their hike.

Jack asked, "When you listened to the gospel of John, did you also listen to the book of Acts?"

"No, not yet. I have been enjoying John too much. I've listened to a few sections over and over, and each time it seems like I catch something else."

Jack replied, "The Bible is that way. When you listen or read, ask the

Holy Spirit to open your eyes to new truths.[302] The Holy Spirit is our teacher."[303] In John's gospel, John wrote from his own personal experience with Jesus. Acts is a follow-up history, covering the first generation after Jesus. The book of Acts covers the period from the church's very beginning through the life of the apostle Paul. Acts was written by Luke, who was Paul's physician and companion. Just as John was there during Jesus' ministry, Luke was there during much of Paul's ministry. Though Acts is primarily the history book of the New Testament, a particular story is related in its eighth chapter. The story takes place within the very early years of the church and is relevant to baptism."

"What is the story?" Sam asked.

"The apostle Philip was prompted by the Holy Spirit to get up, go into the desert and head south along the road that connected Jerusalem with Gaza.[304] When he reached the appointed place, the Holy Spirit prompted Philip to go to a specific chariot traveling on the road.[305] Philip ran and caught up with the chariot. When he got to it, he found an Ethiopian dignitary, who happened to be the Ethiopian queen's treasurer. The dignitary was on his return trip from Jerusalem, where he had gone to worship. When Philip caught up with him, the Ethiopian dignitary was sitting in his chariot reading a passage from Isaiah 53."[306]

"What's Isaiah 53?" Sam asked.

"Isaiah was one of God's numerous Old Testament prophets who prophesied of two comings of the Messiah. One coming would be that of a mighty Messiah who would rule over all the earth.[307] The other would bring salvation[308] by laying down His life to become the atonement for our sin.[58] The fifty-third chapter of Isaiah's writings foresaw Jesus as the sacrificial lamb, healing us from our sin.[309]

"Two Messiahs?" Sam asked.

Jack replied, "Actually, one Messiah, two unique arrivals. Two thousand years ago Jesus came meekly to bring us God's salvation.[308] Then He will return one day in the future as the all-powerful conquering[310] King of kings and Lord of lords."[311]

Sam stopped and pulled his phone out of his pack. In the notes app, he typed, *Read Isaiah 53 and Acts 8.* Just as quickly, he slipped his phone back into his pack, and they were hiking again.

Jack continued, "When Philip caught up with the Ethiopian, he asked the dignitary if he understood what he was reading. The Ethiopian responded, 'How can I without a teacher?' Then he invited Philip to join him in his chariot.[312]

"The Ethiopian sounds like a humble person who was just interested in getting a better understanding," Sam commented.

"If there is truth, it will stand on its own. If there is no truth, then it's better to find the flaw and move on. The Ethiopian was genuinely seeking, and God wanted to reward him for his diligence."[313]

"Sounds like he had a God-thing moment." Sam smiled.

Jack replied, "He sure did. The Scripture the Egyptian was reading was this: *'He was led as a sheep to the slaughter; And as a lamb before its shearer is silent, So He opened not His mouth. In His humiliation His justice was taken away, And who will declare His generation? For His life was taken from the earth.'*[314] The Ethiopian asked Philip if the prophet was speaking about himself or speaking of some other man.[315] Starting with that Scripture, Philip instructed him about Jesus.[316]

"Go Philip!" Sam cheered in a subdued voice.

"They had been traveling together for a while and came to a river. The Ethiopian asked Philip if there was anything hindering him from being baptized.[317] Philip replied that if he believed with all his heart he could be baptized. The Ethiopian replied to Philip that he believed that Jesus is the son of God.[318] The Ethiopian ordered his chariot to stop. They both went down to the water, and Philip baptized him.[319]

"So, what happened to the Ethiopian?" Sam asked.

"When they came out of the water, the Spirit of the Lord suddenly took Philip away, and the Ethiopian never saw him again, but he went on his way rejoicing.[320] Luke didn't say any more about him, but I'm certain he went back to his people and shared the good news. I have no doubt we will meet both Philip and the Ethiopian in Heaven," Jack added with a slight crack in his voice and tears welling in his eyes.

"I see the big picture, Jack. I believe Jesus Christ is the Son of God. I understand my sin, repented and asked Jesus to come into my life."

"I was there and would stand as your witness." Jack felt joy in his spirit. The seed of the gospel had taken root, and he could see a new life sprouting in Sam. "John the Baptist,[321] Jesus[271] and later Peter each said repent and be baptized. [322] Jesus said believers should be baptized in the name of the Father, the Son and the Holy Spirit.[269] Your next step is getting baptized."

Jack continued, "There are some conditions for baptism."

"Conditions?"

"Repentance must proceed baptism.[271] You must be a believer or it will have no effect.[271] Lastly it must be done of good conscience."[291]

"Good conscience?" Sam asked.

"Having a good conscience means that you confess your faith in Jesus,[120, 323] honestly and humbly acknowledge and repent from your sin. The question to ask yourself is if you understand and did you honestly mean it?"

"Yes, I did," Sam stated proudly.

"Then Jesus said that you should be baptized in the name of the Father, the Son and the Holy Spirit. Afterward Jesus instructs us to be disciples of what He has taught."[269]

"Well, I have a good conscience and the more I learn, the more I'm in. Maybe I should get rebaptized?" Sam asked.

"If you were too young to understand or even to remember, then what you experienced was more of a baby dedication or christening, than a baptism. Mary and Joseph also had Jesus dedicated."[324]

"So a baby dedication and baptism are the same thing?"

"No, they are not. A baby being dedicated to God shows the will of the parents. Adult water baptism shows the will of the individual. Having met the conditions for water baptism, you should be baptized as an adult—just like Jesus was.[325] It's not the baptism that saves you; rather, it's an outward sign that your 'old man' with its sinful nature has died and has been buried and a 'new man' has been birthed."[326]

"I guess that leads to where?" Sam asked.

FILTERS TO FIND A CHURCH

"THAT LEADS TO discussing churches."

"I knew that was coming," Sam lamented.

"As far as baptism goes, the simple answer is to find a Bible-believing church with a minister who will baptize you in the name of the Father, the Son and Holy Spirit."[269]

"Don't all churches believe the Bible?" Sam asked.

Jack replied, "Churches are like ice cream, and all ice cream is either dairy or imitation dairy."

Sam laughed. "Over the years, I've sampled some tasty faux ice cream."

"Well-made faux can be a challenge to differentiate from the real. That's a problem when you are looking for the real and do not want the faux. It's like bank tellers who are trained to identify counterfeit bills by only handling genuine bills. I've heard that the bad bills do not feel the same as the good ones."

"I knew a bank teller," Sam replied. "She said that when handling money, if a bill does not feel as it should, they are told to put it aside. Often, they discover that there is a problem with that questionable bill. As for the imitation ice cream, it does not digest the same as real dairy." Sam put his finger in his mouth in a theatrical display of forcing himself to throw up.

Jack responded. "All Christian churches like to think of themselves to be the true house of God, even when different churches have varying concepts of who God is or what God is?"

Sam remarked, "The smorgasbord of churches does seem to be endless. How can you tell?"

"The benchmark for any church is how they feel about the Bible." Jack let the statement hang in the air before continuing. "The Bible is God's Word; its where God teaches us how to live and why. The Bible provides lots of illustrations, both historical and spiritual. None of its words are trivial. The Bible is true,[327] and you can believe what it says. If it were not true, then why bother with any of it? The first filter for determining if a church is worth considering, is to ask if they take the Bible seriously or if they consider it to be just a collection of fables. The immediate follow-up question is to ask if they consider the whole Bible to be inerrant.[166] Some churches cherry-pick God's Word for what they like and discard what do not care for. Some denominations even edit the Bible to suit their own particular doctrine or add extra stuff that supports something different than what the Bible teaches. They consider their additions to be par with or even greater than God's own Word."

Jack paused, then continued. "There are some other basic filters. Do they believe Jesus is the Son of God? Do they believe Jesus came to earth in flesh and blood,[328] lived, died and rose from the dead?[329] Did God create everything in six days?[234] If a church cannot say yes to all these questions, then they do not believe the Bible. Move on till you find a church that does."

Sam nodded as they walked side by side.

Jack resumed, "People are people. Everyone has some kind of an opinion. When it comes to churches, you want to use to base your decision on the church's core beliefs and teaching. The ideal church will be a balance of half teaching and half community. No church is perfect. Just because people may be born again does not mean they are perfect. But the people will honestly be pursuing God and that's who to flock with. In the best of churches, you will see God's Word reflected in the body of the church's congregation."

"It keeps coming back to the Bible, eh?" Sam asked.

Jack replied, "Yes, God's Word is the standard—our benchmark for measuring."

When Jack felt that Sam had comprehended the primary church filter, he added. "Think of church shopping like going into an ice cream shop with lots of different flavors."

Sam laughed. "Well, that's an interesting analogy. I'm lactose intolerant."

"Oh?" *Oops,* Jack thought. *Maybe that was not the best parallel?*

"It's not as bad as it sounds. I can tolerate chocolate ice cream and chocolate milk," Sam replied. "Hard cheeses are okay, but nothing white or too milky."

"I bet that limits your options at the ice cream shop!"

"Yeah, it does limit the selection when choosing a flavor, but there are usually multiple chocolate options. I've learned that it's not unusual for people who cannot tolerate white milk to be okay with chocolate milk. One of my daughters is also lactose intolerant. Her favorite breakfast is cereal is soaked in chocolate milk."

Jack laughed. "That sounds decadent, but tasty. I always thought chocolate milk was invented to bribe kids to drink their milk."

"I guess for most kids it is a bribe. To the ones who cannot digest white milk, it makes a world of difference."

"In that case, maybe ice cream is an even better analogy and more appropriate than I had initially thought. Churches come in lots of flavors and types; some are good and healthy while others can be indigestible. Applying that to churches, you could say that some churches are healthy and spiritually edifying, while some are spiritually toxic."

"It's not like I can walk up to the counter and select a church by color. How do I find the 'chocolate' church?" Sam chuckled. "Is there a guideline to follow?"

"Before we talk about churches, let me be clear in saying that there are all kind of churches and in them, you will find all kinds of devoted people. Some churches have sound doctrine, and some do not. Because a church has bad doctrine does not necessarily mean that the people you find attending there are bad. They are just being led astray by bad teaching.[330] Satan only has to distract and divert a person from the true gospel of God's salvation in order to score another soul. All people were born tainted with the curse of Adam's original sin. By God's grace, each of us will at some time have the opportunity to meet the Creator and get saved."[179]

"I'm confident in my salvation. When we prayed, I felt something in me change. I know I'm not the same person I was before,"[331] Sam stated.

"I could tell something happened when we prayed. You are my brother in Christ," Jack replied.

"Thanks, yes, I feel that way too," Sam beamed.

The trail opened to an old-fashioned city-like street with curbs. A mid-twentieth century streetlight stood in the distance. Sam saw Jack look questioningly up along the street. He pointed in the direction of Jack's gaze. "Up past that streetlight is the historical district and the HQ of the old Army base—the yellow buildings we saw earlier. We've been hiking around them." Crossing the street, they continued on the loop trail and were once again deep into the woods.

"Okay," Jack nodded and pulled out his phone to check the map he had photographed earlier.

"Let's run through some red-flag filters."

"Knowing what to avoid is a good place to start weeding," Sam agreed.

"To re-cap, the primary filter in church shopping is asking if the church you are considering believes that the Bible is truly God's Word—not just another good book. Ask if the church believes that the Bible is the inerrant, inspired Word of God.[166] If they truly believe that the Bible is the inerrant, inspired Word of God, then they will not try to change it or add to it. The Bible says that there is a penalty for those who change the Bible to suit their own purposes. The Bible is very clear that anyone who adds to or deletes from the Bible will go to hell."[32]

"Oh, that is severe!" Sam commented.

Jack replied, "It's a provision that maintains the Bible's integrity."

"That would be a strong deterrent," Sam replied, "...if they believe what the Bible says."

"People who do not believe that the Bible is inerrant would not worry about any penalties it proscribes," Jack replied.

Sam started laughing. "Arguing that a law is invalid or not believing the law is not much of a defense in any court of law."

"Ignorance of the law is not much of a defense either," Jack added.

Jack asked, "How do you feel about people who twist your words to alter their meaning and make your words something other than what you had intended."

"I hate that! A person who twists another person's words for whatever purpose is a corruption," Sam responded harshly. "That's intentionally misleading and really just another form of lying!"

"Yes, it is. God feels the same way about having His own words twisted. The corruption may be subtle, or it may be overt. The fact is that corrupting the meaning of God's Word deceives people[20] and fertilizes the ground for the spiritual cancer of sin to grow. They like the label of Christian; they would better be labeled as 'Cultural Christians.' Their teachers cherry-pick God's Word, and the people in those churches follow along. They may know some aspects of God but will deny the power of God and the power of His Word."[333]

"How can you tell?" Sam asked.

"A church, denomination or body of believers which believes that the Bible is God's inerrant Word will be proud to say so. If a church does not believe the Bible to be God's own inerrant words, then they tend to waffle on the question. You can expect them to justify any number of exceptions. Some sects may do so subtly, yet they intentionally misinterpret God's Word. Some others are very open about their modifications to God's holy Word. Then there are some others who may say that God's Word is incomplete and requires fresh infusions."

Sam nodded. "Maintain the integrity of the Word. *Sola Scriptura*."

"There is one major sect known for their idols. To justify their idols, they redefined God's Ten Commandments to omit God's condemnation of idol worship."[221]

"I'm fairly certain I know which one that is." Sam remembered the religious statues that he had seen over the years. People had them in their homes, at the head of processions and on car dashboards. "When you mentioned God's commandment about not having any idols, I was actually thinking of those statues. I was going to ask how they fit in."

"Those idols do not fit in. They have no place with God-fearing Christians. The idols are a violation of God's Ten Commandments.[221] If you want to keep God happy, don't have anything to do with any kind of idols."

Sam confessed, "A realtor once advised me to bury one in the lawn in front of my house. The realtor said it would aid in selling the house."

"Employing an idol to assist in the sale of your house is a sin. You should talk to God about it." For a few steps, Jack thought about what he had just said and felt it was not enough. "You need to talk to God about what you did and ask Him for His forgiveness. Then be repentant by never employing idols for any purpose in the future." Jack looked at Sam. "God wants us to be good repenters."

"Actually, I think that trick backfired. It took almost a year to sell the house. In my opinion, the idol did not make any difference at all. It may have even delayed the sale. Whatever, I feel foolish for having done it. I felt weird planting a little statue in the lawn, and I have no intention of doing that again. I purposely forgot about it all until just now. I certainly didn't want to let anyone know what I did. Yeah, I'll talk to God about it. I feel bad that I did that at all. By the way, you're sworn to secrecy."

"No problem. The matter is between you and God. I already forgot you told me." Jack could tell the incident bothered Sam. *Thanks, God, for connecting the dots for Sam.*

"Yeah, I'd prefer to completely forget ever having done that. I will talk to God and ask His forgiveness. Then I'll let the incident fade from my memory."

"God keeps a tally of what we do in this life.[334] When we confess our sins to God and ask for forgiveness, He will be faithful to forgive,[150] forget[335] and remove that forgiven sin from us."[336]

Sam stopped in the trail, put his hands together, held them to his chest and looked up. "Dear God, I did not understand what I was doing. When I did it, I felt it was wrong—even though I did not know why. Now I understand why what I did was wrong. Please forgive me. In Jesus' name, Amen."[197]

Sam looked at Jack. "If some strangers see me pray. I don't really care what they think. What concerns me is that I want to be on God's good side, and I don't want to offend God and risk losing what I've found."

"Neither do I," Jack agreed lightly with a nod. "Neither do I."

They stopped where the trail opened up at another old-fashioned city street. Sam saw Jack looking up the street to his right. Sam pointed down the street and said, "The north parking lot is down there." Jack looked to his left and saw the street descend. Turning to the right, the street led out of the woods. On the other side of the street, the loop trail continued through the woods.

Standing on the curb, Sam commented, "There have been things which made me feel weird, but I never understood why. Since meeting you and hearing about Jesus and inviting Him into my heart, some of these things, like the idol planting, have come to mind. In reflection, it seems like, at the time, I had some inner voice telling me not to do something that I went ahead and did regardless. Now when those memories come to mind, I feel like saying 'oops' and asking God's forgiveness—partly for what I did and partly for being so stubborn and doing what I felt that I should not have done."

"That's the Holy Spirit enlightening you."[227]

Crossing the street and continuing on the trail into the woods, Jack resumed his teaching. "Another major sect has their own set of 'bonus scriptures.' They consider those extra so-called scriptures to be divinely inspired and on par with the Bible. The teachings in those bonus scriptures take their adherents on a salvation path very different than what Jesus taught. Jesus said He was the truth and only way to God.[4] They forgot the verse that says not to add or delete from God's Word."[32]

Sam chuckled. "I think I can tell who they are. I've had their people knock on my door more than a few times over the years. They always look so clean-cut, but they leave me unsettled, and I prefer to avoid them. Once a coworker invited my wife and I over for barbeque. He was always such a nice guy in the office. After dinner he wanted us all to watch something on television. It didn't take long before we realized he was one of those door knockers." Sam comically shuddered and began laughing. "The food was good, but we could not get out and away fast enough."

"You may have had some spiritual discernment." Jack chuckled.

"I sure did that day." Sam kept on laughing.

Jack said, "The next red flags are cults. They tend to believe they have an exclusive on some truth that's usually built around a charismatic leader with a unique interpretation of Scripture. They get tend to get dogmatic and insist that they are the sole keepers of truth."

Sam winced. "My antennae go up whenever I hear people say that they are right and anyone who disagrees with them is wrong."

Jack shook his head. "Any group that holds a leader's special insights or an obscure interpretation too highly needs to be questioned. The filter test is that cults do not like their leader's special insights or obscure interpretations questioned. They demand blind obedience. Sometimes they may even become irritated or upset when they are questioned. Cults by nature are authoritarian over their followers. They demand allegiance to their own unique and unquestionable doctrines."

Sam looked down, and with a deep breath, slowly shook it from side to side. "Talking politics can get like that. Some people say they are right; therefore, everyone else is wrong. When you question their positions, they become defensive and attack you for even asking. I just figure that if someone cannot explain why he believes what he believes, then he really is admitting to being ignorant and displaying that he lacks a foundation for what he claims. My policy is why waste my time with someone who does not or cannot think for himself?"

Jack replied, "The Bible instructs us to test all things and hang onto what is good.[3] That instruction extends beyond just looking at churches. Any group that demands blind obedience gets a red flag. When the leader says that he has special truth which nobody else has, he just waved a red flag. When the followers insist their leader is beyond questioning is another waving red flag. Those groups are cults—not just because of their doctrine, but because they exhibit abusive and controlling behavior. Their followers are blind and being led astray."[20]

Jack continued, "God wants us to be free thinkers. His management structure is flat. It's just one step between us and God. That one step is Jesus.[118] Jesus is the only way to God. Jesus is the way the truth and the life.[4] Anyone who says anything else is wrong."[330]

"So, the Bible has a cult-proofing feature?" Sam asked.

Jack replied, "Yes, know the Bible, hold it as your standard and use it to challenge any and all teachings.[337] Don't simply take someone's word that what he says is scriptural truth. Look it up for yourself in the Bible.[166] Look at the verses, examine their context and verify what's truth.[3] Too often erroneous teaching comes from verses taken out of context."

"I don't think I'll have any problem navigating through those red flags. You've given me more reasons for owning and using a hard copy Bible."

"It's meant to be read and used. And don't be afraid of making notes in the margins. It's all about knowing your Bible."

Jack noticed the clearing to their left. "I assume that's also the north parking lot?"

"Yeah, it's much bigger than the south lot. Being closer to the bluffs, I think the south lot makes for a better launch point."

Jack stopped and pulled out his phone to check the map. "I'm glad we're doing the full loop."

Sam agreed.

Jack slipped the phone back into his pack.

Sam asked, "It doesn't sound like you've been struggling since we came off the bluff."

"Ground that is level or rolling is not much of a problem. The climbs can get challenging. Thanks for reminding me of the Lamaze breathing technique. For the climb up the bluff, it made all the difference. I will keep that in mind when I do future climbs."

Sam chuckled. "Sometimes I catch myself breathing to rhythms and song lyrics. I'll do it even when I'm walking on level ground."

"I was just doing that." Jack chuckled. "It goes with the rhythm of the steps."

I want to do this again, Sam thought. "So, Jack, I have a suggestion for our next hike. Have you heard of Wallace Falls?"

"Oh, I did that in my mid-twenties. When I first moved out here, Wallace Falls was my first real mountain hike. That year had an exceptionally warm Christmas. A new friend wanted to show me the different waterfalls and the vista from the top. Yes, that would be a fun hike to look forward to doing. It would be another good hike to practice the Lamaze breathing." Jack snickered but thought, *I remember that trail with a lot of ups and downs. I'm going to have to condition myself more before we do that one. I'm glad Sam is not scared off from our going hiking together again.*

"Think about it," Sam added.

They walked quietly through the next bend.

"You gave some filters for church finding. Before there is such an abundance of churches, what was it like? In the beginning, wasn't Christianity an underground movement?"

"The ancient Romans were a very religious people with an entire spectrum of gods. The Romans considered appeasing their gods to be integral to their culture and government. The Roman pantheistic spectrum included their emperor, whom they also accepted as a god. They worshiped their Caesars as prominent gods. Christians were monotheistic and rejected polytheism. Since the Christians refused to worship Caesar or any of the Roman gods, the Romans considered the Christians to be atheists. Atheism in ancient Rome was a capital crime. Under some of the more tolerant Roman emperors, Christians were free to operate above ground. Other Roman emperors, such as Nero and Diocletian, violently repressed and attempted to purge Christianity from the Empire. In the times of persecution, Christians were forced underground. There were no casual cultural Christians in those days. Believers were either all in or not in at all."

"If it was so dangerous to be a Christian, how did the Christians connect with each other?"

Up ahead, Jack saw a small patch of loose dirt. He stopped in front of the patch and used the toe of his right boot to draw a concave arc. He then drew a mirroring convex starting from the same point but crossing about two thirds of the way between start and finish.

Sam looked at the drawing and remarked, "I've seen that symbol that looks like a fish."

"When a Christian met a stranger and wanted to inquire if that person was a Christian, he would draw an arc—in the dirt with his foot—like I just did. If the other person then drew a mirroring arc to complete the outline of a fish, the two arcs forming a fish was a confirmation they were both Christians."

"If the other person did not match the first arc with his own mirroring arc?" Sam asked.

"The unspoken question had been answered. The sign of the fish was their password. Secret meeting places were often identified by a fish on a doorpost or wall. Where you recall seeing the fish is probably a business or organization operated by Christians who used the fish on their sign as a logo. It's an ancient symbol to let others know they are Christians."

"Why the fish and not a cross?"

"For the first Christians, the fish attracted less attention by those whom Christians did not want to be noticed. In the fourth century, when Constantine decriminalized Christianity,[265] he adopted the cross as his symbol. In time, the cross eclipsed the fish as a common symbol for Christians."

"I like the fish," Sam commented

"I do too."

Jack lowered his left shoulder to let his pack slide off, catching the strap before the pack hit the ground. He knelt down, lowering the pack to the ground. From its front pocket, he pulled out a stuffed flattened baggie. He gave it a cursory glance and re-shouldered his pack.

Jack left the clean arcs of the fish and turned to walk away.

"You left your fish behind."

"It'll let other Christians know that a believer was here." Sam saw Jack's grin as they walked away.

Below and to their left through the woods, they could see a spur from the trail leading to a building with a small parking lot. Sam saw Jack looking. "That's the east lot and the visitors' center."

"I'll have to put that on my to-do list." *Next weekend when I return to build up my endurance for the Wallace Falls hike,* Jack thought but did not say aloud.

"You could say that the fish got them through the door. Once in the door, they knew they were safe and free to break bread, share communion[270] and have church. The Bible had not yet been compiled. To assure doctrinal consistency within the church, the believers developed a creed. The oldest known creed, the 'Old Roman Symbol,' dates to those times.

"Here take this." Jack handed the stuffed baggie to Sam. "I was recently reviewing church history and thought it seemed like a good idea to print out the early creeds so I could review their core tenets."

Sam took the baggie, opened it and took out some folded papers.

"Old Roman Symbol, the Apostles' Creed and the Nicaean Creed." Sam read the titles aloud as he paged through the three sheets.

"The early church fathers wanted to filter out heresies and keep Christians on the same page."

Sam looked at the sheets. "The Roman one is the simplest," he noted.

"By the end of first century, Christianity had grown from a sect of Judaism and become its own religion. The Old Roman Symbol dates to the second century."

"So this was one of the earliest efforts to attain consistency in the basics of Christianity?" Sam looked at the creed and began to read aloud.

I believe in God the Father almighty;
and in Christ Jesus His only Son, our Lord,
Who was born from the Holy Spirit and the Virgin Mary,
Who under Pontius Pilate was crucified and buried,
*   on the third day rose again from the dead,*
*   ascended to heaven,*
*   sits at the right hand of the Father,*
*   whence He will come to judge the living and the dead;*
and in the Holy Spirit,
the holy Church,
the remission of sins,
the resurrection of the flesh
(the life everlasting).

"The Old Roman Symbol was later rewritten as the Apostle's Creed," Jack commented.

Sam shifted the top sheet to the bottom of the stack, revealing the Apostle's Creed, which he also read aloud.

"I believe in God, the Father almighty, creator of heaven and earth.
I believe in Jesus Christ, his only Son, our Lord
He was conceived by the power of the Holy Spirit and born of the
*   Virgin Mary.*

He suffered under Pontius Pilate, was crucified, died, and was
   buried.
He descended into hell.
On the third day he rose again.
He ascended into heaven and is seated at the right hand of the
   Father.
He will come again to judge the living and the dead.
*I believe in the Holy Spirit, the holy **universal** [catholic] Church,*
   the communion of saints, the forgiveness of sins, the resurrec-
   tion of the body, and the life everlasting.
Amen."

"Catholic?"

"The Apostles' Creed dates to the fourth or fifth century. By the way, that is catholic with a small 'c.' I picked up on the same thing when I first read it. *Catholic* with a small 'c' means 'universal.'"

"*Catholic* means 'universal'?"

"The Romans loved to standardize things. Under Constantine, an effort was made to corral the various Christian sects under one umbrella and call it a universal church. Before the word *catholic* came to identify as the Roman Catholic church, there were growing number of sects within the church. The early Church Fathers were trying say that there was only one universal church. The title stayed, and that is where the Catholic church got its name."

"So, they really wanted their church to be known as the *universal church*?" Sam asked.

Jack replied, "A priest once told me that Catholicism is like a pine tree with a single stem and many branches. He contrasted that to the Protestant church, which he likened to a mixed forest. Every disagreement over doctrine sprouted a new church."

"I guess they like to think of themselves as the mother of all churches." Sam chuckled.

Sam shifted the papers to the Nicene creed. "This one is a lot longer."

"The Nicene creed became the standard creed of the church until the Protestant Reformation came along. The Protestant Reformation was driven by the Protestants translating God's Word into the common vernacular. With Gutenberg's help Bibles were mass printed so everyone could have their own copy, in their own language. People being empowered to read their own copies of God's Word in their own language, drove literacy for the next few hundred years. The rest is history."

Sam slowly nodded in acknowledgment, then read aloud the Nicene Creed.

We believe in one God, the Father, the Almighty, maker of heaven and earth, of all that is, both seen and unseen.

We believe in one Lord, Jesus Christ, the only Son of God eternally begotten of the Father, God from God, Light from Light, true God from true God, begotten, not made, one in Being with the Father.

Through him all things were made. For us men and for our salvation he came down from heaven:

By the power of the Holy Spirit he was born of the Virgin Mary, and became man.

For our sake he was crucified under Pontius Pilate; he suffered, died, and was buried.

On the third day he rose again in fulfillment of the Scriptures;

He ascended into heaven and is seated at the right hand of the Father. He will come again in glory to judge the living and the dead, and his kingdom will have no end.

We believe in the Holy Spirit, the Lord, the giver of life, who proceeds from the Father and the Son.

With the Father and Son he is worshiped and glorified. He has spoken through the prophets.

*We believe in one holy **universal** [catholic] and apostolic Church.*

We acknowledge one baptism for the forgiveness of sins. We look for the resurrection of the dead, and the life of the world to come.

Amen.

"The creeds helped make it easier for the church to define itself. The takeaway from the creeds are their key points."

Sam paged back to the Apostle's Creed. "Let me guess. The first is that God is the Father, and He created the heavens and the earth."

"The very first verse of the Bible makes it clear. *'In the beginning God created the heaven and the earth.'*[7,26] A church must believe and teach that God is the Creator. If they deny God created the heavens and the earth, they deny God's Word and they are disowning God.

Sam took it in and nodded. He looked back to the paper. "The next line is that Jesus is the Son of God and that Jesus was conceived of the Holy Spirit and born of the virgin Mary."

"The Bible teaches that Jesus is God and became flesh to dwell among us.[26] The prophet Isaiah prophesied that Jesus would be born of a virgin.[131] The gospels tell us that Jesus was born of a virgin, conceived by the Holy Spirit.[338] To deny the virgin birth is to deny the Bible."

"Remind me again why the virgin birth is so important," Sam urged.

"All humanity has been born under the curse of Adam's sin. Consider it humanity's corporate spiritual birth defect.[55] God made it clear that He would not accept defectives for sacrifices.[129] By being born of a virgin, Jesus did not inherit Adam's original sin.[339] Being sinless allowed Jesus to be the acceptable sacrifice[340] for God to atone for our sins.[127]

Sam looked back at the paper. "If Jesus did not die and get resurrected, then there would be no salvation or life everlasting, right?"

"Communion of saints? What does that mean?" Sam asked.

"The universal church and communion of the saints means that we are all basically singing from the same song sheet, and one day we will all be together in heaven. The original idea was that the creeds would be the sheet music to keep the choir singing in harmony. I have a copy taped inside the cover of my Bible. My relationship with God is very personal. Seeing that reminds me I'm part of something much bigger."

Sam thoughtfully folded up the papers and stuffed them back into the baggie. He held it out to Jack who refused. "Keep them as a reminder that you are part of something much bigger than ourselves."

Slipping the baggie into a flat pocket on his pack, Sam said, "Thanks. I'll keep it for some of my twilight thought."

"There remains one last major test to filter out toxic doctrine."

"I think you've given me a whole toolbox so far."

"Ask the minister if he really believes that God created the heavens and the earth in six calendar days and rested on the seventh."[234]

"Why?"

"The Hebrew word for *day* is the same word used in Genesis which literally means a 'twenty-four-hour period.'[341] If he agrees, then he believes the Bible. If he waffles, you'll probably get justifications and mental gymnastics to merge evolution into the Bible. In that case, he really does not believe the Bible, and you should politely thank him for his time and walk away."

"Okay, I'll make a point to remember the seven-day question. Real teacher don't mind being put on the spot when it comes to core subject matter," Sam replied.

"After filtering out the red-flag churches, it's just a matter of checking if a church has good doctrine. However, testing to see if the teachers really believe God's Word is the best place to start. The Bible is a bottomless well of wisdom and insight—the rock on which to build our lives."[342]

"Filters and flags. Thanks for the toolbox."

"The last thing about finding a healthy church is it will stand firmly and equally balanced on the two legs of discipleship and community. It should be balanced between solid Bible teaching and discipleship training within a community of likeminded believers who are supportive of each other in their corporate pursuit of God."

"I'd like to find a place like that."

Jack said, "It's the essence of the Great Commission."[269]

"What's that?"

"Jesus told us to share the gospel and to make disciples of all people, teaching them disciples what He taught us. If we do so, He will be with us. Going, winning, baptizing and teaching is referred to as the Great Commission."[269]

Ahead, through the trees, the south parking lot came into view.

"Thanks, Jack. I'm feeling even better about what I've gotten myself into."

"It's not just feeling; it's knowing. That's what faith is all about."

"Thanks for the history lessons. When I learn the story behind the story, I feel more secure in my steps."

They walked up behind their vehicles. Jack was about to drop the tailgate to his truck when he stopped and looked at Sam. "I'll look into churches so you can get baptized."

"Thanks, I want to follow through with what God wants me to do. I have the girls next weekend, and we have some longstanding plans. I'll be free the weekend after. Would you like to plan on hiking Wallace Falls in a couple of weeks?"

"Yes, I would," Jack replied.

"Okay. I'll text, and we can work out the rendezvous."

HIKE 3
The Hike to
ANOINTING

PROLOGUE

JACK OPENED HIS phone to Sam's text. He reviewed the rendezvous time and retrieved the address, which he noticed was in the same part of town as his apartment. The address copy pasted easily into the phone's GPS. Factoring in enough time to allow for a leisurely breakfast, he selected a route that took him past his favorite local bistro. Breakfast at the bistro was consistent and had proven itself to be the perfect foundation for a day of hiking. Walking up to the door, he could see that his favorite window table was available.

A waitress spotted him coming through the door. She recognized him and came over to his table with a cup of their morning blend. "The usual?" she asked.

Jack confirmed his order with a smile and nod. He asked, "Can I also get some milk for the coffee?" Picking up the cup, he rested his elbows on the table. Using both hands, he held the cup below his nose, inhaling the rich mellow aroma.

From one end of the country to the other, biscuits and gravy were a culinary adventure. Always inconsistent, the dish could vary from deliciously savory to blandly inedible. Trying any new eatery spun the breakfast roulette wheel. One cold morning in early winter when hunting for a hearty warm breakfast, Jack had randomly stumbled into this bistro. The following weekend it was the first place he thought of. Some may say a cook has chops. This one had the skill and the taste buds. The biscuits were light and fluffy and generously covered with a savory gravy infused with hot spicy sausage, sautéed onions and sage. The first taste led to the next. Then it was hard to pause—even to rinse the palate with their nearly perfect coffee.

Eyes closed and leisurely sipping his coffee, Jack heard the plate arrive on the table. He inhaled deeply of the pleasing aroma rising from his breakfast. "Mmm-mmm-mmm." He opened his eyes, confirming the source of the aroma.

He bowed his head, closed his eyes and prayed quietly. "Thank You, God, for this food. Purify it, sanctify it and bless it for my body. In the name of Jesus. Amen." The first bite only set the path for the next and the next. *I'll miss this place when I go back home. I'm going to have to figure out how to make this gravy myself.* Jack savored every bite of his breakfast.

The waitress returned to Jack who was sitting behind a clean plate, looking out the window. His father had been a detective who had taught him the art of people watching. This table was ideal for people watching.

"Refresh your cup?" the waitress asked.

Turning his head from gazing at the kids passing by, Jack replied, "Can I get it in a to-go cup?"

The GPS directed Jack to a side street where a gate barred entry. Waiting before the closed gate, Jack rechecked Sam's text. *Yep, this is the address.* He texted back, "I'm at the gate."

Jack saw man in uniform walking the fence line. He waited for him to return. Beyond the gate was a large open parking area. On the far side of the lot near a large building, Jack saw a handful of vehicles. The plant guard came walking up to Jack's truck.

"Can I help you?" The guard asked as he peered past Jack into the truck.

"My name is Jack; I'm here to meet with Sam," Jack spoke confidently while feeling somewhat awkward.

"Wait here while I call." The guard stepped back and spoke on his cellphone.

Jack sipped his coffee. He spotted Sam's distinctive VW in a cluster of vehicles at the far end of the parking lot.

"Sam said you would be coming. He told me what to look for and asked me to watch for you. He will be out in a minute. Go park over by his VW." The guard spoke with friendly authority, pointing to the cluster of vehicles Jack had noticed earlier. Then he stepped over to the gate, touched something and like an enormous pocket door, the gate slowly slid sideways.

The guard waved him on with one hand, while burying his cell-phone in a pocket with the other. In his mirrors, Jack saw the guard watch his truck as it crossed the lot.

Jack pulled his truck into a spot beside the VW. When the truck came to a rest, he wondered, *What now?* Before he could answer his own question, he saw Sam emerge from an open door. Sam saw Jack, waved and then held up his right hand with an extended index finger in the universal "Wait-a-minute" gesture. Jack nodded and watched as Sam went to his VW's side door. He could see that Sam was moving around some items, then emerged carrying his pack and boots. Sam locked up and walked over to Jack's truck.

"Is it okay if you drive? I've been hearing some funny noises in the VW, and my cousin says I shouldn't take it outside of the neighborhood until he can check it out."

"No problem. I was going to suggest that for hikes out of town, we really ought to carpool. I figured we would talk about that today."

"I guess we are. Today is your turn." Sam grinned broadly and threw his gear into the back seat.

"The driver has the final say over what's played on the radio." Jack liked to let his passengers play with the radio, but he reserved veto rights.

Sam heard the Ninety's alt folk rock playing. *I can listen to this without any problem.* "Fair enough, and I'll have a veto vote too?"

"Fair enough." Jack threw the truck into gear, pulled out and headed toward the gate. Ahead the guard was reopening for them to exit.

They exchanged waves with the guard. "He knows everyone and does not miss anything. I know my vehicle will not be molested in there," Sam commented.

Five minutes and twice as many blocks later, they were on the ramp heading onto I-5 North. When he had comfortably merged onto the interstate, Jack brought his truck to pace with the flow of traffic and set the cruise. He glanced quickly at Sam but kept his attention on the vehicles and road ahead. "So, how're you doing today?"

"I feel great." Sam stretched and settled into the seat. "I have had a real adventure since I saw you last."

"Your text said that you had something to tell me about? Is everything okay?"

"More than okay. Since I last saw you, I had a business trip that took me to Chicago."

"Cool! I was a kid there." Jack's mind flew through childhood memories and settled on the unique Chicago foods that could not be found elsewhere.

"The Monday after our last hike, my boss pulled me aside and said that there was a crisis with our flagship product. An important client needed on-site support. He said the trip should take about a week. Then he asked me to talk with the client, determine what needed to be done and make the necessary arrangements. This would be my first trip to that particular client, but my predecessor who had been there before had kept good project notes. Our office manager knew the drill and took care of all the travel arrangements."

"Did you get good pizza?" Jack asked.

"I had a feeling you'd ask. I was schooled on pizza when I was there. The genuine Chicago-Style deep dish is not like any pizza I've had before. The Italian Beef hoagies are addictive too."

"My father liked to refer to deep dish pizza as cheesecake, since a single slice could hold so much cheese." Jack unconsciously licked and rubbed his lips together.

Sam smiled. "Lots of everything and the crust was more like a cornmeal pie crust than the bready or leathery thin crusts I'm familiar with."

"Wherever traveling for work, ferreting out the best of unique local cuisine is a fun bonus."

"And I did and did and did." Sam' comically rolled his eyes, holding his gut in mock pleasure of the savory memory. "But that's not what I wanted to talk to you about."

"What a tasty way to start!" Jack squinted his eyes, drew in a deep breath and breathed out long and slow, his thoughts gorged with Chicago-Style, deep-dish pizza. Inhaling, he picked up his cup and allowed the memory to be washed away with the coffee he had brought from the bistro.

Sam could tell Jack was lost in a pleasant memory. When Jack put the cup down, Sam resumed, "After my boss spoke with me, I looked up details on our client. After I called and spoke with the client, it was clear that this was work that had to be done on site and in person. I figured that it should take a week with a couple of days to sort out the problem and a couple more to implement a solution."

Jack nodded.

"That evening when I had dinner with my mom, I told her about my trip. She reminded me of our cousins who live in Chicago. When I was a kid, our families lived on the same cul-de-sac. Johnny was in the same grade at school as I was. We were inseparable from playing with Legos to getting into mischief. It wasn't the same if we weren't doing it together. While we were in middle school, his dad got a job in Chicago, and they all moved away."

"That's too bad. Did you keep contact?" Jack asked.

"Mom and Cousin Sue did. I remember Johnny was very unhappy about the move. We both were, but we were kids and were told to be tough. Johnny and I drifted apart. I heard that he fell in with a bad crowd. Through high school, he was known as the family druggie."

"Changes like that can be hard on kids." Jack flashed on childhood friends who, for whatever reason, had found themselves on similar roads in life.

Sam shook his head in agreement. "He got in trouble for something stupid, and someone in the family called him 'Rotten Johnny.' Sadly, the label stuck."

Jack looked straight ahead. "Words are powerful. Good words can bring life, and bad words can crush."[226]

Sam suppressed a chuckle. "To Johnny, the 'rotten' label became an identity. Mom kept me posted with random Rotten Johnny reports. He had a natural talent for music. In high school, he became a punk rocker, using Rotten Johnny as his stage name. At some point he formed a band with some other guys who all happened to be named John. They named their band the 'Rotten Johnnys.'" Sam chuckled at the memory.

"I had a couple of their CDs. They were okay. The band became a local sensation on the Chicago garage band circuit. Mom said that Johnny met a girl who was as crazy about him as he was about her. She actually got him to stop doing the drugs. They got married and had a couple of kids. He focused on his day job, and his life became stable. I guess he grew up…"

"It sounds like she was good for him," Jack commented.

"My mom says that Cousin Sue loves his wife like the daughter she never had."

"Mom gave me Cousin Sue's number, and I gave her a call. She invited me to come visit. I explained about my trip, and she asked if I could extend the trip over a second weekend. She suggested some family time and a little tourism. Having never been to Chicago before, a little sightseeing sounded like fun. Reconnecting with family sounded harmless enough."

Jack had an ah-ha moment. "Ah, that's why you cancelled our hike two weeks ago. I got your text saying you were out of town on business and could not make it."

"Postponed, not *cancelled*," Sam corrected Jack.

"I stand corrected," Jack replied. "By the way, glad we're out today. I've been looking forward to the falls since Discovery Park."

"All's good," Sam replied, then continued. "My estimate was that the job should take five days. I gave my boss the estimate and asked for a couple of extra days to cover contingencies in case the issue had legs. He said to make sure the client was content and that a couple of extra days as insurance was acceptable. The company would cover my stay through the second work week. But the second weekend would be on my dime. Monday would be a travel day, and we planned for me to be back in the home office the following Tuesday."

"It sounds like you're blessed with a reasonable boss," Jack noted.

"He knows I can be meticulous and always complete projects I'm given. He always has a firm pulse on everybody's workload. So, I had no doubt that he would have the next project waiting for me when I got back." Jack could tell that Sam felt comfortable with his job.

The interstate crested the last hill south of Everett. A full panorama of the Snohomish River Valley opened to their right. In the distance Highway 2 could clearly be seen crossing the valley and snaking up toward the Cascades. Jack drew another sip off his coffee. "Did you have a nice visit?"

Sam's eyes were fixed on the river valley. "I flew out that Wednesday. Thursday was a long day with solid progress defining and working the problem. On Friday, their whole office closed early in the afternoon, and nobody wanted to stay or work over the weekend. I called Cousin Sue, and she invited me over for dinner. I asked about Johnny, and she said he could use a friend. Something had happened, and he was not with his wife anymore. She also knew of my divorce. With our deep family ties, I guess she was thinking that I could be that friend."

"Did you see your cousin Johnny?" Jack asked.

"Sue called him. He had heard I was coming to town, and we met for lunch the next day. Johnny turned me on to his favorite local deep-dish pizza. It was the best pizza I've ever had. By the time we had finished our slices, I felt like we were brothers again. It was a warm spring afternoon, so he suggested a walk down by the lake, saying it would help the pizza settle. I was feeling unusually full and walking sounded like a good idea."

"Pizza and a walk by the lake. Now you are really making me homesick." Jack patted his stomach.

"I didn't realize that lake was so big." Sam turned to look at Jack. "You can't see the other side."

"When I was a kid, I thought Europe was on the opposite shore. I still remember the day my dad showed me a map and gave me a geography lesson." Jack laughed at the memory.

Sam turned to look out over the valley. "After looking out and not seeing the far side, I can understand a kid thinking that. Johnny and I walked along those big steps at the water's edge."

"We called those 'The Rocks,' and I know them very well. Most of the waterfront has those steps. They are breakwaters placed to preserve the shoreline. In some places they are covered with graffiti. At least then it was the primo local art." Jack smiled.

"At the end of a jetty, we stood looking out over the calm waters that surrounded us. Johnny said, 'I have something to talk to you about.'"

"I braced myself as I thought, *Here we go, marriage problems. Thanks a lot, Sue.*"

Sam turned completely in his seat to look directly at Jack. "I could tell that Johnny wanted my full attention. I was his captive audience at the end of that jetty. So Johnny looks me in the eye and asks, 'Have you met the Creator of the universe, life and everything?' I almost fell in the water."

"Awesome!" Jack quickly turned toward Sam, met his eyes and as quickly returned his gaze to the road ahead. "And?" Jack was liking the direction Sam's story had taken.

"Johnny went on to tell me how the previous summer, he had met up with some of his old rocker buddies, and they had gotten high together. A girl who once had a groupie thing for him was there, and she seduced him. His wife discovered what had happened and vehemently kicked him out of their home."

"Stumbling when he was high cost him what mattered to him the most. He was absolutely crushed—almost but not quite suicidal and was struggling to keep it all together. He had a coworker who knew what had happened, and this guy really liked Johnny and could tell that he was hurting bad. One cold snowy weekend sometime around the holidays, his friend asked Johnny to join him and his wife for a concert. Johnny said, 'Why not?'"

"He was blessed to have a friend who would care enough to want to lift his spirits," Jack commented.

"It gets better. The concert was at a dry venue featuring a couple of Jesus rock bands. When the last band was done with their set, one of the musicians remained on stage and began speaking to the audience. When he was done, he challenged the audience to meet Jesus for themselves. Something registered with Johnny. The speaker invited those who wanted to meet Jesus to come to the front. Johnny said that he went forward and prayed with one of the band members who had been waiting at the front to meet anyone who chose to come forward. That night he said his life changed. He said it was like going from black and white to living color."

"Your cousin had a real God moment. What happened then?"

"That was a Friday night. On Sunday morning, his work buddy brought him to his church. It wasn't too long before he parted ways with his old druggie friends."

"That sounds like repentance. What about Johnny's wife?" Jack asked.

"She was and still is dubious. At first when he fell, she was cold, mean and told him to stay away. Since then it sounds like she has been studying him. Late winter, she began to let him see the kids on a limited basis. When she saw that the change in him was more than theater, she began to let him see more of the kids. Now he sees his kids more than I see mine. I think, overall, she is slowly warming back to him. The fact that neither of them dated anyone else while they were apart speaks volumes of how they feel about each other." Sam's face brightened with a warm smile.

Jack said, "God is the healer of broken hearts."[343]

"That's what Johnny said." Sam looked down. "I wish that could happen in my own home."

"Talk to God about it."[191] Jack glanced at Sam.

A right turn brought them onto the Highway 2 causeway that led across the river valley. The mountains towered ahead. Jack finished his coffee. "I like your Johnny story. It sounds like he had a real 'God-can-change-a-life' experience."

"Oh, I'm not done yet. Lately he's been asking her to join him." Before Jack could respond, Sam added, "He asked me to go to church with him."

"Did you?" Jack asked, completely caught off guard.

"Yes, I did. The next morning, I picked him up at his place, and we drove in together. When we got there, standing in the doorway was a big bear of a guy who looked like he could have been a linebacker for the Chicago Bears. He looked at us with real warmth, grinning from ear to ear. He boomed, 'Welcome! This is where Grace meets Broadway.' My first impression was genuinely feeling welcomed by this giant. 'The address is on Grace Street, and the cross street is Broadway. We worship Jesus here. Come on in!' With that greeting, he extended one of his great paws to me. Johnny turned to me and said, 'This is Dwayne, the guy who took me to that concert where I met Jesus.' I remember liking Dwayne right away. Before we could say anything, this beautiful lady came up and put her arm as far around Dwayne as she could. She looked at Johnny and me with an equally glowing smile. 'Johnny, bring your friend, and let's all sit together.' When we settled into our seats, I looked all around. The place had seating for hundreds, and only a few open seats remained unoccupied. The crowd was a genuine mosaic of people. Every ethnic group and nationality must have been represented. The common thread was a glow on their faces and a sincerely warm look in their eyes. I could see why Johnny liked it there."

"The music had soul, and the preacher talked about spiritual armor.[344] By the way, I really want to know more about that," Sam added.

Jack replied, "The apostle Paul used the physical components of a Roman centurion's armor to illustrate how we should be prepared for spiritual battle."[39]

"That's what the preacher said, and then he elaborated for at least half an hour. After the service, the preacher met us at the door and was very welcoming. Johnny told him that I had recently met the Lord and had gotten saved. The preacher looked me in the eye and asked if I had given my heart to Jesus. I said, 'Yes, I have.' He followed up by asking if I had been baptized in water. I remembered our conversation and the difference between infant and adult water baptism. I replied, 'No,' and then quickly added, '…not yet.' The preacher gave me an inquiring look and asked, 'Will you be returning next Sunday?' I told him that I was on a business trip and would be in town through the next weekend. He handed me his card and said that the next Sunday they would be having water baptisms in the morning service."

"Really?" Jack blurted out.

Sam knew he had caught Jack off guard. "The pastor added, 'Give me a call, and I'll work you in. Before baptizing a convert, I require a meeting with every candidate to make sure the person understands what he or she is doing.' He wasn't really asking; he was telling me that is just the way it is. I felt okay with that, so I told him I would call when I knew my workload, and we could schedule time to talk."

Jack nodded approvingly.

Sam continued, "Monday, when I was back at the client's, things went terribly. I realized I had underestimated the scope of the problem. That night, I retreated to my hotel room. I remembered what you said about bringing our problems to God,[345] so I did. I prayed, but ours was more like a one-sided conversation. I brought up all the issues that seemed so impossible to resolve—one thing after another. Somehow, I felt like I was being heard. By the time I fell asleep, I felt better, but I still did not know what to do. When I woke up, I felt almost like someone was coaching me. 'Try this and do that and do it this way, but not like that.' Puzzling pieces seemed to fall into place. When I got to the client, I felt like I had a plan. I kind of felt like I was grabbing a wave and surfing to shore. All day Tuesday and late into the evening I worked smoothly and efficiently. Wednesday morning, I was done before lunch. That afternoon when I called my boss, he said that he had already spoken with the client who was impressed with my work and very happy with the results. My boss said that it looked like I'd earned a little free time. I should go enjoy myself, and he'd see me Tuesday morning. Thursday and Friday, I met with the preacher. Sunday, I was in the water."

"So your trip brought you favor with your boss, reconnection with family and getting yourself baptized in water."

"Yes, it did. I have more physical family than I did a month ago. I also feel like I have spiritual kin." Sam grinned from ear to ear.

Jack gave him a thumbs-up. "God blesses obedience.[346] I think the breaking point for you was that Monday night when you took your situation to God and talked it out with God.[347] His Holy Spirit is our helper[227] and often speaks to us in the early morning hours.[348] God also says that those who seek Him early shall find Him."[349]

"I think the Holy Spirit orchestrated things so that I would get baptized.[350] That Monday, I was feeling very down, thinking I might have to pass on the opportunity to get baptized." Sam looked down. "That thought became the real driver prompting me to pray. I prayed specifically asking God for things to work out, so I could get baptized at Johnny's church."

"It's God working in you."[351]

Sam looked up just in time to see the small brown sign. "This is the turn." Sam pointed ahead to the left to the next side street coming into view.

Jack scanned the signs. Low and to the right, he saw a little brown sign. "Thanks eagle eye, I would have missed that one."

Jack turned and took the street to a T-junction. Another little brown sign pointed to the right. After a few blocks, they took the left fork and passed through the entrance to Wallace Falls State Park.

∿

With his boots securely laced and double knotted, Jack began a series of stretches.

Sam began his series of stretches. "I see you're developing the habit of stretching before we hike?" Sam kidded Jack.

"Some wise guy once said I'd last longer if I did." Jack grinned broadly at Sam.

"Wise indeed." Sam reached for his toes to do a standing hamstring and calf stretch.

At the far end of the half-full parking area stood two small buildings. Between them was the trailhead and a plaza adequate for staging group hikes. At the far end of the plaza stood a large flat signboard. The near side of the signboard held a plexiglass-encased large topographical map of the Wallace Falls trail. They both stopped to examine the map. Jack took out his phone to take a photo for reference. Sam stepped around to the far side to find another plexiglass picture frame. Posted within the picture frame was information on the geology, flora and fauna to be seen along the trail.

Jack studied the map for distances and elevations. "The round trip to the lower falls will be a little more than three miles. That's about the same distance we did at Discovery Park."

"Except for a few hundred yards of cleared trail under power lines, the rest is wooded," Sam added.

Jack continued studying the map. "The map says net elevation gain from here to the lower falls is about five hundred feet. Continuing from the lower falls to the upper falls will be another eighth of a mile in pure elevation gain."

Sam came back around to the map side. "The view on top is great," he offered as an incentive.

"I do want to see that again. That's the part I remember best from when I was here." Jack looked up at the sky. "That hike was on a day much like today. It was the first time I'd hiked up a mountainside with aggressive switchbacks. I felt so accomplished standing at the top and looking out over the valley. It was one of those great life moments, and that was the day I truly fell in love with hiking."

"Those are great moments in life," Sam agreed as he looked at Jack. "I love seeing my girls discover things for the first time. I love as much seeing them rediscover something in a new and deeper way. Then I relish seeing them groove on it. My fathering motto is: 'A father's job is to pack his kids' heads with positive enlightening memories.' That must have been a great moment for you to have been eager to return."

"I've wanted to return. This is the first opportunity I've had in many years. Now I get to see if I can make it up to the top." Jack looked at the trailhead, adjacent to the sign.

DIVERSITY

JACK TURNED TO the patch of grass below the sign. "Here's a discovery thought for you…" He dropped his phone into the cargo pocket of his shorts and reached past his pocket to the patch of grass. He took hold of a single blade of grass near its base and plucked it out of the clump. The blade separated just shy of its fleshy base. He looked at it as he finished, "…grass." He handed the grass to Sam.

"A blade of grass? Big deal," Sam said as he looked at the blade of grass.

"Each one is unique," Jack replied. "They always have been and always will be."

"It looks like just another blade of grass to me."

"Okay, pick one type of grass," Jack suggested.

"What about the grass that covers the American prairie?"

Jack smiled. "What about the grasses that cover the Eurasian steppe or African veld?"

"What about Pampas or Savannah or my lawn? Okay, Jack, there's lots of kinds of grass."

"In each variety of grass, every single blade is unique from every other blade. They always have been, and they always will be—through all of time."

"Okay, that's a powerful statement," Sam replied.

"From high school biology, we learned the complexities of living cells: their molecular structure and the proteins and enzymes that comprise them."

Sam looked at Jack, then looked back at the simple blade of grass he was holding. "But, Jack, there must be billions upon billions of blades for any specific variety of grass. Surely there must be duplicates?"

Jack replied, "Count the variables." Jack extended his right hand in a fist. "Cell shape…" Jack raised a finger. "Cell count, cell arrangement, cell composition, the duration of the growing season, soil profile, nutrients, season, rainfall, drought and sunlight. Let's add wind, too. Breezes always make for heartier stalks." With each variable, he raised a finger until all ten fingers were raised. "Each blade of grass is stamped with its own fingerprint of uniqueness.[352] God does that to His pleasure."[27]

Sam rolled the blade between his fingers. "Each blade has so many cells. even if you got every cell identical in shape, configuration, number and size, the soil, sunlight and water would affect their chemical composition. That would also vary from one location to another—even with blades near each other, shading each other while they are growing and developing."

Jack started walking past the trailhead with Sam following a step behind him.

"Wow!" Sam looked at Jack. "God does not copy and paste, does He?"

"God pays attention to even the minutest of details. He tailors everything—right down to dressing the blades of grass."[352]

"That's a paradigm changer. Even the simplest things in nature look a bit different now."

"And?" Jack looked at Sam.

Sam looked at the trees they passed. "Tree rings tell us that some years provide more rain while some years are dryer. Whatever decomposes in the ground affects soil quality which, in turn, affects the chemistry of their cells." Sam looked back at the blade of grass between his fingers. "Total uniqueness per blade is realistic. You could have an almost perfect match. Except one cell shape would be different or the quality of a single enzyme within one of the cells would vary. Any factor could qualify a blade for uniqueness." Turning the blade between his fingers, he said, "When you think about it deep enough, it's actually easier for each blade to be unique than for them to be identical."

Jack replied, "God dresses the grass[352] and wildflowers[353] and feeds the birds.[174] While He does, He respects individuality and understands their specific needs. Imagine how He values us.[354] God knows how many hairs we have on our heads.[355] God loves diversity[356] and designed His creation to exist in harmony."[357]

"Deep thought." Sam nodded, looked at the blade and let it go. His eyes followed its path as it lightly fell to the ground.

Jack smiled. "Now you have that look."

"Thanks, I guess I do. "I've never thought of grass that way."

"Then think of pine needles that way too."

"Yeah, it would be the same." Sam chuckled.

The canopy opened to a grassy trail. Power lines appeared overhead. Like a reverse Mohawk, the clearing drew a line from where they walked down through the valley ahead and up across the far mountainside. "Impressive!" Jack tried his hardest to focus on the vista while ignoring the power lines.

The trail proceeded along the middle of the grassy clearing. Where the trail crested the next rise, they met a fork. The right fork was a spur that led to a picnic table. The table provided a place to rest with a full open vista of the valley fanning out below them. A family of four occupied the table. The adults were surveying the valley while the children played in the grassy field surrounding the table. Jack and Sam took the left fork to reenter the forest.

CREATION MEETS EVOLUTION

BACK UNDER THE canopy, Sam resumed. "Okay, I have another deep thought about the six-day test. While I was in Chicago and I spoke with Johnny's minister, I recalled your six-day test. So I asked him if he believed God created the world in six days. He grinned really big and gave me a hearty 'Amen! That's my God!' He said he could recommend some books so I could learn more."

Jack enthusiastically replied, "Good! It sounds like Johnny's minister gets it. You seem to have fallen into good hands."

"I may be having a mental pause...I understand the six days, but why was that an acid test?"

"I can give you two reasons why. First of all, the Bible says that when Adam sinned, he brought death into this world.[55] Therefore, there was no sin and no death prior to Adam."[358]

Sam considered what Jack had just said. "But Darwin's theory of evolution says that there was life and death for billions of years before man entered the scene."[359]

"The theory of evolution is in direct opposition to what the Bible says. The Bible says that God created the heavens and the earth in six days.[234] Man was created on that sixth day.[8] And Adam's sin in the garden is what brought sin and death into the world."[55]

"At the beginning, who was there?" Jack asked.

"Well, the book of John began with stating that God was there at the beginning,"[26] Sam replied.

"But who does the theory of evolution say was there? Who are the witnesses? Who are the people we can ask what happened?" Jack asked. "Where did the first speck come from?"

"Nobody was there to document what happened. The beginning happened before people happened," Jack continued. "Since people were not there to be witnesses to either the Creation or evolution, discussing Creation versus evolution becomes like solving a crime when there were no witnesses. We look at the evidence. What does the evidence testify?

"Well, there was supposed to have been a *Big Bang* to form the cosmos," Sam offered.

"Have you ever blown up stuff with fireworks? Put a big firecracker into something, light it, run and then watch the object suddenly go from one piece to countless pieces?"

Sam replied, "What kid hasn't? When I was at that age, Johnny and I would make models of things. Once in a while when we got some M-80's, we would build them into the models. Then for fun, we would blow them up."

"Did the pieces re-form in the air and reassemble themselves into something greater than they had been prior to the explosion?"

Sam laughed. "We could never find all the pieces. All the bits were trash."

"Sam, do you know the 'Second Law of Thermodynamics'?"

"Sure, entropy. Things decay over time, energy is lost. It's why a perpetual motion machine is impossible. It's why we need to put gas in our engines, paint our houses, whatever."

"Entropy technically is death—the loss of energy. All physical things eventually break down to the point where their very molecules go their own ways.[107] The world we live in is a case study in entropy. What if I told you that I have a pile of dirt in my backyard and that I'm waiting for it to turn into a red sports car, with a key in the ignition and a tank full of gas?"

Sam laughed. "I would say, 'That's not going to happen!' The most that pile of dirt will do is erode."

Jack laughed with Sam. "That's the difference between evolution and creation. The evolutionist will expect the red sports car to just happen by itself. The creationist will extract the minerals from the dirt and make something out of them. *Creationism* is also referred to as *Intelligent Design*. There had to be some intelligence behind the design."[26]

"So then, the honest answer would be that both creationism and the theory of evolution are religions. It takes faith to believe either way."

"I would venture to say that it takes more faith to believe that things happened from nothing, than to believe that there was a Creator who used intelligent design to make the world we live in. Consider air. There are so many elements and trace elements that it could not just have happened. In perfect balance, air is what we need to survive."

"More than a few minutes without this precious perfect mixture, and we would die," Sam acknowledged.

"Or consider the human eye. How does it see? Our noses smell by picking up particles floating in the air. But the eye is different; it's a wonder. That didn't just happen."

"I see your point. What about the layers of history the evolutionists have told us about?"

"Wouldn't you think that if animals had lived and died on the earth for hundreds of billions of years that there would be a lot more bones? The earth is big, but that's a long time. Shouldn't there be more than the rare fossil bed?" Jack asked.

"Well, hair, fingernails and bone decay at a much slower rate than flesh. However, there are places on Earth so dry and arid that flesh naturally mummifies."

"Especially in places like that." Jack asked, "After billions of years of animal life, wouldn't the soil be overflowing with fossil remains? Maybe every time you put a spade in the soil?"

Jack continued, "When rivers overflow their banks, they blanket the flooded land with silt. Upscale that to Noah's flood. All dry land was covered with water,[359a] and every breathing creature that lived on dry land drowned."[289] Jack paused for effect. "There was silt, lots of foliage and corpses. The saturated waters settled and then receded."

"That would explain why sedimentary rock covers roughly three quarters of the earth's surface while it only composes about five percent of the earth's crust." Sam gathered his thoughts. "That would also explain fossil fuels. When the corpses were done bloating, they would settle to the bottom, get covered by silt. They would compress under the weight of the silt and pressure of how many fathoms of water. *Voilà!* You find fossil fuel pockets trapped within layers of sedimentary rock. That would also explain the jellyfish fossils. I could never accept how they could say they happened over eons of time. But if masses of silt sloshed over them, trapped them and hardened, that would explain why today we can find perfect fossils of jellyfish."

"Oh, it keeps going. I'd recommend following up with Johnny's minister and get some titles on Creation Science." Jack looked to Sam. "Be the detective. You will find that honest science supports creation. While evolution is supported by continuously evolving theories, purposed to negate God. The biggest driver behind evolution is the intent of excluding God from the process.[359] To say God did not create the earth by intelligent design is like saying that sunshine does not affect climate. Personally, my faith had a firm skeleton, but when I learned about intelligent design, that put flesh to my faith."

"So then, any minister who supports the theory of evolution is willingly being ignorant of what the Bible says?"[359]

"A minister who cannot believe and teach that God did what God said that He has done when God said that He had done it does not believe the Word of God. Neither will that minister trust God to do what God promises to do."

"Ouch!" Sam commented. "Yeah, that's a disconnect."

"To say that things lived and died before Adam is in direct contradiction to how the Bible teaches that the world began. That minister will not be preaching the God of the Bible and will lead people astray.[360] That minister's god is limited. Our God is omnipotent."[24] Our God is the One who created life, the universe and everything."[27]

"That's the God I signed on with," Sam interjected. "Why bother with anything less?"

"Secondly," Jack continued. "God made it repeatedly clear that He created everything and that everything that was created;[26] He also created it all in six days.[234] The omnipotent[173] God of the Bible has that capacity, none other.[361] For a minister to teach a compromise between creation and evolution is simply diluting the gospel. A compromised gospel is no gospel at all. If you ask him and he concurs to things that contradict Scripture, shake the dust off your feet and walk away.[362] Who knows what other heresies he has bought into."[360]

"I guess the six-day test is a quick way to tell if the minister believes the Bible," Sam commented. "It's really quite binary. Their answer will be a firm yes or a waffling no."

"It's a fast check that gets immediate results." Jack laughed. "Everyone has opinions. The six-day test gauges how ministers honestly feel about God's Word."

"What about people?" Sam asked.

"People are always a product of their teaching," Jack replied.

"Which goes back to the pastor or minister or vicar or priest or whoever. Test the teacher to see if he is worth hearing,"[337] Sam replied.

"Always test everything,"[3] Jack commented.

For the last few hundred yards, they could hear the creek below sing its melody. The continuous brush that had obscured the creek opened at a stile. Jack stopped at the stile and took out his phone to review his photo of the trail map.

"Let's take a hydration break." Sam dropped his pack and pulled out a water bottle. "High road or low road?"

Looking up the trail they had been walking on, Jack took a refreshing drink of cool water. The wide railroad grade trail climbed steadily uphill. Below, past the stile, a narrow footpath led down the hillside to a bridge crossing the creek below. Past the bridge, the trail rounded the mountainside. "The woody trail looks prettier."

Sam added, "The woody trail has lots of ups and downs while the railroad grade is a consistent slow climb."

Jack looked past the stile that led to the woody trail. He drew another drink from his water bottle and returned it to the side pocket of his pack. "Since our last hike, I've been doing some uphill climbs. My apartment is near Picnic Point. From the beach to the parking area, that's about a four-hundred-foot elevation gain. I've hiked that trail more than a few times to build my stamina. I'm thinking that I should be okay."

Sam re-shouldered his backpack and looked over at Jack. "Lead the way!" First Jack then Sam squeezed through the stile and trekked down the narrow path that led toward the bridge.

Jack stopped on the bridge to look downstream and then turned upstream. He breathed deeply to fill his lungs with the rich cool air rising from the stream. "I love this stuff!" After voicing his thought aloud, he turned back toward the onward trail and resumed hiking. "Sam, how are you feeling about being baptized?"

"Jesus said I should,[158] and I did. I feel that I did the right thing."

"God promised us that we are obedient to His Word, things will go well with us."[363]

"I had a couple of one-on-one meetings with Johnny's minister. Each time we met, we talked for over an hour. The first time, he made sure that I understood what God's salvation was and that I had truly received Jesus into my heart. He explained how prayer and Bible reading are the nutrients of spiritual growth."[364]

Jack interjected, "Relationships are built by intercommunication.[365] Talk to God,[183] read His Word[166] and He will speak to you."[163]

"He said something like that. I told him I had not yet purchased a Bible." Sam paused. "I told him that I had been listening to an audio Bible through my phone. He said I needed a hard copy and that everyone who gets baptized in his church gets a new Bible. Then he went over to a box in the corner of his office and took out a Bible. On the inside cover, he wrote my name and the date of my water baptism. With a genuinely warm big ol' grin, he handed it to me, saying, 'It's also a good size to carry to church, making it easy to follow along with the minister's sermons.'"

"What version did he give you?" Jack asked.

"It's a New International Version Bible with Jesus' words printed in red. It's got a black leather cover, and the pages are softer than regular book paper. Later, I followed the text of Luke and Acts as I listened to the audio. I used my mechanical pencil to bracket and make notes in the columns. I brought it along to show you when we sit down for lunch up at the top of the falls."

"Cool! I look forward to seeing it." Jack immediately began to think of verses to highlight.

Sam continued, "That afternoon when I left his office with my new Bible, I felt comfortable with my decision to proceed with getting water baptized at his church. He insisted on our meeting again the next day. He said that he wanted to give me a toolkit for helping me live a victorious Christian life."

"Toolkit?" Jack's curiosity was sparked.

THE TRINITY

"WHEN I CAME in for the second meeting with Johnny's minister, I noticed the obvious plant at the far end of his desk—a lush, bright-green clover. After we had done a few warm-up formalities, he looked me in the eye and said, 'When I baptize you, I will be baptizing you in the name of the Father, the Son and the Holy Spirit.' Then he paused. I could tell he wanted the next words to stand for themselves. 'Do you understand what the trinity is?' I confessed, 'Not well enough to explain it to anyone.'

"'This will help you,' he said as he reached for the bushy plant and plucked the largest clover on it. He looked it over and then handed it to me as he proceeded to tell me the story of an early Church Father, who employed the clover to explain the trinity. 'Three leaves on a single stem. Three unique facets of God—all united in one.'"

"I appreciate that he wanted to make sure you knew what you were yourself getting into. You and Johnny appear to have fallen into good hands."

"I feel like we did."

Jack was curious to hear what Sam had gleaned. "Tell me about it."

"Thanks for the pop quiz!" Sam kidded. "Tell me if I've got this right."

"Go for it." Jack grinned.

"Johnny's minister said that when Jesus rose out of the water, the Holy Spirit in the form of a dove landed on Him. When it did, a voice spoke from heaven, saying, *'This is my son in whom I am well pleased.'*[366] When the Holy Spirit descended onto Jesus, God declared Jesus to be His Son. That puts the three of them together."

"Yes, that is the event recorded in three of the Gospels—Matthew, Mark and Luke,"[366] Jack replied.

Sam counted on his fingers. "God is the Father.[367] God is the Holy Spirit.[368] God acts through His Spirit.[369] God became flesh, and that's Jesus.[5, 118] Jesus said He and the Father were one."[370]

"Three in one and one in three," Jack commented. "God's concepts are always simple—'A+'!"

"I opened the new Bible to somewhere near the middle and laid the clover to press between the pages. Later in my room, I opened it to see where I had laid it. The clover was on Psalms 33, underlining the sixth verse. The verse said that God made everything by His breath."[371]

Jack stopped and extended his arm to stop Sam. Jack inhaled a long deep breath and slowly let it out. "In Hebrew, the name of God has four letters which can be pronounced as either Jehovah[372] or Yahweh." Jack looked at Sam. "Take a deep breath and listen to the sound your breath naturally makes as you inhale."

"Yah," Sam inhaled, audibly.

"Okay, now exhale and listen to the sound your breath makes when you exhale."

"Whey..." Sam audibly exhaled. "No kidding!"

Jack started walking again. "With every breath you take, you are calling out the name of God in Hebrew."

"In the language where it was first spoken!" Sam exclaimed.

Thanks, God! That'll be a reminder for Sam, Jack prayed under his breath. "The first recorded mention of breath is when God breathed life into Adam."[113]

Thanks, God, for giving me breath.[373] Sam paused his walking and looked out through a break in the trees.

Parallel with the trail and far above the treetops, Sam pointed at a bald eagle gliding along the valley.

Jack stopped to look. "What a great photograph or clip!"

"Some things are meant to be experienced when they happen: bluegrass, jazz, a bald eagle gliding across a vista.... Such a majestic bird gliding before a backdrop of forest, mountains, and puffy white clouds spotting a sapphire blue sky is one of those moments that just happens. Soak them up when they do."

"Tonight, when Marie and I video chat, she will love hearing about the eagle. Sam, are you an artist?"

"Everybody needs some kind of art in their lives," Sam replied. "I see pictures."

"*They that wait upon the* LORD *shall renew their strength; they shall mount up with wings as eagles; they shall run, and not be weary; and they shall walk, and not faint.*"[374]

Sam asked, "Jack, are you a poet?"

"No, I see illustrations of God's Word. The prophet Isaiah wrote that verse, which is part of a longer passage. God told him what He wanted His people to hear. The passage is the last verse in Isaiah chapter 40."

Sam, who was walking behind Jack, pulled out his phone and paused to type. "After I left the meeting with Johnny's minister, I found myself thinking about those people who audibly heard God's voice. What does God's voice sound like? Approaching thunder? Waves crashing against a rocky shore?"[375]

Jack nodded. "Power, with a tone of majesty."[376] I'm certain anyone who hears it would instinctively know whose voice it is. Someday we will all hear it."

"On a different point…didn't a dove bring the twig to Noah?"

Jack replied, "The dove brought a freshly plucked olive leaf to Noah.[377] That was how Noah knew the waters were receding."

"Coincidence?" Sam asked.

"There are no coincidences."

The ribbon-like trail hugged the contours of mountain. Each rise in the trail became a higher crest. The slopes grew steeper with each bend. Rounding the bends, the canopy shrank to its thinnest. The steep slopes limited the reach of the tall trees below. Sunlight filtered through the trees in streaks. Each emerging vista showed more of the snow-peaked mountains pouring themselves into the green valley below.

Using stepped breathing for the elevation climbs, Jack kept himself from getting winded. Talking was easier on the declines. There was just more gain than loss.

THE HOLY SPIRIT

AT THE TOP of a crest, Jack dropped his pack and retrieved his water bottle as he marveled at the jagged, snow-covered mountain peaks. After another long sip, he spoke. "The secret to living a victorious Christian life is cultivating a positive relationship with the Holy Spirit."

"If we let Him, the Holy Spirit can be active in our lives, teaching us things[227] and guiding us in truth.[378] He will give us inner strength[379] and boldness[380] and let us know what to do with it.[13] He will give us the power to be His witnesses,[381] living holy lives.[382] The Holy Spirit prays for us and helps us when we pray.[300] He is our access to God."[383]

Sam looked at Jack. "That's what the minister said. He went on to say that there was another baptism—a baptism in the Holy Spirit. On the return flight, I listened to Acts. Following along with my new Bible, I came across numerous mentions of a baptism in the Holy Spirit."

"Sam, the Holy Spirit was very visibly active in the early church," Jack explained.

"What happened?"

"People who didn't understand it told others they should not have it. Traditions developed, and the Holy Spirit became suppressed.[384] That's why some churches feel dry and dead when you enter. On the other hand, where the Holy Spirit is, there is liberty."[369] Those churches feel vibrantly alive."[381] Jack took another sip and slipped the bottle back into the side pocket of the pack. Standing up, he eased the strap over his left shoulder, and they resumed walking.

"When it comes to the perspectives on the Holy Spirit, you'll find a split among believers. The split parts on whether or not they believe the Bible is inerrant. Of all the people who believe the Bible, the old-line denominations say that workings of the Holy Spirit recorded in the book of Acts were for then—not for now. They say that if the Holy Spirit acts now, it's quietly and in subtle ways. Then there are churches that believe God is the same today as He was yesterday and will be forever.[92] They claim the Holy Spirit is as active and relevant today as it was in the first century. These churches pursue the baptism of the Holy Spirit and all it entails."

"Johnny's church felt alive with a warmth I could not explain. I felt at home there."

Sam continued. "To that minister, the Holy Spirit sounded relevant for his day-to-day living. When we met, he also spoke of spiritual gifts, spiritual fruit for spiritual growth and spiritual armor being essential for prevailing in spiritual warfare. He made it clear that he wanted me to understand that there was a lot to the spiritual. The minister's take-away for me was that when I came to Jesus, it was because the Holy Spirit drew me.[2] When I accepted Jesus as my personal Savior, the Holy

Spirit became my guide.[378] One of his takeaways for me was that life will go better when I make the Holy Spirit my friend."[385]

"I have a car analogy…"

"Okay, let's hear it."

"You see a car that catches your interest. It's available[386] and afford-able.[387] The price of the car is abandoning detrimental activities.[103] You are invited to sit in it.[157] That's when the Holy Spirit awakens you to the gospel.[2] When you are offered the key,[106] you take it and turn over the engine. That's when you accept the gospel and invite Jesus into your heart.[120] The gas in your tank is your living in repentance[145] and having fellowship with God by praying[183] and reading His Word.[166] When you put the car into gear and step on the gas, how does the car respond? Some people are content if their vehicle putters enough to get them about their daily business. Others want their vehicles to have the power for heavy lifting and the handling to tackle rugged terrain."[388]

Jack waited to let the analogy settle in.

"That would enhance my walk with the Lord?"

"Baptism in the Holy Spirit gives you a deeper walk. Did you notice in Acts that whenever the Holy Spirit was active on the scene, there was more spiritual energy?"

"I would describe what I read in Acts as high-octane Christianity."

Jack smiled, glad that Sam had picked up on that. "It could be said that the book of Acts was powered by the Holy Spirit."

Sam stepped up, onto and over a series of natural stairs formed by live tree roots crisscrossing the trail.

"The book of Acts opens with Jesus, who had died, had been buried and had risen from the grave.[389] For the next forty days, He was actively engaged with His followers. He told them about the kingdom of God and provided proof that He was alive.[390] In one incident, there were over 500 eyewitnesses.[155] After 40 days, Jesus ascended to be with God in heaven.[391] But before He did, He told His disciples to linger in Jerusalem for a promise to come from God the Father.[392, 393] He said they would be baptized with the Holy Spirit.[394, 381] Jesus said the Holy Spirit would empower them.[381] The apostle Paul said that the Holy Spirit is the earnest of our salvation[395]—a down payment on what's to come."[396]

"So, I already have the Holy Spirit?" Sam asked.

"Yes, Sam. When you accepted Jesus as your Savior and invited Him into your heart, Jesus gave you the Holy Spirit as a tangible guarantee on your future with Him.[395] We pray to God and Jesus. Jesus opened the lines of communication with God, and the Holy Spirit maintains them.[383] The Holy Spirit is the member of the trinity with whom we interact the most.[227] Receiving the baptism of the Holy Spirit empowers the Holy Spirit to work in the person's life."[381]

"A spiritual upgrade?" Sam asked.

"More like a spiritual enrichment,"[397] Jack responded.

The woody trail continued to wind through one horseshoe bend after another. With the modest elevation gain, Jack did not feel any strain worthy of mention.

As the trail rose to become new level ground, Jack continued, "Jewish holidays are related to feasts. Passover was the first and is the highest of all the Jewish feast days. In ancient days, devout Jews would crowd into Jerusalem for the Passover observance. Passover is the feast for remembering when the Israelites left Egypt.[398] Considered the holiest of all of the Jewish feast days,[399] the high day is the fifteenth. A Passover lamb is sacrificed the fourteenth.[400] Jesus was crucified and buried the day before[401] the commencement of Passover."[402]

"Coincidence?"

"No, prophetic fulfillment," Jack answered. "Jesus was the Passover Lamb."[403]

"The incident in Acts happened on the day of Pentecost, the harvest festival that comes seven weeks after Passover. Pentecost is the feast day for celebrating the first harvests.[404] Pentecost was another special day when devout Jews crowded into Jerusalem."

Sam considered the timing with feast days. "Maximizing the number of eyewitnesses retelling the same event would filter out discrepancies and reinforce the accuracy of the narrative."

"Yep." Jack looked out into the valley. "A deeper significance links these New Testament events to those Old Testament festivals. But that's a study all to itself."

Sam continued, "Acts said that Jesus followers were of one mind gathered together in one place[405] when the promise arrived. The place where they gathered was filled with the sound of a rushing wind[406] and they saw what looked like flames on top of each of them."[407]

Jack interjected. "They were filled with the Holy Spirit, which enabled them to speak in languages different from their own."[408]

Sam continued, "The author said that every known nation was represented among the witnesses.[409] When these witnesses heard the commotion, they came to check it out. When they got there, each one recognized his own native language being spoken."[410]

Jack added, "It must have been really something to see the many people and all the different languages all declaring the wonders of God.[411] Some of the languages must have been uncommon in Jerusalem—something the hearers would not have thought the speakers could have known.[412]

"What a sight-and-sound show nobody would forget!" Sam grinned.

Sam finished the story. "Peter spoke to the crowd and said that if they repented and were baptized in the name of Jesus Christ, they too could receive the gift of the Holy Spirit."[322]

Jack commented, "The release of that octane boost was a turning point for Christ's followers.[381] Over three thousand people heard, believed and got saved that day."[413]

They came to a marker identifying a fork in the trail. One path led to the falls and the other to the lake above the falls. Sam was in the lead and stopped at the fork. He slipped off his pack to pull out his water bottle. "How are you feeling?"

"So far so good," Jack replied.

"I heard you doing some stepped breathing earlier."

"Every rise!" Jack chuckled. He dropped his pack and pulled out his water bottle. "Overall I'm feeling pretty good—no straining in my chest."

"I'm glad to hear it." Sam raised his bottle in a toast. "The lake is past the upper falls. At the upper falls, we can consider doing the full loop to include the lake, return through this juncture or use the railroad grade."

"Let's stick with plan 'A' and head to the falls." Jack pointed with his bottle to the continuation of the woody trail. "We can think about plan 'B' for the return," Jack replied, returning his bottle to his pack.

With their thirst sated, they shouldered their packs and resumed their trek to the falls.

A trail runner came from behind and politely passed them. Ahead they could see a group of people who were apparently returning from the falls. "It's a beautiful day, and I had been expecting to see more people on the trail," Jack commented.

"The day is still young. I'd rather be here earlier than later."

Sam stopped a few yards short of the bridge. "This brook is fed by runoff from Wallace Lake."

Jack watched the single-file hikers. Not wasting energy on courtesy, they maintained their stride, stepping onto the narrow footbridge, crossing, passing and disappearing about the bend. "Let's take a look at that," he replied. He stepped onto the bridge and stopped in the middle. Pointed upstream, he closed his eyes and inhaled. The cool mountain water misting off the brook felt so fresh. Sam stopped and stood next to Jack.

Jack turned to look downstream. "God gave us two books to help us know Him. One is perfect, and the other is flawed. Of course, the perfect one is the Bible.[166] The flawed one is nature. The earth was perfect[48] before Adam's fall.[55] God's fingerprints are inescapable."[414]

Off the bridge and back onto the dirt trail, Jack resumed his breathing cadence for ease in climbing the gradually rising slope.

Sam recounted more of what he remembered from reading Acts.

"Another incident that caught my attention was about Paul traveling and finding some believers. When he asked if they had received the Holy Spirit, they said that they were baptized followers of John and unfamiliar with a Holy Spirit.[415] Paul explained that John the Baptist was the warmup for Jesus and that they should be baptized in the name of Jesus Christ. When they heard this, they understood and were baptized in the name of Jesus. Then Paul laid hands on them, and they were also baptized in the Holy Spirit."[416]

"That incident took place in Ephesus," Jack interjected. "Paul was traveling in Asia Minor. In what we know today as Greece and Turkey. Ephesus, at the time, was one of the largest cities in the Roman Empire. During the two years Paul resided in Ephesus,[417] many people became Christians and abandoned their pagan ways. Many of the new believers had a wealth in occult books, which they renounced and burned in public."[418]

"How much wealth?" Sam asked.

"A piece of silver weighs a bit more than half an ounce." Jack replied. "Paul's accounting has the books valued at fifty thousand pieces of silver. At twenty dollars an once, that would mean the new believers burned books valued at over a half million dollars.[418] The idol makers in Ephesus became irate when they experienced such a reduced demand for their occult paraphernalia that they rioted against Paul."[419]

"Sounds like the new believers exhibited some of that higher octane!"

"Jesus said they would receive power when the Holy Spirit came upon them.[381] The word He used for power is *dynamis*,[420] which is also the Greek root word for dynamite."

"Dynamite is high energy! I want some of that kind of energy! Why wouldn't any Christian want that?" Sam asked.

"It's all about the teaching or the lack of teaching. [421] As you read in the book of Acts, the baptism of the Holy Spirit is available to believers, and it will be dynamic in their lives. Somewhere after the earliest days of the early church, people who did not understand the *dynamis* of the Holy Spirit developed the doctrine of a passive Holy Spirit.[422] Their teaching is that the Holy Spirit exists but not the dynamic Holy Spirit of the first century."

"Another tradition—like Sunday and tolerating idols?"

"A yellow flag," Jack replied.

For the last couple of bends in the trail, a low natural-sounding drone had grown to become identifiable as the sound of rushing waters. Jack strained to listen. "I'm hearing something. We must be getting closer."

A couple came from the opposite direction. In passing, they volunteered some welcomed information: "You're almost there!"

"Over time, teaching on the Holy Spirit has become one of primary doctrinal dividers within the various denominations of the church.[423] Some denominations maintain a passive perspective of the Holy Spirit. They teach that God's Holy Spirit enters you when you get saved and water baptized or sprinkled as an infant. They see it as just another part of the process of attending a church. For them, the Holy Spirit is more like a conscience or guiding force. For all of us, prior to accepting Christ as our Savior, our conscience was morally relative—like a compass without a magnetic north. Then after accepting Christ as our Savior and tempering ourselves with God's Word, our conscience becomes more like a moral compass with a *true north*."[424]

"What about the *dynamis*?"

"Then there are other denominations with a more active view of the involvement of the Holy Spirit in our daily lives. They believe that what the New Testament described is active and relevant today. These denominations teach a separate baptism of the Holy Spirit that happens after you have accepted Christ and have been water baptized.[425] To them, conversion, water baptism and the baptism of the Holy Spirit are unique events—usually in that sequence. Conversion and water baptism are critical to salvation,[271] while the baptism of the Holy Spirit is a bonus.[381] For them, the baptism of the Holy Spirit is recognized as releasing an active and dynamic component of God into their lives."

"So, one group wants to be like the first-century Christians and the other group prefers to stick with tradition?"

"It's a matter of living a Christian life or having a more abundant Christian life."[426]

Clearing the final bend, a picnic area and a platform deck came into sight. Approaching the deck, Jack and Sam became aware of a group of people rapidly coming up from behind. Everyone converged on the deck at the same time, crowding the deck which already had people lingering at the railings. Down the trail, another group was coming into view from behind.

To look over the railing at the waters crashing below, Jack had to squeeze past the lingerers. Sam followed in Jack's wake, stepping up to the railing next to Jack. "The view is better higher up."

Jack looked around at the other people on the platform. "This must be the most crowded part of the whole trail. Let's go for the middle falls."

Sam looked at the crowd around them. "I was hoping you'd say that." Without another word, Jack and Sam pulled away from the crowded railing and eased off the deck. They left the crowd and returned to the trail, commencing their ascent to the middle falls.

"I had been thinking of lunch at the picnic area." Sam pointed.

"If I had not been feeling well, that would have been a good idea."

"We'll find other spots to picnic up higher. We might as well work up more of an appetite." Sam chuckled.

"I remember the view from the upper falls. I want to see that again." Jack pulled out a baggie from a cargo pocket, shook out some raw almonds and offered the baggie to Sam, who shook out a few.

The trail wound up the mountain. Sam could hear the cadence of Jack's breathing as they climbed. Jack wasn't saying anything, which told Sam that Jack was concentrating on how he was feeling as they climbed. He decided not to say anything, but instead monitor Jack's breathing. It seemed logical enough that any breathing irregularity would precede a potential crisis.

It didn't take long before the trail crested, and the middle falls viewing deck came into view. Sam passed Jack at the crest and was the first to step onto the viewing deck for the middle falls. Jack, who had stopped briefly at the crest, came up behind him.

"Just like I remember, the view does improve." With the deck to themselves, Jack stood at the railing. "I see more treetops than I saw at the lower platform."

Sam heard noise and turned around. The noise came from the same large group of people they had seen on the lower falls viewing deck. "How are you feeling?" Sam asked Jack.

Jack turned to respond and saw the approaching crowd. "Good enough to attempt the upper falls."

"Glad to hear it," Sam replied.

Seeing the group's rapid approach to the platform, Jack looked to Sam and said, "Let's go all the way to the top." They exited the platform before the first of the next wave of occupants arrived.

Beyond sight of the platform, the upward trail became a series of switchbacks cut into the steep mountainside. The rushing sound of the middle falls dissipated as they climbed. Stopping at the fourth switchback, Sam dropped his pack and took out his water bottle. "This part of the trail is almost all switchbacks. Are you up for it?"

"I'm just a little winded." Sam noticed Jack's sentences were getting shorter. "I do foresee a lot of breaks."

"I'm okay with lots of breaks." Sam stood and began climbing the ramp toward the next switchback.

Except for the rhythmic cadence of Jack's Lamaze breathing and the crush of gravel below their boots, the trek upward was quiet. Sam led the way and stopped every other switchback, allowing Jack to catch up. At one switchback Jack parked himself on top of a big rock. "If this trail were to go straight from bottom to top, it would be a ladder." Sam smiled to a flash memory of a hike when his four-year-old Chloe was climbing tree roots as if they were rungs on a ladder.

"That's why this leg allows for lots of breaks. Switchbacks thin the herd. The upper falls will be the least crowded of the three," Sam noted.

Below them, scattered people were climbing the switchbacks. Above, others could be seen descending. Seeing Sam and Jack sitting on a rock sipping water, one sightseer sauntered downward, offering a word of encouragement. "The falls are just over the next rise." Before either could respond, the hiker turned through the switchback and was already steps down the next ramp.

Sam looked at Jack and started to laugh. "There is only one rise left; this one crests right in front of the falls." They both laughed.

When they crested the rise, the trail leveled, and they could hear the rushing waters of the upper falls.

Nearing the falls, the trees thinned and opened into a vista. From the upper platform, they could see over the falls and into the whole valley. "This was so worth it," Jack breathed. Standing at the railing, he closed his eyes. *Thank You, God, for the strength to make it to the top and a hiking partner patient enough for all my rest breaks.* Opening his eyes, all he could do was soak up the view. Jack did not notice when Sam slipped away.

Sam left to look around for a semi-private spot with an optimal view so they could sit, eat and talk. He headed off the platform and onto the trail leading above the falls. He paused at a signpost. Stepping away from the signpost, Sam headed back toward the water above the falls. Jack turned to see Sam wander over to an exposed rock surface, drop his pack and plant himself. Jack lingered for one more long look over the railing at the falls below. Exiting the deck, he headed up to where Sam had parked. Crossing his legs, he set down on the rock surface an arm's length from Sam. Their perch had a better view over the valley than the viewing deck had offered. The muted sound of rushing waters filled the air.

Jack pulled out one of his water bottles and consumed a third in a single drink. "After the heart attack, I felt damaged. Stairs were some-where between difficult and impossible. With every physical activity I did, I became hyper-vigilant regarding how my body was feeling. One day when things did not feel like they were going to get any better, I remembered God said He would heal the brokenhearted and bind up their wounds.[343] He said that He is the One who heals us,[427] so I knelt and asked God to heal me. Jesus said whatever we ask in prayer, we will receive—if we have the faith."[195] Jack straightened his back and took a deep breath. "Today at this very moment, I feel just as lousy as I did when I did this hike at twenty-seven!"

Sam looked questioningly at Jack.

Jack burst into laughter. "Actually, I feel better today, right now, than I did way back then."[428]

"You climbed like a champ."

"I always keep a vial of nitroglycerine on my keychain. I probably always will. Today is a milestone on my road to cardio recovery. There was never a point in our climb that I felt the need for a nitro. I could not have done this even a couple of weeks ago." Jack lifted his half-full bottle of water for a toast.

Sam reached over with his water bottle, clinked plastic to fulfill the spirit of the toast. "It'll be easier going down than it was coming up." Sam pointed to the signpost. "The notice on the sign says the trail from here to the lake is closed. That means we've peaked, so no loop today. It's all in and out, which means downhill from here. You may not need your nitro at all today."

"I can live with that. I'm feeling accomplished to have made it up here. What a great workout!" Jack said as he pulled out one baggie con-taining a sandwich and another stuffed full of carrot and celery sticks.

Soaking on the vista, they leisurely consumed what they had brought. From where they sat, the upper platform was visible below them. The voices of the people on the platform were covered by the waters cascading over the falls.

Upon finishing his lunch, Jack stuffed all his trash into one of the used baggies. Sam likewise gathered his trash and stuffed each piece into an empty water bottle, which he deposited in the main pocket of his pack. From a side pocket, he pulled out a full water bottle. Taking a sip, he rinsed his mouth and then he swallowed a bigger sip. He set down the water bottle and fished a bigger gallon-size baggie out of the pack's front pocket. "Check this out," he said as he handed it to Jack.

Jack took the package. "This looks nice!" He opened the bag and lifted out the Bible. "Leather, nice, gold-edged pages, nice." He thumbed through it to the gospels. "Jesus' words in red—nice."

"Yeah, isn't that cool? The first night, I just paged from one red-lettered verse to another."

"It does not have any of the extra helps I saw in other Bibles. The minister cautioned me to always rely on God's Word directly, rather than leaning on commentaries with opinions that attempt to interpret or reinterpret God's Word."

"It sounds like he wanted to make sure you started off on the right foot."

"He said that, in time, I would probably be getting a couple of different kinds of Bibles. Some with a commentary toward a particular focus. But for having a Bible to bring to church, having one that was plain and simple felt good."

Jack leaned over to his pack and from the front pocket took out a pad of paper and a pen. "Would you mind if I gave you a few verses to chew on?"

"I expected you would."

Jack wrote the book, chapter and verse number and then quoted the Scriptures.

Proverbs 3:5-6, *Trust in the LORD with all your heart and lean not on your own understanding; in all your ways let yourself be instructed by Him, and He will make your paths straight.'* [429]

Matthew 6:9-13, *In this manner, therefore, pray: Our Father in heaven, Hallowed be Your name. Your kingdom come. Your will be done On earth as it is in heaven. Give us this day our daily bread. And forgive us our debts, As we forgive our debtors. And do not lead us into temptation, But deliver us from the evil one. For Yours is the kingdom and the power and the glory forever. Amen.*[190]

"These are all fundamental verses to commit to memory. They will remind you how to listen and how to pray."

"I think I'll be sharpening my red pencil," Sam commented.

"I use one of those checking pencils that's red on one end and blue on the other. The blue is nice for underlining Jesus' words," Jack replied. He paused to look at the peaks in the distance. "Here's a verse for Bible validity—2 Timothy 3:16-17." Jack looked down at the paper and wrote, *"All Scripture is God-breathed and is useful for teaching, rebuking, correcting and training in righteousness, so that the servant of God may be thoroughly equipped for every good work."*[166]

"*Sola Scriptura.*" Sam nodded.

"It's also the guideline for applying 2 Corinthians 9:8." Jack quoted as he wrote. "*And God is able to make all grace abound toward you, that you, always having all sufficiency in all things, may have an abundance for every good work.*[73] And Ephesians 2:8-10 says, '*For it is by grace you have been saved, through faith and this is not from yourselves, it is the gift of God not by works, so that no one can boast. For we are God's handiwork, created in Christ Jesus to do good works, which God prepared in advance for us to do.*'"[111]

"Training, budget and mission," Sam remarked.

"Here is a favorite for directional stability."

Psalm 1, *Blessed is the one who does not walk in step with the wicked or stand in the way of sinners or sit in the company of mockers, but whose delight is in the law of the Lord, and who meditates on his law day and night. That person is like a tree planted by streams of water, which yields its fruit in season and whose leaf does not wither whatever they do prospers. Not so the wicked! They are like chaff that the wind blows away. Therefore the wicked will not stand in the judgment, nor sinners in the assembly of the righteous. For the* LORD *watches over the way of the righteous, but the way of the wicked leads to destruction.*[247]

Jack paused and looked out at the farthest peak. "The first Psalm is a good one to commit to memory. It goes well with Romans 6:23, which says, *'For the wages of sin is death, but the gift of God is eternal life in Christ Jesus our Lord,'*[103] which Jack added to the list. "There are so many good verses."

Sam said, "Those sound like good places to start."

Jack was not done, but neither did he want to overwhelm Sam. "And here is your sonic screwdriver that will save you when you feel like you are about to cave to temptation: 1 Corinthians 10:13. *'No temptation has overtaken you except such as is common to man; but God is faithful, who will not allow you to be tempted beyond what you are able, but with the temptation will also make the way of escape, that you may be able to bear it.'*[38]

Jack tore the page from his pad, folded the paper and placed it between the pages that opened to Galatians 1. He held the Bible open to show Sam to show where he had inserted the paper. "This is a good place to start reading Paul's letters." Jack slipped the Bible back into the baggie and handed it back to Sam.

"Thanks." Sam took the Bible, bled the air out of the baggie and resealed it. "I'd been wondering where to read next."

"I have a solution for that."

"What's that?"

"I'll show you when we get back to the truck."

"Okay, I'm curious."

"You'll like it." Jack replied with a grin.

Baptism in the Holy Spirit as Evidence

Sam returned the baggie containing his Bible to the front pocket of his backpack. "Before the climb, we were talking about the baptism of the Holy Spirit."

Jack replied, "Whereas water baptism is immersion and symbolizes the death of the 'old man'[430] and the birth of a new creature in Christ,[179] the baptism in the Holy Spirit is more of an anointing than an act of getting wet."

Sam burst into a laugh. "When I was baptized, I got completely soaked. The pastor and Johnny told me to bring a change of dry clothes. I'm glad they did because I needed them. It didn't sound like anyone got wet when they were baptized of the Holy Spirit."

"Don't worry; I'm not going to suggest we get into that pool of water." Jack pointed to a calm pool of water separated from the river by a long island and a dammed channel.

"We'd watch ourselves turn purple if we did." Sam laughed. "The water in that river is snow melt off. It must be just above freezing." Jack laughed along with Sam.

Sam resumed, "Baptism and anointing are more of those words that sound so religious. Now you're merging them?"

Jack sipped his water. "Baptism is immersion,[273] and anointing is the act of smearing a dense liquid, like oil, onto and into a surface.[431] The visual I use for something being anointed is applying and working oil into leather to rejuvenate and preserve the leather. Anointing takes the leather from being dry, stiff and brittle to making it as supple as living hide."

Sam looked over at the falls. "So, water baptism is for the symbolic washing away of our sins, and the baptism of the Holy Spirit is an anointing to preserve, protect and enhance?"

"After the day of Pentecost, the word *anointed* took on an entirely new meaning.[432] It referred to Christians who were infused with the power of the Holy Spirit,[433] empowering them to do what God wanted them to do. When we invited Jesus in to our hearts,[157] we asked the Holy Spirit to take up residence. When we gave our hearts to Jesus and were saved, He gave us the Holy Spirit as the earnest of our salvation.[395] From that moment on, the Holy Spirit took up residence[434] and became our guide,[378] teacher and helper."[227]

"Guide, teacher and helper?" Sam repeated.

"When we drove out here this morning, you told me about the problem you were having with the project on which you were working. You said you asked God for help before you went to sleep and woke up with the solution."

"I knew the elements, so it's not like I was trying to reinvent the wheel. But I would never have thought to put the elements together in the way that I did."

"You asked,[266] and the Holy Spirit brought back to mind[435] what you needed to develop the solution. The Holy Spirit then showed you how to put it together.[436] By the way, did you thank God?[437]

"Ummmm…" Sam bowed his head. *Thanks, God, for the incredible solution only You could have given me.*

"I don't think things would have gone so well a couple of months ago." Sam realized that he had actually experienced a spiritual assist with a tangible real-world problem. *Thanks, God, for proving Yourself.*

"You got an appetizer. The baptism of the Holy Spirit gives you *dynamis* and comes with gifts and fruit. The baptism of the Holy Spirit is more of an anointing—an immersion in God's Spirit."

Sam rocked slightly, nodding his head. "I see. That's why Johnny's pastor advised me to learn more about the Holy Spirit and recommended that I make the Holy Spirit my friend. So, how do I receive the baptism of the Holy Spirit?"

"The simple answer is ask, believe and receive.[195] The longer answer is to do a heart check, then ask, believe and receive."

"Heart check?" Sam questioned.

"The question to ask yourself is 'Do I want this for myself or do I want this for God?' Acts 8 contains an account of a sorcerer who got saved named Simon.[438] When Simon saw people getting baptized with the Holy Spirit, he offered money to buy the gift so that he, like the apostles, could also impart the Holy Spirit.[439] Peter rebuked Simon, telling him that his heart was not right with God.[440] Peter went on to say Simon's heart was captive to sin, poisoned by bitterness and generally wicked. The solution was first for Simon to repent of his wickedness."[441]

"After the heart check?" Sam asked.

"Ask, believe and receive."[195] Jack pulled out his pad and pen to write something and handed it to Sam. "Here is a prayer you can pray after you've done a heart check."

Sam accepted the paper and read:

Heavenly Father, I come today in total repentance of all my sins and seek to know You in greater measure. I seek You and ask for You to impart to me the gift of the anointing of Your Spirit. I humble myself before You, submitting myself, and yielding myself in total obedience to You only. In doing so, I ask for You to baptize me now. Anoint me in the power of the Holy Spirit to receive gifts of your anointing to use for God's kingdom. Come, Holy Spirit, I receive You to mold me, melt me, fill me and use me now for God's glory only and not my own. I receive by faith the baptism of the Holy Spirit. Thank You, Lord Jesus, for baptizing me in Your Holy Spirit. Amen.

"Thanks, Jack. I will save that for my quiet time." Sam folded the paper, took out the baggie holding his Bible and slipped the prayer between some pages in his Bible. Resealing the baggie, he returned it to his pack. "Jack, when I asked Jesus into my heart, I felt something that I cannot put my finger on. But it felt genuine, and I knew something good had happened."

"What you felt was the Holy Spirit. Right after Jesus says that anything we ask in His name, He will do it.[197] He says that if we love Him and keep His commandments, He will give us the Holy Spirit[442] who will dwell in us.[443] The Holy Spirit is the earnest of your future with God[395]—a down payment[396] on the next level of our walk."[303]

TONGUES

SAM STARED OUT across the peaks. "If I already have the Holy Spirit, then how do I know when or if I've been baptized in the Holy Spirit?"

Jack said, "In the book of Acts, the accepted proof of those who were baptized in the Holy Spirit was that they spoke in tongues."[444]

"Tongues?" Sam asked.

"Jesus said that a new language would be a sign of those who believe.[445] With a private prayer language with God's Spirit praying through us,[446] our tongues have the power of life and death.[200] The Spirit gives life,[447] so praying in the spirit is speaking life over a situation. When you come to God in prayer, you come with petitions and supplications and thanksgivings. When you pray, your mind is conscious of what it is praying about, driving you to pray about the problem. When you pray *in tongues*, the Holy Spirit is praying through you. The Holy Spirit knows all things.[13] When you pray to God in tongues, His Holy Spirit is assessing the situation and discussing the solution with God."[300]

"That's a paradigm shift!" Sam turned to look at Jack. "When I prayed about that problem at work, all my mind could see was the problem. All I could remember was churning over the details that were not coming together. In the morning when I woke, everything seemed arranged differently, and I walked right through the solution."

"Sam, God saw the solution before you knew there was a problem."[448]

"So, where do I learn this language?" Sam asked.

"You don't. You just let go and let God. I think of body surfing. You see the wave, jump into it and let it take you to shore. When you are anointed with the Holy Spirit, the Holy Spirit wells up inside of you.[436] If you allow, it will percolate to the top and manifest itself in the speech of a different unknown language.[449] At some time when you're praying, you will find different words wanting to come out.[149] That's perfectly acceptable. There will be some kind of structure, syntax, syllables, etc., but you won't be able to interpret what you're saying.[300] Most importantly, your personal barometer is that you will feel peace[450] in your spirit, and deep inside you'll know it's right. When you get comfortable with speaking in tongues, it's becomes like releasing a valve or opening the throttle. Part of our spiritual armor is that we are directed to pray for each other 'in the spirit.'"[451]

"When my sister and I were little, we had our own private language. It was fun to be in public or even with our parents saying stuff, and nobody else knew what we were talking about. Having that kind of a relationship with God would be incredible!"

"Sam, on a personal level, praying in tongues is spiritually edifying for the speaker[446] because it's the power of the spoken word,[200] and it's the Holy Spirit speaking life through you."[445]

Sam took another drink and secured his water bottle in his pack's side pocket. "I will definitely be thinking about this."

"Do that; it's a worthy meditation." Jack sealed his gear, stood and stretched. "It's the effective solution for an empowered[452] Christian walk."

Sam stood, and before shouldering his pack, he performed a set of full body stretches.

"So praying in the Spirit is part of spiritual armor?[451] You've got to tell me more about this armor."

Jack reshouldered his pack. Before stepping onto the trail that would take them back down the mountain, he stood straight, breathed deep lung-filling breaths and gave the valley a long final look to commit the vista to memory. "Relationships are built on communication. Prayer is talking to God. Praying in the Spirit is God's using our own mouth[453] to send a coded message[149] to Him.[454] Our struggle is not with the physical but with the spiritual.[45] Praying in the Spirit is the battlefield communications[451] of spiritual warfare."

"Oh, that makes sense. Battlefield communications are one of the most important elements in any soldier's toolkit. On a battlefield, comms are essential for victory and for maintaining order to keep the battle from dissolving into chaos and defeat. One of the primary objectives in battle is to disrupt or corrupt the comms of the opposing force to put them into confusion."

"The principles in spiritual warfare are not that different from strategy on the physical battlefield. Bad comms[6] lead to confusion.[423] We need to maintain optimal communication with God.

"It's about building that personal relationship with God, eh?"

"Exactly," Jack replied. "The early Christians were no strangers to persecution. They understood that even though the persecution was physical, the driving force behind the persecution was always spiritual.[45] Paul gives us a complete spiritual toolkit for how a Christian should be prepared for engaging in spiritual warfare."

SPIRITUAL ARMOR

"THE FIRST TIME I heard Johnny's minister, he spoke about spiritual armor. Later in our meetings he said spiritual armor would be critical to my spiritual survival."

"You'll love this," Jack said. "To illustrate the elements of the spiritual toolkit, Paul compares the spiritual elements to the physical components of armor that a Roman soldier would have worn and used when going into combat. Paul encouraged us to be sober and strong in all of the elements so that we could withstand the wiles of the Devil[455] who is like a hungry lion prowling for its next meal.[18] Like a soldier is trained for hand-to-hand combat, we should have all the elements in place so we can stand firm when a bad day comes[39] because God wants us all to be overcomers."[456]

Jack stood at the crest of the trail, looking down at the descending switchbacks. Sam joined him at the crest.

"It'll be easier going down than it was coming up," Sam noted. "How are you feeling?"

"I feel like I just had a long lunch following a full workout." Jack answered with a laugh.

"Well then, let's do it." Sam stepped past Jack and began the first ramp descending to the first switchback.

Jack lagged only a few yards behind Sam. "All this down may be a little tough on our knees. Let's plan on a rest at the lower falls before the last leg."

Sam set a leisurely pace. "By armor, you're talking about shields and swords and stuff?"

THE BELT OF TRUTH

"BY ARMOR, PAUL is referring to everything the soldier wears when going into battle. Starting with the fabric that is in contact with his body."

"Didn't everyone wear a toga back then?"

"Togas were outerwear fashion that spoke of class and rank. Not everyone wore togas, but everyone wore tunics, the underwear or the fabric in contact with the skin. The simplest tunic was a rectangular piece of cloth with a hole for the head. The wearer had a belt of some kind to keep the tunic from flowing in the wind and revealing the wearer's body. Traditionally, men wore their tunics short for mobility, and women wore their tunics long for modesty. The belt set the height for the tunic. At night they would remove the belt, and the tunic became a nightshirt."

"Let me guess. The first article of armor is the belt so that a soldier is not running out into battle with his nightshirt flapping in the breeze." Sam snickered at his visual.

Jack joined Sam's snicker with his own. "Not only would it look ridiculous, but his legs would become entangled in the fabric, and he would literally be tripping all over himself. That problem would not be effective in battle or anything else demanding mobility."

Sam began to laugh heartily. "Warriors in nightshirts, tripping on themselves and falling on their faces…." As Sam's laughing died down, he added, "…great visual."

Jack waited for Sam to join him mentally. "Sam, the soldier's dress was all about function over form. The belt Paul spoke of is truth."[457]

Sam went quiet, then let out an "Oooo…ouch! If you don't have truth, then you trip on yourself and fall on your face."

"Ain't that the truth!" Jack replied. "It all starts with being purified by God's truth[165] and then by standing on His truth."[458]

"Standing on truth always provides the firmest footing," Sam chimed.

The Breastplate of Righteousness

"After the tunic is adjusted and locked in place by the belt of truth, the next piece of spiritual armor is the breastplate of righteousness.[457] The breastplate would protect the vital organs. Injury to any one of them in battle would be an end to participating in any battle."

"But, Jack, isn't righteousness just knowing right from wrong?"

"God loves righteousness[458] and hates lawlessness.[459] We live by physical laws like gravity or that you are what you eat. They affect our physical world. Survival is dependent on learning what is beneficial and what is toxic. It's the same parallel with our spiritual beings. The way that you stay away from physical toxins, your spiritual health hinges on your staying away from things that are spiritually toxic."

Descending the mountainside switchback by switchback, they watched the canopy rise. The tall hemlocks and fir trees allowed them to see through the straight trunks into the valley below. Ahead Jack saw the same rock where he had rested on their ascent. "Let's break at the big rock above the next switchback."

"Sounds good. The view is too good not to take a moment to enjoy it again," Sam called back.

"Sam, I'd also like to add another verse to that list I gave you."

"Okay." Sam reached the rock first and set his pack on it. Jack watched him retrieve the packet, place it on the rock and get his water bottle out before setting the pack on the ground and sitting on the rock.

Jack took out his pen and grabbed his water bottle before setting his pack on the ground and joining Sam. "Even though we are looking through trees, the view over the trail below with all of its switchbacks is spectacular."

Jack took the packet and opened the Bible to Galatians where he found the list of verses he had compiled above the falls. "Philippians 4:8 is another good verse to commit to memory." Jack quoted as he wrote, *"Finally, brethren, whatsoever things are true, whatsoever things are honest, whatsoever things are just, whatsoever things are pure, whatsoever things are lovely, whatsoever things are of good report; if there be any virtue, and if there be any praise, think on these things."*[460] Once he had finished writing, Jack refolded the paper and returned it to the page open to Galatians. He put the Bible into the baggie and handed it to Sam who sealed the baggie and returned the packet to his pack.

"That sounds like a good verse to meditate on at night."

"It's about where we park our thoughts." Jack looked far into the valley. "To be *righteous* means being just in one's ways, lawful, correct and vindicated by God.[461] The servants of sin are free of righteousness[462] and those who have been freed from sin are servants of righteous-ness.[463] Living righteously is living by God's law to please God.

"Righteousness is a heart issue. Our heart, the seat of our primary emotions,[83] is where we believe. Righteousness is the armor to protect our hearts," Jack explained.

"Sounds like righteous living becomes a restraint to sinning."

"Jesus said that He did not come to call the righteous, but sinners to repentance.[464] Jesus also says that those who hunger for righteousness will be satisfied,[465] and those who are persecuted for righteousness' sake will have a place in heaven.[466] However righteously we live our lives,[467] God refers to what we do 'as filthy rags.'[468] God said that none is righteous, no not one,[469] but God's righteousness is available to us through Jesus.[470] Who by his death on the cross,[358] took our sin onto himself, that we might exchange our unrighteousness and self-righteousness for his righteousness."[340]

"Another benchmark? We get a clean slate? Then how do I learn what is righteous?" Sam asked.

"God's Word is the plumb line He uses to measure righteousness.[166] The first usage of righteousness in the Bible was to describe the char-acter of Noah, the only man who God considered worth saving from the worldwide flood. Noah's righteousness bought him and his family passage on the ark. The next incident was Abraham, whose faith God counted to him as righteousness.[471, 472] When Jesus died on the cross, His blood washed away our sin,[473] and we were credited with His righ-teousness.[339] In practice, to be *righteous* is 'to think and live according to that which is right according to God's Word.'[166] It means taking seri-ously the admonitions to take off the old man,[430] put on the new man[179] and to begin renewing the mind.[492] Ideally, Christians should think in the same way Christ Jesus does[474] and remember that God's righteous-ness endures forever."[458]

As Sam walked through the next two switchbacks, Jack could tell he was reflecting. "So, there is nothing we can do to earn God's righteousness, but we get it from Jesus as part of our salvation.[340] We learn about it and how to maintain it through Scripture?"[166]

"Yep. It's a gift for us to grow and to grow into. Righteousness is one of the fruit of the Spirit."[475] Paul refers to it as walking in the light."[476]

Sam noted, "The soldier's breastplate would protect their heart and vital organs. Spiritually, that would be done by living a righteous life according to God's Word?"

Jack smiled. "You know a tree by its fruit."[477]

"Not many walnut trees grow apples," Sam kidded.

GOSPEL SANDALS

"THE NEXT ITEM in a soldier's armor is his footwear." [478] "Your favorite topic!" Sam kidded Jack.

Jack remembered his grandfather's words about shoes. "My grandpa used to say we should take care of our feet because that is how we get around. Paul likened good footwear to being prepared[479] to share the gospel anytime and anywhere."

Good time for my sandal story, Sam thought. "A few years back, I needed a new pair of hiking sandals, so I went sandal shopping. People have been wearing sandals for a long time, so I figured that there must be more than what I saw at the mall stores. In my research, the ones that caught my eye were the sandals of the Roman soldiers. My bent has always been more toward function than form. The Roman soldiers spent their waking hours in their sandals, so they must have been very comfortable. They crossed deserts, climbed mountains and fought battles while wearing those sandals."

Oh, this sounds quite interesting, Jack thought. "I've thought about getting a pair of hiking sandals. What made the Roman soldier's sandals so good for walking?"

"The basic sandal was their combat boot. It was made of a single piece of leather, sewn up the back and from bottom to top tied in the front. The leather had lots of slit-like openings so when bound, they would conform to the wearer's foot and allow their feet to breathe. As the leather was broken in and conformed to the wearer's foot, they became like a second skin. Even in cold climates, they wore the same sandals. For insulation, they wrapped wool fabric around their feet."

"I read that they could march twenty-five miles every day after day. I just thought of them as being fit and healthy. But marching like that would require good footwear."

"The soles had two more layers, and all three were nailed together with hobnails. The hobnails gave traction, reduced wear and were effective for stomping on a fallen foe. Hobnails were the original cleats runners and athletes use to maximize their traction."

"Thanks, Sam, you shed a whole new light on that verse. We should be prepared with the gospel—like wearing a comfortable well-fitting pair of sandals tough enough to cross deserts and with the traction required to climb mountains. The gospel also stomps on Satan."[480]

"Glad to contribute." Sam raised his palm to do a virtual high five.

They met a large group of teens who were straggling through the remaining switchbacks. Some of them wore hiking boots, and others wore sneakers; each carried a daypack. Jack and Sam nodded when they met eyes of the passing hikers. After the parade of teens came two pairs of adults walking and talking together. Obviously, they were leaders holding up the rear of the parade.

As they approached, Jack asked, "Are you all on some kind of school outing?"

The lead man replied, "Church youth group from the city. We like to get the kids out into God's creation a few times a season."

"Isaiah six three," Jack threw out the reference.

"Amen! That's the theme verse for our church youth program."

"Glad to hear your perspective. God bless you all." Jack called as he waved when they passed.

"God bless you too," each of the youth group leaders greeted as they passed Jack and Sam.

When they had all passed each other, Sam looked back at Jack. "What's Isaiah six three?"

"It's my favorite hiking verse: *'Holy, holy, holy is the* LORD *of Hosts. The whole earth is full of his glory.'*[169]

"I can see why they said 'Amen.' Can you remind me of that one the next time we take a break so I can make a note of it?"

When Sam did not hear footsteps behind him, he stopped and turned around to see Jack looking at his phone. *Ping.* Sam's phone alerted him of an incoming text.

"I just did," Jack said as he pocketed his phone.

"Thanks, Jack."

To the left they could see a crowd at the middle falls. Without comment, they walked past the trail spur that led to the falls and continued down the trail toward the lower falls.

THE SHIELD OF FAITH

"SHIELDS. WHAT ABOUT shields?"

"Paul told us to take up the shield of faith to be able to quench the fiery arrows of the enemy."[481]

Oh, Jack is going to love this! Sam thought. "Did you know that the Roman shields were made of plywood?"

"No, I did not. I thought plywood, laminates and adhesives were modern." Jack could tell Sam knew something he was eager to share.

"I had a project which required the fastening together of some components. I wanted to use nuts and bolts. My supervisor directed me to bond the components. I replied that I was uncomfortable using adhesives. He directed me to stop what I was doing, study the history of adhesives and then get back to him."

"What did you learn?" Jack asked.

"Glues have been around for as long as people have been around. The first glues were made from tree sap. Later glues were made by rendering animal connective tissue. Archeology has shown that the Egyptians used glue to repair pottery and make furniture."

"I thought glue was a modern invention. But then again, the Romans knew about steam power and only used it to impress people by opening the massive temple doors without the use of manual labor." Jack laughed.

"Glue making was another of those lost skills—lost after the Roman Empire fell—only to be resurrected in relatively modern times. The fact is that the Romans made better use of glue than they did of steam."

"How does that relate to their shields?" Jack was curious.

"The Roman shields were advanced composites in an ancient world. The shields were made of three thin sheets or layers of hardwood, usually oak or birch. The plies were glued together with their grains alternating horizontal and vertical, which gave the shield great strength and prevented any splitting along grain lines. The shields then had a layer of leather glued on and usually metal trimmed the shield perimeter. The finished product was about a centimeter thick at the edges and two centimeters thick at the center. The leather had to be oiled to keep the leather supple and waterproof. The leather coating also hindered the shields from splintering in battle."

"Oiling the leather is the act of anointing,"[431] Jack noted.

"Yeah, if the leather was not oiled, it would get dry and crack. Cracks would expose the wooden inner structure to rot."

Jack made the spiritual connection. "Yes, in the physical world, oiling preserves the leather. In a spiritual context, oil also keeps us supple, enabling us to do the tasks that God has set before us. In the Bible, oil is often used as a metaphor for the Holy Spirit. In the Old Testament, there was an holy anointing oil[482] that was used to anoint the priests[483] and the tabernacle.[484] The tabernacle was where the Israelites went to worship God. In the Old Testament, the tabernacle was God's dwelling place on earth.[485] In the New Testament, the Holy Spirit dwells in us,[434] making our bodies the temple of God.[486] God's Holy Spirit anointing empowers us[303] so that we will not fail."

"Oh, I hadn't seen the connection, but that is the definition of anointing." Sam let the thought sink in. "Flaming arrows were a common element in battle. To quench the fire of the arrows in battle, the shields were also doused with water prior to and during a battle. The shields got wet, but not heavy."

Jack was thinking aloud. "There are lots of different kinds of oils. I wonder if the oil they used could also have been somewhat friendly to water on some level or could it also have been a flame retardant?"

Sam remembered a pair of leather winter boots that required constant maintenance. "When I was younger, I had some stylish cowboy boots I used in the winter for walking in deep snow. Those boots required regular oiling with mink oil. Without the oiling, they would absorb water like a sponge. Once the oil was reapplied, they became water repellent again. I never thought of it, but I'm certain if I had put a lit match into the mink oil, it would have extinguished the flame."

Through the next bend Jack digested what he had just learned. "I had only thought of a shield as a barrier. How the shield could stop flaming arrows is the story behind the story. The Roman shield tells us that our faith should be in plies. Faith comes by instruction in the Word of God,[166] and the Bible reinforces itself.[303] No matter how many plies, each strengthens the others.[487] They are held together[488] with the glue of the Holy Spirit.[489] The leathery skin, regularly maintained by being anointed with oil, remained supple and in optimal condition for repelling arrows. The supple leather will also hold water without letting it penetrate to the wood, preventing rot. In battle, the oil and water work together to stop the fiery darts.[481] God's Word tells us that we are to be cleansed and sanctified with bathing ourselves in the Word of God.[490]

The lower falls became audible, and the trail leveled out. Ahead

Sam could see a group of people preparing to leave the picnic table. He stepped up his pace and arrived at the table just as they abandoned it. He threw down his pack on the tabletop and sat next to it with his feet on the bench.

Jack arrived a minute later, and at the other end of the bench, he assumed the same position. "Nice move."

"Carpe momentum. If you don't, someone else will." Sam smiled. "I thought I'd grab it before someone else got the idea. It'll be nice to have one last sit with a view before the final leg."

Jack looked around. He saw a handful of people milling around and some at the viewing deck taking selfies. "I think we have it until the next mob passes through."

THE HELMET OF SALVATION

"Do you have any insights on helmets?" Jack asked while pulling out his water bottle.

Sam replied, "Nothing special or more than helmets are for brain protection. In our case, we could say protection for the mind?"

"Paul directed us to receive the helmet of salvation.[491] The prefrontal cortex is where upper level reasoning happens—what the Bible refers to as the mind. The apostle Paul understood we were in a battle for the mind. He encouraged us to use God's Word to renew[492] and refresh our minds.[490] God's Word even directs us where to park our thoughts.[460] I wrote down Philippians 4:8 for you, and this verse helps to keep your head in the right perspective for righteous living."

Sam thought for a moment and said, "On our first hike, you made a distinction between the heart and the mind. Aren't they the two primary thought centers of the brain, fight or flight and higher reasoning?"

"The limbic system, which is the seat of our emotions, is where we love, hate, fear and have our flight-or-fight response. The limbic is well established in childhood. The Bible refers to that part of our brain as our heart, and we are told to guard it.[493] The prefrontal cortex is the higher-level reasoning part of the brain. The Bible refers to the prefrontal cortex as your mind, which should be fully developed by the mid-twenties. The Bible makes a clear distinction between thinking as a child and thinking as an adult."[82]

Sam digested what Jack had just said while Jack stared at the valley before them.

Jack continued, "We get our righteousness from Jesus,[150] and it's our responsibility to maintain it. Protecting our primary emotions and thoughts[492] is why we put on the breastplate of righteousness.[457] Protecting our higher-level reasoning is why we put on the helmet of salvation. Guarding this reasoning keeps us from being lured away from our salvation."[90]

After a long silence, Jack turned to see Sam staring out into the valley. "Helmets and chest protection are usually made from the same material. Would that mean that learning about God's righteousness and pursuing it builds both our helmets and our body armor?"

"Yep." Jack nodded. "There are spiritual gifts and spiritual fruit. We should talk about that on our next hike…"

Sam replied, "Foundations and basics. I don't want to go on any tangents until I have my basics in order."

Jack replied, "They are basics too. Spiritual gifts and spiritual fruit are spiritual growth basics. Think of the basic Christian growth plan like a curriculum. Understanding sin and salvation and accepting Jesus Christ as your personal Savior is the 100 level. Water baptism is graduation from the 100 level to the 200 level. The 200 level is shoring up the foundation, getting to know the Holy Spirit and building spiritual armor. The 300 level is learning and using the spiritual gifts God has individually given each of us. The 400 level is cultivating spiritual fruit.

"For instance, one of the fruit of the Spirit is peace. There is a special peace when we follow the Holy Spirit's leading.[60] The peace of God is a barometer for us with respect to guarding our hearts and minds.[494] On the other hand, there is a noticeable lack of peace when we sorrow the Holy Spirit[495] by doing what He warns us not to do.[496] Above all, do not quench the Holy Spirit[384] by choosing sin over repentance. That's like cheating on a fiancé."

"Ouch!" Sam winced.

"Yeah, it keeps coming back to relationship…" Jack let the words hang for emphasis. "On earth we get courted.[2] When we accept God's salvation, we commit to each other.[395] Jesus is the bridegroom; believers in Christ are the bride.[497] We are promised a marriage feast that will be in heaven.[498] The marriage will last forever.[106] God guarantees His side of the deal by giving us the Holy Spirit as a down payment.[396] The Holy Spirit is jealously protective of us[499] and helps[227] us to remain spiritually chaste.[500] We hold up our side of the betrothment by pursuing righteous living and living in repentance."

Sam commented, "Just like any couple preparing to be married, they do not pursue anyone else because they are not interested in anyone else."

"God's Holy Spirit helps us to live in repentance.[227] When we follow the Holy Spirit's lead,[60] He will keep us out of trouble.[60] The more righteous choices we make, the easier righteous living gets. Think of a guy who is engaged. He is committing himself to his fiancée. One day they will be married. The proof of their commitment to each other is their remaining chaste to each other.[500] If he wants to keep the betrothal, he ignores enticements from other women[38] because entertaining enticements[90] would offend the fiancé."[495]

Sam lightly chuckled to himself with an "I-got-it" kind of a chuckle. "The woman in the red dress was fun before you met your fiancé. The fiancée discovers the woman in the red dress has returned and warns you to stay away from her, making it clear that you cannot have them both. You will have to choose." Sam paused.

Before Jack could pick up the thread, Sam continued with a smile.

"Pursue righteous living, and the Holy Spirit will provide an escape—if you need it."[38]

"Without the breastplate of righteousness and helmet of salvation, we're vulnerable to mortal head and heart wounds." Jack looked at the ground. "If you're not done in by a mortal head or heart wound, then at best, you're out of the fight."

Sam looked over at Jack and then past Jack. "And I think we're done here too."

Jack looked up and saw Sam's gaze and turned to look toward his left. What looked like an outing of an extended family poured out of the trailhead for the woody trail. Two pairs of guys emerged from the pack. Each had coolers hanging from shoulder straps.

Jack said, "Yep, I think so too."

After Jack slipped his water bottle into the side pocket of his pack, he took out a baggie with a small chocolate bar. Sam took a long sip of his water and put the half-empty bottle into the side pocket of his pack. Jumping off the table and turning toward the trail, Jack could see the mob heading directly toward them. "Well, it was nice while it lasted."

"Looks like they need it more than we do," Sam said as he stepped past Jack and away from the table.

Jack followed behind Sam, walking toward the trailhead. They passed the newcomers. When they got to the trailhead, another string of people came into view. Watching them round the bend, Jack took out the chocolate and offered it to Sam who broke off a piece. "Thanks," he said as he returned it. The trailhead cleared, allowing them entry.

The trail was not wide enough for adults to walk comfortably side by side. People walking in opposite ways had to step off the trail to yield passage. Jack observed that more often than not, Sam would stop before meeting an oncoming group. This time, standing there waiting for a long caravan pass, Jack had to ask. "Why did you stop for them rather than wait for them to stop so we can pass?"

"This part of the trail is quite narrow. One group or the other would have to stop. If they had stopped, and I had to pass them, then I'd have to watch every one of them not to bump into them. If I stop first, then I can pick the spot of passing, and all I have to do is make enough room for them to comfortably pass." After the caravan had all passed by, Sam reentered the trail. "Be polite and everybody wins."

Jack replied, "It looks awfully courteous, and I have to admit, it's the easiest solution."

"Especially when there are dogs in the group." Sam laughed.

"It sure looks like more people coming than going."

"It's a pretty day," Sam replied.

Clearing the bend, they entered the first horseshoe. At the far end, a couple with two young kids also entered the horseshoe. Meeting at about the midpoint, Sam stepped aside to let them comfortably pass. The man carrying a pack nodded and said, "Thanks." The woman looked up, only to see whom they were passing. The kids passed by, oblivious of the courtesy Sam had extended.

THE SWORD OF TRUTH

WHEN THEY WERE out of earshot, Sam said, "So far, all the armor has been defensive. What about offense? An unarmed soldier is an oxymoron."

"Time for the sword," Jack replied.

Sam took his cue. "When I studied the Roman shields, I learned about their swords too."

"I know they used short swords. Good for close quarters combat?" Jack commented.

"The Romans used a double-edged sword that was about two foot long. They were designed for close quarters hand-to-hand combat and were common to every soldier. On the battlefield, the Romans would approach their enemy behind a wall of shields. In essence, they were the battlefield tank of the ancient world. When the enemy was physically close enough to be beating on the Romans' shields, the Roman kept moving. The Roman short swords would be thrust out from between the shields. As the enemy fell, the Romans would walk right over them with their hobnail sandals. When the enemy were drawn in close and crowded together so tight that they could not properly swing their own weapons, the Romans would continue moving in on them, dispatching them by thrusting, cutting and chopping them with their short swords. Those short swords required extensive training in technique and lots of practice."

Jack added, "Jesus' Word is alive and more powerful and sharper than any two-edged sword.[501] The word of God, pierces to the division of soul and spirit, and of joints and marrow. It even discerns the thoughts and attitudes of the heart."[502]

"So, it keeps coming back to reading the Bible and learning what is in it?"[166] Sam asked.

"Indeed, it does. The Word of God is the sword of the spirit.[491] And faith comes by learning the Word of God.[163] Sharpen your sword and build your shield."

"The first thing the Roman recruits did was build their stamina. They would march about thirty clicks in five hours, carrying about twenty kilos of gear. For combat, they trained with over-weighted equipment."

"Sword training happens by learning God's Word:[166] spiritually condition yourself[503] and build endurance[504] to be able to apply the Word of God correctly in any situation."[505]

Praying for Other Christian Brothers and Sisters

"The last item of spiritual warfare is prayer. Paul encourages us to pray without ceasing.[183] Bring our prayers and requests to God. Pray for other believers. Pray on every occasion.[451] Pray beyond your own issues."[506]

"Comms…" Sam replied. "Battlefield communications is where we began."

"It's not this item or that item. You need a full toolkit of spiritual armor because each of the items has its own purpose, but they are designed to work together."

Up ahead approached another group of people. The leader stopped to allow Sam and Jack to pass. This bunch included a dog sitting alertly and obediently by its owner's side. Sam turned to look at Jack after they passed. "That was a very well-behaved dog."

For the remainder of the return leg, there was not a section of the trail that did not contain people within earshot. The leisurely hike from earlier in the day had become more like mall walking on a weekend afternoon.

"I'm glad to see people out enjoying nature, but this trail is over-crowded," Jack lamented. "For our next, let's pick one where we can enjoy more of nature rather than hiking on a highway."

"I know just the hike—Oyster Dome. It's on the far side of Mt. Vernon and somewhatt off of the beaten track."

The railroad grade split happened before they knew it. The trail was now wide enough to walk side by side. *Rrrringgg!* Both turned around to see a mountain bike coming downhill and heading directly toward them. Jack jumped to one side and Sam to the other as the bike passed between them. Three more bikes followed far enough apart to be separate passing events. A fifth biker courteously rode around them in the cleared area below the power lines.

The canopy closed above them, but the flow of uphill traffic did not abate. The trail was level, and when it began a descent, they could see park buildings and the parking lot ahead. A dozen people were milling around the trailhead, apparently waiting for their fellow hikers using the restrooms.

Jack used the clicker to open the doors, and they both tossed their packs into the backseat and got their sneakers. Jack dropped the tailgate, sat on it and unlaced his boots. "Mind if I join you?" Sam jumped up onto it and began unlacing his boots.

"The cars circling the lot look like sharks hunting prey," Sam said as he massaged his bare feet.

Jack started to laugh. "In a couple of minutes, one of them is going to feel like he won the parking lottery."

Sam pointed to the entrance of the parking lot. "Look. More people are walking in. They must be the ones who quit the hunt."

Jack turned to see random people walking up the middle of the road that led to the entrance to the park. "This place has filled up since we arrived this morning."

"I'd say it's overflowing," Sam added.

With his Chuckies firmly wrapped around his feet, Jack jumped off the tailgate to join Sam who was already on the pavement doing some after work-out stretches. "Let's make someone happy."

The next "shark" saw them getting into the truck and stopped to see if they were leaving.

A CHRONOLOGICAL BIBLE

J ACK TURNED THE key and let the truck idle long enough to suck oil up into the block. He reached behind his seat to check if the package was secured in the footwell behind his seat. After a sip of water, he shifted into gear and backed into the aisle where the shark had not left much room for him to maneuver. Before he turned out of the aisle to head toward the gate, he checked his mirror and saw that the shark had claimed his former spot. The shark parade had already resumed.

Vehicles lined the sides of the road from the park entrance to the post with signs alerting drivers that they were entering the city limits and that the city did not tolerate street parking. Passing the signs, Jack took the first left and drove for another quarter mile. At the stop sign, he reached for the package and pulled it up between the seats.

"You'll like this." Jack handed the package to Sam.

Jack saw an opening and took a right. They were back onto Highway 2, heading west.

Sam unfolded the paper bag that resembled a package. "A Bible?" he questioned.

"Yes, but it's a little different. It's called a chronological Bible. From the beginning until the end, it's a very smooth and cohesive read."

Sam looked questioningly at Jack. "A *different* Bible? Doesn't the Bible contain a stern warning that no one should add or subtract anything from it?"[507]

"Nothing is taken or added. It's just a matter of organization. Traditional Bibles are arranged topically: the books of Moses, Judges, major and minor prophets, gospels, letters and so on. A handful of books like Acts, Kings and Chronicles provide historical context to tie the others together. To grasp the big picture within the sequential historical context, traditional Bibles can be a bit challenging."

"I noticed topical formats and was wondering about that. But I hadn't gotten to the point of how or what to ask."

"This one is arranged chronologically, which makes it much easier to tell who wrote what and when they wrote it. For example, open to the early part of the New Testament."

Sam tore off the plastic from where it was slit at the bottom. He let his thumb fan the pages to where he saw "New Testament" and tried to find the book of John. Stopping on a random page, he saw, *"Jesus said…"*

"Here's something: '*Jesus said…*' and there are references from Matthew, Mark, Luke and John."

"The four gospels are all told in the order that things happened. Go farther, and you'll see that Paul's letters are woven through Acts.

Written chronologically lets the reader know where he was, what was going on and when he wrote what to whom. This Bible leaves no question as to when Paul wrote to Timothy, the Galatians or any of the other letters. This type of perspective and connection was something only scholars had a handle on. Now it's plain to see for anyone who reads."

"I thought about that when I was listening to Acts. I'd looked ahead and knew that there would be letters following Acts. I found myself wondering at what point Paul wrote each of the individual letters."

Jack said, "When you read the Bible chronologically from cover to cover, the whole story builds with a crisp clarity."

Sam closed the book and thumbed through it from the beginning. "I see mixed-up references here in the Old Testament too."

"Same thing. When chronologically arranged, the Old Testament becomes a more cohesive read—almost like a novel. It's all there; don't worry. Nothing is added other than some historical commentary for support, which is easily distinguished from the Scriptures they support."

Continuing to thumb through the pages, Sam stopped where the text had a different color and type. "What's this?"

"Notes and commentary for historical background are set in a different type style than the actual words of the Bible. This was the author's tool to assist the reader in distinguishing content from comment."

"When I was Bible shopping, I saw Bibles with commentaries and what looked like teaching materials printed right in them."

Jack said, "This one has commentary that provides cultural and historical context to better understand what was happening when a particular passage was written. It also fills in gaps, like the time period between the last prophet of the Old Testament and the opening of the New Testament. In my opinion, it's the only commentary that's useful and not distracting or somebody else's opinion on what you should be figuring out yourself."

"I'd already decided that I want to read the whole Bible. This might be the one for me to read?"

"The author put marks on every few pages. They guide the reader with daily readings at a one-year pace."

Looking at the Bible, Sam spoke what he was thinking. "This might go well with breakfast. Starting the day with God[508] could frame my mind for the coming day."[349]

"Then in the future when you read certain passages, you'll understand what leads up to what you read. It becomes pretty apparent that the Bible really is the greatest story ever told."[487]

Sam paused and opened the front cover. "You wrote that for the inscription inside the cover."

> *To Sam, my brother-in-Christ,*
>   *The Bible is the greatest story ever told, the foundation*
> *of our faith and life manual.*
>   *Your brother-in-Christ,*
>   *Jack*
>   *2 Timothy 3:16-17*[166]

"Yeah, and I wrote it in ink." Jack smiled.

"Sam, the Bible is the greatest adventure story you'll ever read. It's true, real, relevant and the manual for us to live by.[509] As you read from the beginning through to the end, the chronological Bible makes for a smoother grasp of content in context. But if you want to find verses quickly, I'd recommend using that handsome leather-backed Bible the minister gave you. That's the indexing scheme everyone uses. It's handier and more practical."

"Cool!" Sam said softly while nodding his head in agreement.

Upon crossing the valley, the first major exit ramp put them on I-5.

"Plans for next time?" Jack already wanted to firm up their hiking plans.

"Oyster Dome is about as far north as we drove east. It'll give us a nice view of the San Juan Islands."

"Should we text to set up a time and place to meet?"

Sam continued paging randomly through the Bible. "Let's just do the same as we did this morning. That worked for me."

"Worked well for me too," Jack replied.

Sam put the Bible back into the bag, folded the bag and slipped it into the main pocket of his backpack. "Thanks very much for the new Bible. It looks like it will be raining tomorrow, and I'll be having my first day in a month without any plans. I think I'll relax and do some reading."

"From page one, you'll have a hard time putting it down," Jack added with a smile.

"By the way, how did you inscribe it when it was still sealed in plastic?"

"We all have our talents!" Jack laughed.

"That we do." Sam laughed with Jack as they pulled up to the gate.

HIKE 4
The Hike to
VICTORY

PROLOGUE

J ack pushed back his plate, woke up his phone and texted Sam. "How do you like your coffee?"

"Black, thanx," Sam responded.

"CU in 15," Jack texted in reply.

The waitress noticed that Jack had finished his breakfast. She came over to the table to pick up the empty plate. "Coffee to go?"

"Yes, please; make it two."

A couple of minutes later, the waitress returned with the bill and two large paper cups topped with sipping lids. She paused to see him pop one of the lids and inhale the aromatic steam rising from the open cup. "You have the best coffee in town."

"That's what they tell me," she answered with a knowing smile. "The owner is the head chef. He stocks the pantry and is very picky about everything served to his customers." She picked up the bill along with Jack's card. "We're glad you like it and glad to see you return."

"My pleasure," Jack replied through the steam.

Jack poured in a splash of milk and dropped three sugars into his cup. The waitress returned with the card and receipt. He used the pen on the resealed cup, moving it up and down as he rotated the cup. The pen drew a continuous sine curve on the upper half of the cup. Before putting the pen down, he signed the receipt, leaving a generous tip.

Ten minutes later, Jack pulled up to the gate. The same guard who had engaged him on his previous visit exited the shack and sauntered over to the truck. Jack removed his sunglasses.

"I recognize you from a couple of weeks ago." The guard scanned

---

the interior of Jack's truck. "Nice truck," he commented. "I didn't know these came with a stick."

"They are rare. But they are out there." Jack accepted the guard's comment as a compliment.

"Sam said you'd be by about this time. I'll ping him to let him know you've arrived. Pull up to that building with the cluster of cars." The guard pointed to same building from where Sam had exited the last time they met. This time, though, there was no microbus.

Jack drove up to the cluster of cars. Before he pulled into a parking spot, Sam exited the building and waved. Jack waved in return.

Midway, Sam stopped at a non-descript sedan, opened the trunk and retrieved his pack and boots. A click in his wake, he walked over to Jack's truck and opened the rear passenger door. He set his pack on the back seat and dropped his boots in the rear footwell. Sam closed the rear passenger door, opened the front door and slipped into the passenger seat.

"I checked the weather. We are in for an absolutely perfect day for hiking."

"We're blessed."

"Your coffee is hot and waiting. It's the one without a mark." Jack held up and turned his cup the show his mark.

"A sine wave, I see." Sam clicked and adjusted his seatbelt.

"Just getting the morning started with the right frequency," Jack quipped.

Sam elicited a fake moan to accompany the slow shaking of his head. Picking up his cup, he popped the lid, closed his eyes and brought the cup up to right below his nose. He slowly inhaled the liberated steam escaping with the open cup. "Awesome aroma, corny humor."

"We do what we can." Jack chuckled.

Sam took a small sip to gauge how hot the coffee was. "Yeouch, that's hot!" Sam snapped the lid back on and returned his cup to the holder in the console between them.

232 | The Hike to Eternity

Jack had been waiting for Sam to snap the lid back on before he put the truck into gear. Sam pointed toward the gate.

"No microbus?" Jack asked. "You traded your microbus for an unmarked police car?"

"My cousin has the VW, and he gave me that car for a loaner." Sam turned to look at his loaner. "I had not thought of it looking like one."

"On the open road, you may notice other cars near you driving slower."

"I'll have to keep that in mind." Sam laughed. "That would be my cousin's sense of humor and why the other cars make way for me. In heavy traffic, I think of Moses parting the Red Sea."

Jack saw the gate open. Passing the guard, they each waved.

Sam did not venture another sip until they had joined a smooth section of I-5 north.

Jack was quickly up to speed. He punched two buttons and set the cruise. Sam picked up his cup, popped the lid and started blowing gently over the top of the steaming cup. Sam skimmed a light sip off the top. "This is really good coffee. Is their food as good as the coffee?"

"I like what I've had," Jack replied. "The owner runs the kitchen and stocks the pantry. I'm convinced he has exceptional taste buds. Others must surely agree because the place is always busy."

"So where is this bistro?" Sam asked.

"On 164th above the public spring. There is a cluster of small shops on the corner that holds the box store. The cluster looks like a small-town center. The bistro is on a corner."

"I know right where that is. I always see people in there. I've thought about trying it. Since my last road trip, my workload has eased. Would you like to do lunch sometime this week?"

"I thought you'd never ask." Jack smiled as he reached for his cup.

Sam replaced the lid and put the cup back in the cupholder. "I've been enjoying the chronological Bible you gave me."

"It makes for a good read, eh?" Jack asked.

"You were right. It does read like a novel," Sam replied.

"Where you able to follow?" Jack asked.

"The historical commentary really did help to put the content of what I was reading into a timeline perspective."

"Yeah, it does. Where are you?" Jack asked.

"Joseph is in Egypt, and he's been reunited with his family. What an awesome divulgence! When he told his brothers who he was, they all experienced the fulfillment of his dream.[252] He could have had revenge, but he chose to be kind and generous."[275]

"Through the years, lots of parents have named their sons Joseph. His character is worthy of emulating, and Joseph was worthy of being a patriarch," Jack commented. "Later, when Moses led the Israelites out of Egypt, they carried Joseph's bones with them into the Promised Land."

"Thanks for the spoiler!" Sam nodded. "I'm glad he made it home."

"Joseph is a good example of how God speaks to us through dreams."

Sam said, "I put a pad and pen on my bedside table. I noticed that when I make notes, I tend to remember more. Last night I had a dream that you and I were cowboys riding horses in the mountains. We crossed a pass and descended into a valley. Beside a stream in the valley, we saw an old prospector who seemed to have lost his way and needed some help. We helped him and camped out there for the night. I vividly remember sitting around the campfire talking. I don't remember what we were talking about, but it was good. When I woke up, I felt I should write down as many details as I could recall."

"When the dream stays with you after you awaken and you remember a lot of detail, there is probably some meaning. Do you have any interpretation?" Jack asked.

"Not really." Sam shrugged.

"Glad to see you develop another good habit. When a dream stays with you, it's a good practice to write down as much as you can remember. Time will tell."

"Tonight, when we get back, I'm going to stop by the office supply store and get a proper notebook for my bedside table. My dreams may be random, but this will put my notes in one place."

"It beats sifting through a shoebox filled with scraps of paper."

Sam laughed. "That was exactly my thinking."

Sam looked to his right to feast his eyes on the Cascades towering over the Snohomish River Valley. "This time we will heading north along the coast to Blanchard Mountain. It's an exit or two past the turnoff for Anacortes and the Friday Harbor Ferry to the San Juan Islands. Along the hike, we will be able to see the San Juan Islands. On the top, we will be able to peek into Canada."

"Cool!" Jack exclaimed.

"Isn't that why we hike?" Sam asked.

"Yeah, and this stuff just makes me feel a little bit closer to God," Jack replied. "I can't get enough."

"Two trailheads could work for us. The one starts at the water's edge of Sammish Bay. That trail climbs the full two thousand feet to the dome. We can cut that climb in half by starting at the Sammamish Overlook. The lower portion of the hike is really just a climb with plenty of switchbacks. It's pure elevation gain. The upper half is more of a hike with about half the overall elevation gain."

"On the map, I saw two trails merge on their way to the dome," Jack said. "I'm okay with the overlook."

"Besides I'd rather walk and talk."

Sam took out his phone and entered their destination into the maps app. "We should be there in about forty-five minutes."

"Sit back and enjoy the ride."

SPIRITUAL GIFTS

SAM SIPPED HIS coffee and looked out at the Snohomish River Valley. "When I was in Chicago, the minister who baptized me mentioned spiritual gifts and spiritual fruit. It sounded like you were familiar with what he was talking about."

"Yes, I am." Holding up his cup and turning it slightly, Jack said, "See, we're on the same wavelength. I thought today would be a good hike for talking about spiritual gifts and spiritual fruit—especially spiritual fruit, which are the basic elements of spiritual growth. People are given spiritual gifts, and fruit is cultivated."

Sam said, "My first bike was a Christmas gift. By New Year's Day, I had fallen more than a few times. By spring, I was an expert." Sam paused. "Over the years, I've grown peppers and tomatoes. You have to be a good steward if you expect a good harvest."

"Something like that," Jack replied.

"Okay, so what kind of gifts?" Sam asked.

"God's gifts are a sign of favor that He shows us. They are favor without any merit of our own.[510] People are gifted by God with various attributes and inclinations. The Holy Spirit intends these gifts to be used for the benefit of the recipient in some way to benefit others.[511] Some of the gifts are community focused such as special giftings toward leadership, administration, teaching, giving, mercy and serving.[512] Then there are gifts that may relate simply to interacting with other people either individually or in the community. These gifts are words of wisdom or words of knowledge, healings, miracles and prophecy, faith, tongues and the interpretation of tongues.[513] God gives them, and we should be good stewards in applying and cultivating them,"[514] Jack explained.

Sam commented, "I've known people who are natural leaders or born teachers. I've also known people who have an uncanny ability to know things before they happen."

Jack kept his eyes on the road as he continued to explain. "The spiritual gifts I'm talking about come from God. He says that He gives freely and that He will not regret having given us what He has given to us.[515] Consider them as seed that God has planted within us. Jesus said that those who grow what they have been given will be given more. Those who do not grow what they have been given will lose what has been given to them.[516]

"There is something to be said about using your skillset—whether it was hard learned or it came easy."

"Use it or lose it," Jack replied. "Or simply fail to reach your full potential."

"Okay, what's the spiritual connection to the gift?" Sam asked.

"God wants us to use the gifts He has given to us for His glory.[514] The Holy Spirit is capable of growing our gifts, bringing them to their full potential.[374] You just read about Joseph and his gift for administration.[517] His gift saved a country and his family.[518] He will give us what we need when we need it to do His good work."[73]

Sam looked at Jack. "Lots of talented people are not Christians."

"Imagine if they met and accepted Christ and allowed His Holy Spirit to grow their talents and gifts.[519] God's growth plan for us is the mustard seed—the smallest seed that grows into the greatest herb.[520] God wants us to do whatever we do with all our heart as if we were doing it in service directly to Him.[521] He promises to strengthen us to do it.[522]

"You listed a whole mouthful of gifts. Can we talk about them?" Sam asked.

FAITH

"Let's start with faith," Jack replied. "Faith is probably the most core of the spiritual gifts. Everybody has some degree of faith and some have great faith. To have great faith is a gift. The character of faith is spiritual. The portion of faith that you already possessed is what got you in the door.[111] Consider faith as the energy and the Holy Spirit as the rudder.[523] The Holy Spirit is your guidance system.[378] By genuinely allowing the Holy Spirit to be your pilot and guide you,[378] He will show you which path to take.[429] Combine the power of faith[524] with the Holy Spirit's guidance, and you will sail smoothly."

"I have known people who have had faith in things that went ka-put—like a rocket without a guidance system," Sam responded.

"Their guidance did not come from the Holy Spirit,[525] Jack replied. "The Holy Spirit is not required to have faith, but the Holy Spirit is fueled by faith. Faith is like a muscle. We start with the faith which God has given us to get through the door. When we seek Him, He takes that seed of faith, and He grows it.[526] Reading God's Word provides the nutrients[163] we need to grow[364] healthy faith and exercise the faith that we already have."[524]

"So, the key to faith and growing one's faith is having faith in God?" Sam asked. "That sounds circular."

"A farmer plants a seed and cares for the seed. When the harvest comes, he harvests more seed. Trust in God, and He will prove himself faithful,"[527] Jack replied.

The highway was engulfed in ruralness as the last of Marysville fell off of the rearview mirror.

WORDS OF KNOWLEDGE AND WORDS OF WISDOM

JACK CONTINUED, "SOME people get words of knowledge, and others get words of wisdom. Some get both; some get neither."
"Words?" Sam asked.

Jack took a sip off his coffee. "John gave an example of a word of knowledge that happened when Jesus was gathering His disciples. Jesus had called Philip who met with Nathaniel to bring him to Jesus. When Philip and Nathaniel arrived, Jesus accurately commented about Nathaniel on his character. Nathaniel responded by asking Jesus how He knew him. Jesus told Nathaniel that he had been sitting under a fig tree before meeting Philip. That Nathaniel had been sitting under a fig tree was something Jesus could not have known except by supernatural means. This word of knowledge confirmed Jesus' identity."[528]

"Okay, but Jesus was the Son of God. Wouldn't He know stuff like that?" Sam replied.

"In another case, Peter and Cornelius each had complementary supporting words of knowledge."

"I remember Cornelius from my reading in Acts. He was a Roman centurion," Sam stated knowledgeably.

"By Roman law, occupied peoples were granted freedom to worship their pre-occupation religions. This allowance permitted the Jews to freely practice Judaism anywhere in the empire. To fly under the Roman radar, the Jews kept their religion to themselves. When Christianity emerged as a sect of Judaism, there were growth pains. The very first Jewish converts retained many of their Jewish ways and traditions.[529] The retained Jewish ways and traditions were an issue with both Jewish and non-Jewish converts. The time had come for the gospel of Jesus to expand beyond the Jewish community. The time had come for the new believers to break free of their Jewish ways and traditions.

"A Roman centurion named Cornelius was a God-fearing man who gave to the needy and prayed to God regularly.[263] But Cornelius did not know Jesus. One night, God gave Cornelius a vision. An angel told him where to find Peter and directed him to send three men to fetch Peter.[530] Around noon next day, God gave Peter his own vision,[531] which told him that none of the things God had made were to be considered unclean.[532] By tradition, the Jews considered all non-Jews to be ceremonially unclean. While Peter was contemplating his vision, the Holy Spirit told him that three men who were downstairs had been sent for him and that he should go with them.[533] When Peter came downstairs, he met the men and said, 'I'm the man you are looking for.'"[534]

"What happened next?" Sam asked.

"The next day, Peter went with the men to Cornelius' house."[535] When Peter arrived at Cornelius' house, the centurion gathered together all of his household and asked Peter to tell them the message God had appointed Peter to tell.[536] While Peter was sharing the gospel of Jesus, the Holy Spirit fell on everyone who heard the message.[537] The Jews who had accompanied Peter were astonished to see and hear non-Jews speaking in tongues. The early church considered speaking in tongues to be evidence of being filled with the Holy Spirit. Peter agreed and insisted that the new believers should be baptized[444] in water in the name of Jesus."[269]

"That was how Christianity grew beyond just being just a sect of Judaism?" Sam asked.

Jack replied, "It all happened because a Jew and a Roman each acted on words of knowledge and the words of wisdom. The words of wisdom let them know when and how to act on their words of knowledge. The Holy Spirit orchestrated the event, and the church was born. It's also a story of how God rewards those who diligently seek Him."[526]

"Words of wisdom are very much like words of knowledge. Both are peeks into what to expect and what to do with knowledge God has make available.[60] The word of knowledge provides us with information we would not have had without it having come from God. The word of wisdom is God's directing us to know what to do with the knowledge we have been given.[538] In another case, when Philip was directed to meet with the Ethiopian, he was told where to go, when to go and what to do when he got there.[304] Peter was told about the three men and when to depart with them.[533] Cornelius was directed where and when to send his men to fetch Peter."[530]

"So Jack, the word of knowledge is like divine intel and the word of wisdom is what to do with and when to act on the intel. That's like getting a good stock tip and being told when to make the move on it."

"You could say that," Jack replied. "The only cap to wisdom is self-imposed. To those who revere God[69] and to those who ask, He is liberal with giving wisdom."[539]

"Here's some knowledge. The next exit is ours. Your wisdom is that missing this exit will mean about fifteen minutes and an equal number of miles to double back for the same exit," Sam said as he looked at his phone.

"Good application," Jack commented. "I'll accept those words of knowledge and wisdom."

"Thanks." Sam looked up from his phone. "At the top of the exit ramp, take a left to cross the freeway. Then take another left and then the third right. That will put us on the last leg, which transitions from a paved road to a dirt road. Our exit is in about a mile or so."

TONGUES

JACK TOOK THE exit and crossed the bridge. "My parents immigrated to this country from a different country that had its own culture and language. We encountered very few people in this country who knew our language. To me, as a kid, I felt like our family had its own private language."

Sam commented, "On our last hike, we talked about God giving us a private prayer language[449] that comes when we are baptized with the Holy Spirit.[444] It sounds like that is what the first non-Jewish believers experienced at Cornelius' house. I can see praying in tongues being like that."

Jack replied, "I like to compare it to battlefield communications. Praying in the Spirit[451] is the Holy Spirit praying through you and communicating on a frequency the Enemy does not understand.[449] This is a kind of praying that is very much an individual thing between you and God."

"Take this right." Sam pointed to the small sign for Blanchard Mountain parking. "Then the next left will put us on the final leg."

Jack took the right and then continued talking. "Praying in tongues is a private prayer language between you and God. The gift of tongues and the gift of the interpretation of tongues is between you, God and other believers. The spiritual gifts of tongues and interpretation of tongues are meant to be exercised within a body of believers. Someone speaks a word from God in a language unknown to them.[408] Then another person provides the interpretation."[410]

"That sounds like it could become a free-for-all," Sam commented.

"To maintain order, Paul laid down some guidelines. He said that there should only be one, two or at the most three messages given in tongues. However, there should only be one person doing the interpretation.[540] If no interpreter arises, then the speaker should keep quiet.[541] The check to the gift of tongues and the interpretation of tongues is that there will be a different person who interprets the word."

"So," Sam let the word hang. If the message falls flat, then either the speaker was not right, the interpreter was not doing his part or the church was unaccepting of the message."

"Any which way, the signal was lost, and the message does not get through. A proof to the validity of the message is the tag team—one verifying the other," Jack replied. "This is not to be confused with speaking in tongues as evidence of Holy Spirit anointing."[444]

Sam held his fist. "We talked about the gift of faith and words of knowledge." Upon saying faith, he extended his thumb and then his index finger with knowledge. "We talked about words of wisdom, tongues and the interpretation of tongues." With each, he extended another finger.

"You're keeping count," Jack observed.

"I don't want to miss any." Sam smiled at Jack.

The pavement ended, and Jack shifted his truck into four-wheel drive. "I don't get to do this enough," Jack said with a laugh as he downshifted and stepped on the gas, leaving a solid plume of dust in their wake.

"Hey, cowboy. This is considered a rough road, and we may meet oncoming cars.

"No problem. My truck was made for it. Besides, it's overdue for a wash," Jack said as he focused on avoiding ruts and potholes.

"Anybody behind us or anyone we meet will need a bath too." Sam laughed, enjoying the feel of the four-wheel drive clawing over the rough dirt road. "This could be addictive."

"It is," Jack agreed as he slowed to enter the overlook parking lot.

⌢

Jack and Sam sat on either side of the tailgate. Jack leaned back, resting on his palms.

Sam had changed into his hiking socks and was slipping on his boots. "Tell me, Jack, how old are you?"

"Why do you ask?" Jack leaned back, wiggling his toes. His Chuckies and sweat socks were lying by one side; his boots and wool socks were on his other side.

"Back there, I thought you were sixteen taking a joy ride."

"*Carpe momentum.*" Jack smiled and replied. "I will accept the responsibilities that come with life, but why should I always have to behave like a grownup?"

"Well, it was fun."

Jack replied, "My goal every time when I drive is not to let anything happen to my vehicle. That's the first line of defense. With the vehicle safe, the occupants are safe."

Sam jumped off the tailgate, nested his heels into his boots and started to lace up. "Can't argue with that. I never felt like at risk."

Sam used the side of the truck bed to lean against while he proceeded to do a series of leg stretches. Looking up, he said, "Not a cloud in the sky."

"We could not have asked for a more perfect day." Jack pulled on his new merino wool hiking socks and slipped on his boots. Hopping off the tailgate, he turned and raised his right boot to the tailgate. With his heel comfortably nested, he laced up and repeated the procedure with his left boot.

Comfortably stretched, Sam walked over to the overlook. Behind him, Jack was going through his calf and hamstring stretches. A minute later Jack stood next to Sam. Silently they both looked out beyond the shoreline below.

"Is that Anacortes?" Jack asked as he went through a set of torso twists.

"See the wake? That's the ferry returning to Anacortes from Friday

Harbor," Sam stated, staring at the fresh wake in the open water between the shore and the islands.

"I've heard that people on that ferry have seen Orcas."

"Not me, not yet. Someday, I would love to see them in the wild," Sam replied. He shifted his gaze to the coastal plain below. "Ready for a hike?"

"Let's do it." Jack returned to the truck to fetch his pack.

Sam caught up with Jack, who was clicking to unlock the truck. "You like that thing?" Sam asked.

"It's a luxury to see the lights blink and to tell me the doors are locked. If I had a choice, I wish I had the old-school option of the five-dollar keys and forego all the anti-theft stuff."

"I know what you mean. The convenience is nice, but fancy keys are an expensive and inconvenient lump in the pocket."

"Every year manufacturers force more superfluous stuff for vehicles on the buyers."

Sam inhaled and comically shook his head. "Don't get me started on superfluous electronics and software. The superfluous stuff just provides additional points of failure. Nobody wants to consider all the energy they require.

"A refresher course in the basics of how things work would do their designers a world of good."

Sam reached the trailhead first. He pulled out his phone and took a photo of the trail map.

"New tricks?" Jack asked as he pulled out his own phone to take the same photo.

"Not too old to learn," Sam said with a smile. "I thought it might make a handy reference."

"That is does," Jack replied.

Beyond the map board, the trail immediately began to descend. After about a hundred feet, Jack stopped and turned around to look up the trailhead. "That was quick; I can see the map board, but I don't see or hear the parking lot."

244 | THE HIKE TO ETERNITY

"I don't hear anything either," Sam said. "We seem to have our own space for talking freely. Let's pick up where we left off."

PROPHECY

JACK TOOK THE lead on the narrow trail. "Prophecy is another of the spiritual gifts. In the Greek of the New Testament authors, prophecy is the idea of foretelling future events or things that can only be known by divine revelation." [542]

"That sounds like fortunetelling to me," Sam remarked.

"Not quite," Jack responded. "We've all known people or known of people who have a natural foreknowing of something about to happen—before it happened."

Sam laughed. "My grandmother was like that. She knew stuff that she could not have known unless someone had tipped her off. It went way beyond her having clocked more life experience than the rest of us. I remember one time when she adamantly told my dad to get all his money out of the stock market. Like a dog with a bone, she would not let it go. He had invested heavily in tech stocks during the tech boom. His gut told him to listen to her—even though he knew that she knew nothing about the stock market. Shortly after he pulled out, the dot-com bubble began to burst. While other people were stressed and gnashing their teeth, Dad sang Grandma's praise. Later, he reinvested, and today he is living a comfortable retirement and makes sure his mother receives the senior care she needs."

"That natural foreknowing is just a foreshadow of a much greater spiritual gift that she may or may not have known that she possessed. Like any other gift, spiritual gifts are given to us, and it's our choice how we choose to use, misuse or waive them. On the one hand, with God, the spiritual gifts can be cultivated to reach their full potential. [543] Without God and without the application of His Word,[166] spiritual gifts tend to get misused or squandered."

"Like a misappropriation of funds, eh?" Sam commented.

"Just like any gift, different people given the same kind of gift will treat the gift differently," Jack replied. "Spiritual gifts are designed by God and given to us with the intent of being used for His kingdom.[544] Satan, on the other hand, is always out to ruin or corrupt[77] things that God has meant for good. Fortunetelling or turning to fortunetellers is one of those corruptions that will spiritually defile everyone involved."[545]

"I always found fortunetelling repugnant," Sam snorted.

"That was the Holy Spirit giving you a heads-up that there is a problem with fortunetellers." Jack drew a deep breath and continued, "Prophecy, on the other hand, is an avenue that God uses for speaking to an individual.[410, 249] Prophecy is for declaring His purposes.[546] The prophetic words may or may not be preceded by tongues.[262] Either way, when the gift of prophecy is properly exercised, it is spiritually edifying."[547]

"So, an interpretation of tongues may be a prophecy?" Sam asked.

"God speaks to us in many ways,"[548] Jack replied. "It's on us to behold."

"How can you tell if someone is getting a message from God or just talking through his hat?"

"A few years ago, someone told me that he had a prophetic word for me. It was at a time when I was between contracts and trying to figure out where God wanted me next. Among other things, the prophet told me that he saw me living in a place with palm trees. Not knowing him personally, I nodded and said, "Thanks. I'll wait for God's confirmation." A few months later, I was working on a contract in San Diego. One evening, looking at the palm trees in the courtyard outside of my apartment window, I recalled his words."

"Did he say anything else?"

"A few personal nature type family details also came to pass," Jack replied.

"Hmmm…" Sam uttered just loud enough for Jack to hear.

"When it comes to prophecy, don't scoff.[549] Test any and all prophetic words to filter for the good."[3]

"How do you know if a prophecy is valid?" Sam asked.

"A valid prophetic word must agree with God's Word[262] and not stray from His character.[550] The foundation for challenging anything of a spiritual nature is knowing God's Word and holding His Word as the standard.[166] Does it conform to God's Word[166] and does it testify to Jesus?[551] A valid prophetic word will come with confirmations of some kind."

"Jack, what was your confirmation?" Sam asked.

"In that case, it was the palm trees first and then the other details."

"What about the palm trees and other stuff that the San Diego prophet said?"

"The palm trees got my attention. When I considered the other elements of the prophecy, I saw them all fall into place. I took the various elements as confirmation of being where I should be when I should be there. While I was there, a family crisis arose. I was where I needed to be. Had I not been spiritually primed by that prophecy I probably would have missed my opportunity to perform my role in helping to resolve a particular crisis. On a non-spiritual note, the San Diego job had been unsolicited. But it was a perfect fit for my skillset. After the crisis was resolved, the contract closed up just as quickly as it had opened. Before I knew it, I was back home, looking for my next contract. Overall, that job broke even. I was no worse off than I was before. But I was richer by seeing God's hand work in my life."

Sam nodded in understanding, then asked. "What about the validity of the prophets?"

"There are both true prophets and false prophets.[552] True prophets will point people toward Jesus to build their faith. False prophets have no light in them. All they do is tickle people's ears.[360] The false prophets do not speak according to God's Word.[553] Jesus called them wolves in sheep's clothing. He said that we would know them by their fruits.[554]

The direct and indirect purpose of false prophets is always to pervert God's Word for the goal of corrupting our relationship with God."[550]

"How do you test the prophets?" Sam asked.

"The first test is whether or not the prophet's prophecies come to pass and the second is if their prophecies lead the hearer to the true God.[555] For the prophet test, both need to apply. Every spirit that professes that Jesus Christ is the Son of God and that He came to this earth in the flesh is of God. While every spirit that does not confess that Jesus Christ is the Son of God and came in the flesh is not of God."[556]

"What about prophecy itself?" Sam asked.

"Prophetic words from God will always be edifying and comforting—never judgmental or condemning.[557] You may not always like the content, but the purpose of a prophecy from God is to point you toward God. Prophetic words may come spontaneously. If you get 'the word' and it's for yourself, it's a word of knowledge or wisdom. If you get the word for someone else, then it's a prophecy. Either way it will comfort, encourage and point the recipient toward God."[558]

The dense canopy opened to a clearing. The absence of the trees on the left revealed that the trail was cut into a steep mountainside. Ahead Sam saw a large flat rock, big enough to be a bench for hikers. "Let's have our first water break at that rock up ahead."

Sam reached the rock first, dropped his pack and removed a water bottle. Hopping up on the rock, Sam sat, sipped some water and stared out at the San Juan Islands. Jack dropped his pack and proceeded to do a series of long slow stretches, alternating between hamstring and calf stretches.

"Let me recap."

"Please do," Jack replied.

Sam drew a long breath. "Faith is the catalyst.[526] When we are baptized in the Holy Spirit, God gives us tongues for the Holy Spirit to speak through us to Him.[444] He also gives us words of knowledge and wisdom when He wants to give us information. The words of knowledge and wisdom are like receiving inside information and knowing when to act on it. He gives us tongues and prophecy when He wants us to speak for Him to others. Another person interpreting the tongues is the confirmation that the communication was successful. If no one interprets, let it go. Whatever you got was meant to be between you and God. Prophecy is a divine communication driven by the Holy Spirit.[262] The primary test of any prophetic word is that it should always direct people toward God."[551]

"*The fear of the LORD is the beginning of wisdom,*"[x69] Jack replied. "The grace to act in these gifts is given to us in proportion to our faith."[559]

Placing his hands on his hips, Jack arched his back as far backward as the center of gravity would allow. Then bent forward to touch his boots. After five repetitions, he stood straight, looking at the islands. Keeping his legs and hips still, he turned at his waist to look up the trail and then turned to look down the trail. "I have one more test. It's a personal one that my dad taught me."

"Go ahead," Sam commented.

"If God has a word for you that may be coming from someone else, He will also confirm it to you."

"That sounds reasonable." Sam snacked on a baggie of granola.

"I'll admit to being skeptical about other people offering unsolicited advice or telling me what to do or whatever. But sometimes that is how God chooses to affect our paradigm. If God wants to say something, He will tell us whatever it is, and then He will provide confirmations. We Christians should never be expected to blindly follow any other people who say they are hearing from God. We should always test[337] and confirm.[505] God may use others for a confirmation or pre-confirmation or just to get your attention and confirm to you that you are where you should be."

"Like the palm tree guy?"

"Yep, like the palm tree guy. I didn't know what to think at first. I filed it away, and the Holy Spirit brought it back when the time was ripe."[227]

Jack reached down to his pack, retrieved his water bottle and sat down on the far end of the rock. "Nice view."

"I had to stop for the view. I could feed my eyes with this all day long."

"How does it compare with the top?" Jack asked.

"Different. Partly because we will be higher up and partly because of how the forest opens at each vista," Sam replied and returned the baggie and water to their pockets in his pack. "Let's get going. We can always stop here again on the return."

Jack took a deep drink of water. "Let's do it.

Sam re-shouldered his pack and did his own set of torso twists while Jack put away his bottle.

With one eye on the trail and the other on the vista, Jack followed Sam along the wall of the bowl.

DISCERNMENT

"DISCERNMENT[560] IS ANOTHER spiritual gift.[513] Discernment is a capability that can be heightened.[561, 562]

Sam laughed. "This morning I went to the fridge for some milk to put in my coffee. I opened the lid and got a whiff of something foul."

"That's *physical* discernment. Be thankful that God gave you a good sniffer. When your spiritual discernment grows, evil spirits will smell just as foul," Jack added.

"In the course of my divorce, I was directed to a particular lawyer, and I couldn't help but notice the wicked look in his eye. No kidding, there was a smell of sulfur in the air about him. He disturbed something in me, and I could not get away from him fast enough."

"That may have been an inkling of spiritual discernment," Jack responded.

"Well, I do feel a peace about talking with you about this God stuff."

"Inner peace is a good sign of being on track."

"Spiritual discernment falls into four general categories: the discernment of human spirits[563, 564, 565] discerning the presence of God's Holy Spirit,[408] discerning the presence of angels[566] and the discernment of the presence of demonic spirits.[567]

Sam commented, "My mom possessed a naturally good discernment of people. When I was a kid, I thought she was being prejudiced. In time, I saw that she had an uncanny ability to see past the trappings that other people would get hung up on. Whether good or bad, she could see something in people that other people could not see. She was as colorblind as a person could be. As I've gotten older, I've found myself seeing something too. Getting older and wiser is one thing, but this is something different—like a radar. I've walked out of making deals because I've felt something was amiss. I've felt something was not right and avoided people who later turned out to be trouble. Last summer, when we met on the roof, I had a positive feeling about you. That's why when I saw you at the store, I chose to follow you upstairs."

"I'm glad you did," Jack responded.

"It's a God thing!" Sam smiled.

"It sure is!" Jack smiled. "You may have an inclination toward spiritual discernment. There is a radar quality about it."

"Over the years, I've found it interesting to see how random people can affect other people's moods."

"How do you mean? Jack asked.

"A few years back, I worked in a company that was a great place to work. We had a small close-knit team working on a black-hole project to develop an all-new product. We worked hard and performed in harmony. That office was truly a well-oiled machine. We all knew each other's roles, and each employee excelled in his or her role. Outside of work, we also enjoyed each other's companionship. Near the end of the project, someone high up on the managerial food chain decided that we needed more bodies for the final push to product release. Two new people were hired, and they started work while the program manager was on an overseas business trip. His lead engineer had accompanied him, and they had left the next best engineer on the team to watch over production while they were gone. When the new hires arrived, one guy accepted his assignment and got right to work. Like adding another gear ring to a sprocket, he slipped right in. The other person made it her business to stick her nose into everyone else's business. She used what she learned to manipulate people. By the second week, people were questioning each other's roles and the manager's choice for interim leadership. Before the bosses returned, relationships had soured, verbal altercations had erupted and work on the project had nearly ground to a halt. When the bosses returned, the manager quickly and accurately surmised what had happened. The bad egg was immediately removed."

"What about you?"

"When she approached me, I ignored her, and she quickly lost interest." Sam shrugged. "That's okay, I'm always professional, and my gut told me to give her lots of distance.

By the end of the first week, I felt like I was in the grandstands, watching a sporting event. Another guy had awakened at about the same time, and together we surmised what was happening. We tried to warn one guy she was particularly fixated on. He was an amiable guy, vulnerable to flattery, more of a lackey than a leader. The two became buddies, and she convinced him that he should have been the interim leadership."

"How was it after the saboteur was ejected?" Jack asked.

"The project succeeded and went to market. Most of us went our own ways. But the group never regained the rapport we had lost."

"Did you ever consider that that person had brought in spirits of confusion and rebellion?"[568]

"Yes, the resulting genuine confusion and minor rebellion seemed as if she had blown magic dust on people. Some people morphed, and our group never quite recovered."

"It's a good thing you listened to your gut. You may have sensed evil spirits, and your gut had enough discernment to tell you to stay away."

"When my gut speaks, I've learned that it does me well to listen."

"Jack, do you think I may have an inclination toward spiritual discernment?"

"Talk to God about it. I liken discernment to radar. When tuned, it helps you skirt spiritual traps that lead to physical downfalls. From what you said about your experience on that project, you may be blessed with some discernment."

"Huh?" Sam grunted.

"I'm certain you have had days that were all bluebirds and butterflies, and you had a bounce in your step. Then you find yourself in a situation where you are forced to interact with someone in an extreme mood. If the person is angry, you cannot help but become angry too. You don't even know why. There might even be some event that precipitated the anger. Afterward, it takes a while for you to shake off your own anger and return to the good mood you once had—that is, if you can."

"Yeah, I hate when that happens," Sam remarked.

"Those were anger spirits having an anger party. The angry person was being ravaged by angry spirits, and one of their angry spirits jumped onto you. Before you realized what was going on, that spirit of anger was steering your responses. An ounce of discernment would have helped you resist the prompting and not given it a place to land. Without permission to stay and not feeding it, the spirit will go away."[37]

"That sounds like the police officers who train to keep their cool in heated situations."

"In the secular, that's a good example. With spiritual discernment, it's like reading a heat signature."

"This is interesting. My gut has a history of prompting me to bypass certain people and transactions. It's also told me to stay away from certain women," Sam added with a chuckle.

"It sounds like your natural discernment has kept you out of trouble, and spiritual discernment *will* keep you out of trouble. By the way, spiritual discernment can be grown."

"How?"

"Ask God. He said He will give it to us.[569] Read and meditate on the Word[166] and soak yourself with God's Word[492]; it's solid food for spiritual growth, and it will improve your discernment."[561]

"Jack, living the Christian life really does keep returning to relationship with God and allowing His Holy Spirit to guide us into what is best for us."[227]

"Make the Holy Spirit your friend and cultivate that relationship. It's the best thing you can do for yourself."

Jack continued, "Another aspect of discernment is being able to tell if the Holy Spirit is active in a situation."

"The trip to Chicago a few weeks ago and the way everything came together made me feel something else was at work—something good."

"From what you told me, it sounds like the Holy Spirit had a hand in how it all came together."

Jack smiled. "On the day of Pentecost, Peter discerned that the Holy Spirit was at work."[570]

"Another facet of discernment is being able to sense or see angels or demons. Zechariah saw and talked with angels.[571] Jacob met angels on his travels.[572] Elisha saw angels and prayed that his servant would see them too.[573] Jesus was seen with angels[574] and cast out demons.[575] Jesus sent out His twelve disciples and told them that they had authority over evil spirits.[576] Seventy other disciples said that the demons were subject to them when they spoke in Jesus' name.[577] Paul identified and cast out demons.[578]

"I guess if you can't discern them to be there, you can't tell them to leave," Sam responded.

"Whether its angels or demons, they are only hidden to those who do not see. Discernment is the radar that lets you fly through the mist. That's part of what discernment is about," Jack replied. "A discerning heart, seeks knowledge."[579]

The trail dipped farther and met a trail coming up from below. "Is this the trail that comes up from the water?" Jack asked.

"It's almost all switchbacks. If we had taken that trail, we would have experienced over a thousand feet of pure elevation gain."

"I don't think I'm up for that steep of a climb—not yet," Jack said as he paused to look down the trail spur.

"This is the low point for the lookout trial. Either way, back to the truck or up to the dome, it's all uphill from here."

HEALINGS AND MIRACLES

JACK SAID, "LET'S wrap up the remaining individual spiritual gifts—healings and working of miracles.[513] Along with faith, they are what I call the power trio."

"That sounds like *dynamis*," Sam paused. "I love that word!"

Jack smiled from ear to ear. "I love *dynamis* too. It's the word for power. It can also be translated as miracle, strength, virtue and mighty. *Dynamis*[420] is a part of what the Holy Spirit gives us for empowering our walk in Christ."

"Faith is the catalyst?" Sam asked.

"Faith enables the *dynamis*," Jack replied. "Jesus was known for His miracles.[580] He said that those who believe in Him could do the works that He did.[581] He said that those who believe could lay hands on the sick, and they would recover.[582] It all goes back to faith. Asking God in faith triggers miracles."[197]

"Faith is the fuel for the *dynamis*," Sam replied.

"Healing is fixing something that is broken. Healings[297] can be both spiritual[583] and physical.[584] The greatest of all healings are the spiritual healings.[297] Physical healings can be immediate,[585] or they can take time to manifest.[586] In a crude sense, our physical bodies are simply organic machines meant to last for only so long. But our spirits survive on into eternity.[587] Just like what we feed our physical body affects our physical health, what we feed our spirit affects our spiritual health. Spiritually, Satan wants to poison our spirits.[588] We can block him by reading and meditating on God's Word. God's promises bring spiritual life and that crosses over into the physical realm reflected in the health of our flesh."[248]

Jack continued, "Miracles,[420] on the other hand, are always powerful. They are often dramatic occurrences."

"Faith is the catalyst for miracles?" Sam asked.

"Things impossible to man are possible with God.[589] When I was a baby, I had scarlet fever; my pediatrician documented that I lost the hearing in my left ear. When I was in third grade, someone with the gift of healing prayed over my ear, and my hearing fully returned. If we dig deep enough, we all have our own testimonies of what God has done for us. That is one of mine."

Sam replied, "The Bible that you gave me starts by saying that God created everything that was created.[7, 26] He made us out of dust,[113] and He made wine out of water."[590]

Jack said, "Dust is just dry earth. Dry earth and everything else for that matter is made of molecules. When you consider dust as molecules, all God did was rearrange the molecules, then breathe into us His breath of life."[113] Jack paused. "As humans, we live in a physical world and like to gauge things by physical standards. Jesus called His disciples together and told them they would be able to cast out demons and cure diseases.[591] Sometimes, sickness is the manifestation of a demonic oppression."[432]

"That's where healing overlaps with discernment? Discerning whether it's a case of natural human decline or demons acting out? [592] I knew a lady who became so bitter after her divorce. She was very pretty, but in her unhappiness, she began to scowl until she developed permanent harsh scowl lines in her face. Then she got cancer and died."

"Bitterness is a demonic oppression that will eat a person alive. For the physical wellbeing alone, it's better to forgive, let go and move on.[138] When Adam and Eve disobeyed God's command, sin and death entered the world.[55] Due to sin, God allows sickness, which is corruption. Either directly or indirectly, Satan is the source of illness."[593] Even death is a spirit, and the good news is that death too will eventually be thrown into hell."[594]

"But Jesus died so we could be healed,"[58] Sam articulated.

"Physical and spiritual healing," Jack replied. "Adam's fall in the garden[51] invited death into this world.[595] The fact that our physical bodies grow and decline from the day we are born comes from Adam's fall in the garden. Sickness is just accelerated decline.[596] The good news is that death will be the last enemy to be destroyed.[597] Meanwhile, physical healing is a reprieve.[427] Spiritual healing brings abundant life."[426]

"Spiritually healed so we can have eternal life with Him!"[106]

"Amen!"[598, 599] Jack continued, "A word of caution though, Sam. Physical healings and the working of miracles are real. Faith is the catalyst. In the gospels and in the book of Acts, signs and wonders were used to get people's attention so they would listen to the preaching of the gospel. What is important to note is that the gospel is the spotlight. Signs and wonders are just the attention getters. The sharing of the gospel is always the message. In numerous places in the Bible, we are warned against false prophets who will use signs and wonders to deceive.[600] Moses gave a stern warning about false prophets.[553, 601] So, you want to keep your discernment dialed to 'high.' It is always about pointing back to God—not to the signs and wonders themselves."

Sam looked at Jack. "So, the same way we put on our spiritual armor, discernment is our radar."

"The spiritual armor is something every Christian should put on every day. Discernment is a gift."

"Jesus told us to be wise as serpents and harmless as doves.[602] We should always be vigilant because Satan is always on the prowl."[18]

Jack's words hung in the air.

With the first switchback, Sam could hear Jack's Lamaze breathing. "Do you want to take a water break?" Sam asked.

"Let's do a few more of these. Look for one with a rock big enough for us to sit on. If not, then at the crest of the next rise."

Ahead, Sam saw the trail disappear in a hundred feet or so. "Okay."

Jack reached the crest first, bent over and took a series of deep breaths. Sam stopped just short of where Jack stood. "Are you all right?"

"Talking and walking uphill just got me a bit winded." Jack looked up the trail. "The trail appears almost level up ahead."

"That was the last of the steep inclines until we do the final push. Let's call this a water break."

"Cool. I could use a drink." Jack dropped his pack and took out a fresh water bottle from the side pocket. From the center pocket, he pulled out a baggie containing small packets.

"What are those?" Sam asked.

"These are flavored electrolyte mixes. I always bring my own swamp cooler."

"I hadn't noticed," Sam lied with feigned civility.

"A couple of these in water replenishes the electrolytes I lose perspiring. Put it in the water bottle, shake and voilà. Would you like to try?" Jack took out two packets and offered the baggie to Sam.

"Sure, I'm game." Sam took two packets and followed Jack's lead.

"Not bad… This is a treat I was not expecting."

"Healthy too." Jack raised his bottle for a toast.

Sam met Jack's bottle with his own, making the dull thunk sound of plastic to plastic.

COMMUNION

JACK STRETCHED HIS neck from side to side. "What do you know about communion?"

Sam replied, "Communion is a sacrament. A priest gives you a wafer and then offers a sip of wine from a chalice to wash it down."

"Well, that does give us a place to start," Jack replied. "Do you know what a sacrament is?"

Sam took a drink of water. "A Christian rite?"

"Hmmm…definitely more than a rite. A *sacrament* is 'an outward sign of inward belief.' Sacraments confirm our interest in Christ with visible signs between those who belong to Christ's church and the rest of the world. When Jesus personally walked the earth, He instituted two sacraments: water baptism[269] and communion.[270] When believers are born again,[182] they should be baptized.[271] Communion should be done as a remembrance."[272]

"I'm glad I was baptized. I felt then and still do that it was right to do. Tell me more about communion."

Seeing Jack take a drink and return his bottle to his pack, Sam followed suit. They each re-shouldered their packs and resumed the hike.

"Communion is also known as the Eucharist and the Lord's Supper. *Eucharist* comes from the Greek word meaning 'to give thanks.'[604] *Communion* comes from the Greek word meaning 'fellowship, association and community.'[605] And the Lord's Supper refers to that last supper where Jesus introduced us to how to take communion. The last supper was the night Jesus was arrested prior to starting the journey to His crucifixion. He met with His twelve disciples and gave them a remembrance for remembering Him by, instructing them to maintain the remembrance until He returns."[606]

"I don't remember that from when I read the gospel of John."

"John was written decades after the other gospels. Matthew,[270] Mark[606] and Luke[272] each give an account of the last supper and Jesus showing us how to do communion. By the time John wrote his gospel, the sacrament of communion was well established. Paul had also written to the Corinthians telling them how to do communion. The very idea of communion has been part of Christianity from the very beginning."

"I would like to take communion," Sam asserted.

"I would too," Jack replied. "I thought ahead and have what we need."

"I know you are an engineer. Are you a minister too?"

"No, I am not ordained if that is what you are asking." Jack chuckled, then resumed. "I'm just another brother in Christ. However, I do have some good news. We qualify to give and partake in communion."[608]

"What?"

"In the Old Testament only people of certain lineage qualified to be priests and offer sacrifices.[609] In the new covenant, His Word says that we are being built into a holy priesthood.[610] In Christ, we are new creatures.[179] It's our responsibility not to conform ourselves to the world but to transform ourselves by the renewing of our minds,[492] sanctifying and cleansing our minds by the water of His Word.

"Okay, we qualify. How do we do communion?"

Jack replied, "Let's start with the purpose of communion, which is to commemorate the death of Christ. To commemorate Christ's death, tangible elements are used. The bread symbolizes His body that was broken for us,[58] and then we drink to symbolize His blood that was shed for us."[124]

Sam meekly asked, "Wine?"

Jack replied, "Some of the old-line denominations use wine; that's a tradition. Before refrigeration and modern sanitation methods, fermentation was the best method for long-term preservation of foods and beverages. That was then, this is now. For us, I brought some juice we could use for communion."

Sam looked down. "My parents divorced because of my father's alcoholism. I loved Dr. Jekyll and hated Mr. Hyde. Mom felt the same. I swore to myself as a kid that I would never be like him in that way.

Honestly, I was a little uncomfortable about communion because I do not want to have anything to do with wine, period."

"Relax, Jesus did not prescribe any specific beverage to be used with communion. He just said eat the bread and drink from the cup.[270] Some churches use grape juice, I brought pomegranate juice. The deep red color reminds me of the blood He shed for me.[473] I also brought a pair of two-ounce glasses I use at home for liquid measurement."

Sam looked at Jack and said, "Thanks."

Jack stopped at the fork in the trail.

Sam said, "The trail to the right is another way to get up here. Down that trail are a couple of lakes backpackers like to camp beside."

"The Oyster Dome is to the left?"

"About a quarter mile up ahead."

"Okay, baptism was a one-time event. Communion is a regular reminder, right?"

"Yes, in the early days of Christianity, believers took communion whenever they gathered together. Paul made it clear that taking communion was a sober decision. He warned that if communion was taken unworthily, the partaker would be liable of nailing Christ to the cross themselves.[611] The unworthy person is literally drinking and eating judgment to himself." [612]

"Wow, that has gravity! Jesus died for my sins. I certainly would not want to be guilty of putting Him up on the cross again or repeatedly. What is taking communion unworthily?" Sam asked.

"That question leads to the process of taking communion. The first requirement for taking communion is being born again. If a person is not born again, communion has no meaning and not only is the unsaved person unworthy of taking communion,[611] he or she has no business taking communion."

"That's a given," Sam commented.

"The next requirement is having a clear conscience.[613] Partakers should examine their own heart to see if there is any unconfessed sin."

"That sounds simple, but potentially is a showstopper. Does that require going to confession?"

Jack replied, "Our confession is to God;[613] there are no intermediaries. Since the last time you took communion or in your case since you asked Jesus into your heart, do any things stand out? Is there anything in your life or has come into your life that would hinder your relationship with God? What does your conscience tell you? Confess what comes to mind to God and ask for His forgiveness."

"What if I can't think of anything?" Sam asked.

"Just like in secular law, ignorance of a law is not an acceptable excuse for violating the law."

"How do I know?" Sam asked.

"As you grow in Christ, you will find some things you thought were okay may no longer be acceptable. It's part of the sanctification process. Just pray to God and ask His Holy Spirit to bring things to your remembrance.[227] Think of it like house cleaning before inviting the Eucharist to come in. To make sure I'm covered, when I pray to God, I ask for forgiveness for the sins I know I've done. Then I go one step further and ask for forgiveness for the sins I did not know that I did. Asking God in prayer to give you a better awareness of what pleases Him and what displeases Him is a very good idea."

"I can do that."

Jack said, "Then enter His gates with thanksgiving.[614] Communion is a serious time of thankfulness[603] and reflection as we do a remembrance of what Jesus did for us."[605]

"Can I summarize what I have learned?"

"Go ahead."

"Before taking communion, do some deep soul searching. Ask God for forgiveness of any sins committed since the last communion. If you cannot think of anything, then ask the Holy Spirit to bring to mind anything for which you should ask forgiveness and repent of. To be safe, offer a blanket prayer by sincerely asking forgiveness for sins you didn't know that you committed. Then take a piece of bread and a sip, all the while remembering what Jesus did for us on the cross."

"Remember, communion is a sacrament—not a ritual," Jack added.

Ahead to the left, the trees thinned, and people could be seen.

"We've arrived!" Sam exclaimed.

The trail ended with a bald rock promontory. The outcropping provided a wide-open view of the San Juan Islands, Strait of Juan de Fuca and as much of the Puget Sound as sight distance would allow. Jack saw people scattered around the exposed granite surface. Some were sitting, some standing and others simply milling about taking photos.

"I wasn't expecting a crowd." Jack's surprise was thinly veiled.

"Well, we did meet two other trails, and other vehicles were in the overlook parking lot."

"I liked feeling that we had the trail to ourselves."

"We did." Sam chuckled.

Jack stared at the vista while Sam studied the outcropping for a spot to sit.

"Over there!" Sam pointed at a place, while staring at a primo spot becoming available that was sure to provide an unobstructed view. Looking toward Jack, Sam nodded toward his left. "It looks like that family is preparing to leave."

To his right, Sam noticed another couple eying the same spot. They began to move, then stopped. Sam looked to the left to see Jack moving in as the family had moved out.

"Quick thinking," Sam said as he dropped his pack and sat down next to Jack.

Jack chuckled. "I saw my opportunity, and I took it."

"That you did," Sam commented with a matching laugh.

"This is as good as a vista ever gets."

Scanning the view to the right, Sam saw the couple park themselves on an equally prime patch of exposed granite.

Jack pulled out his phone and leaned back so far his lower back touched the rock. He framed and took a photo of his boots on the granite surface with the islands as the backdrop. "That's the photo of this hike," he said, handing his phone to Sam.

"You've got a good eye. That would make a great photo for a hiking blog or book jacket."

"Thanks," Jack replied.

Sam pulled out his half-empty bottle of electrolyte mix. Jack took out a baggie of carrot sticks and one of celery sticks. Silently they soaked in the vista. A gentle breeze generated enough white noise for neither to hear anything more than a low din from the other people on the dome.

"Sam, didn't you say we could see Canada?"

"On the north side of the dome," Sam replied. "Are you ready?"

Jack slipped the empty baggies in his pack, took a sip of water and replied, "Let's do it."

Together they got up and abandoned the spot where they had been sitting. Stepping off of the granite face, Jack turned to see their spot was no longer vacant. A man with a long beard was sitting there, deep fishing for something in his backpack.

Sam led the way up a short, unmarked trail spur. Through the trees, they found a smaller outcropping.

Jack stood on the exposed granite, soaking in a grand vista of the North Cascades. "These outcroppings remind me of the granite domes in North Carolina's Appalachians—just different views and foliage."

"I remember in geology class being taught that the Appalachians were an older volcanic range and the Cascades a younger volcanic range."

"We are at about the same altitude as the mountains behind my home in North Carolina. In the Appalachians, it's also common to see the pointy peaks of sleeping volcanoes," Jack said as he enjoyed Mount Baker's snow-capped peak. "Though not as dramatic since all the snow melts each summer."

"Someday I think I'd like to hike on the Appalachian Trail," Sam mentioned.

"I've done portions; you would like it—especially in late spring when the wild rhododendrons are blooming."

"I thought the Madronas around Puget Sound were the only native rhododendron in North America."

"Take a drive on the lower Blue Ridge Parkway, and you will get your fill. They show like green pillows beside the road. In early June, they bloom with the prettiest pink flowers. Whole mountainsides are covered with them."

"That must be some eye candy." Sam smiled.

Jack took his phone out of his pocket and opened the compass app.

"Canada?" Jack asked, pointing due north.

"On the far side of Mount Baker is where Canada starts."

Jack turned to look down the trail spur. "I see we have this spot to ourselves. I think it would be a wonderful place for taking communion."

"Most people go to the other overlook, rest and return. We may or may not get other hikers out here."

"Then let's take advantage of the time we have." Jack sat down and fished in the large center pocket of his pack. He pulled out an insulated thermal lunch bag.

Sam watched curiously. From the bag Jack took out a small size bottle of juice, a packet of crackers and a pair of glasses rolled in a paper towel. "You came prepared."

"I was hoping to do communion with you today. I want to make sure you understand the why and how of this important sacrament."

Sam looked out over the valley. "Thanks for the 'why.' Before today, I had not given communion much thought. After I was baptized, the minister said I was qualified to take communion, and I just said, 'Okay.' I think he assumed we would have been having a third meeting. He said something about the first Sunday of the month."

"Doing communion on the first Sunday of the month is a tradition in many churches."

"That Sunday was mid-month, and I'm certain he could see I was a bit overwhelmed by everything. While we were sitting in our other spot looking out over the sound, I prayed silently to God and some things came to mind that I felt I ought to ask forgiveness for. I did."

"Good, you listened. I did the same. Back home my wife and I do communion together. We each begin with taking some time for soul searching. We each take our turns asking God's forgiveness for sins committed since our last communion."

"Doing some house cleaning seems to be the appropriate way to start," Sam added.

"It's important to make sure that we are taking communion worthily. Housekeeping is most definitely the way to start, and it sounds like we have both done that."

"I have," Sam replied.

"After my wife and I have done our house cleaning, we read Paul's instructions for how to take communion." Jack took his phone and opened to his favorite Bible app. "You'll want to make a note of this passage: I Corinthians 11:23-26."

Sam took out his phone and opened the notes app and began to type. "Okay, got it."

Jack read:

> "For I have received of the Lord that which also I delivered unto you, That the Lord Jesus the same night in which he was betrayed took bread: And when he had given thanks, he brake it, and said, Take, eat: this is my body, which is broken for you: this do in remembrance of me. After the same manner also he took the cup, when he had supped, saying, This cup is the new testament in my blood: this do ye, as oft as ye drink it, in remembrance of me. For as often as ye eat this bread, and drink this cup, ye do shew the Lord's death till he come."[605]

Jack took the juice and poured its contents into the two glasses. He offered one of the glasses to Sam. "Wait for the crackers."

Jack opened up the cracker packet and kept one and offered the other to Sam. Sam looked to Jack to follow his lead. "We've searched ourselves and prayed to make sure we are worthy of taking communion. Do you feel ready?" Jack asked.

"Yes, I do." Sam replied.

Jack bowed his head. Sam did likewise, but he kept one eye on Jack.

Jack prayed, "Dear Heavenly Father, thank You for life and breath and the truth You shine into my soul. Thank You, Jesus, for being the atonement for my sins. Thank You, Holy Spirit, for revealing this to me. Thank You, God, for loving me and wanting me. Thank You, Jesus, for the price You paid for me. Thank You that Your body was broken."

Jack lifted the cracker and looked at Sam who met his gaze. Jack nodded, and both ate their crackers. Jack continued praying, "Thank You for Your blood that was shed for me. Your blood washed me clean and gives me life." Sam picked up his glass when saw Jack pick up his. Jack opened his eyes to see Sam was following his lead. They raised their glasses and drank. "Thank You, Jesus, for giving us communion as a remembrance of what You have done for us. We praise Your Holy name. Amen."

Jack took the glasses and rolled them in the paper towel he had brought. The glasses, empty bottle and cracker wrapper went back into his thermal bag, and he put the bag back into the main pocket of his backpack. "When my wife and I have communion, we usually sing a couple of songs. We'll pass on that part."

"I'm curious."

"Next time..." Jack smiled.

Sam leaned back on the support of both arms. "I feel right."

"Clean?" Jack asked.

"Yeah. I'm glad this is something we should do often."

"The first Christians had communion whenever they broke bread together."

Sam leaned back to look at the sky. "I love You, God. I love You, Jesus. I love You, Holy Spirit."

Jack looked up at the sky. "Thank You, God."

"There is a lot of thankfulness going on," Sam commented.

"That's why communion is also called the Eucharist,"[603] Jack replied.

An eagle flew out from the trees on the mountain to soar over the valley.

"By the way, I looked past you while you were praying. I saw a bearded guy at the trail head. He stood at the spur watching us."

"Hmmm, must be the same guy who took our spot on the other outcropping." Jack turned to see.

"Oh, he's gone now. Whatever, he had an impressive beard."

"Yeah, that's the guy. I had a beard like that once. When the wind blew, I felt like someone was yanking on my face," Jack said with a laugh.

"Why did you shave it?" Sam asked.

"Too many adults said I looked like Santa." Jack laughed.

"I can see that." Sam laughed with Jack.

A little girl came running up from behind them. Jack and Sam turned to see the source of the commotion and saw a family following behind her.

"I think we've had our time here."

Sam nodded, and they both stood.

"Thanks for the 'how.' I'll remember this," Sam promised.

"You better." Jack smiled, turned and led the way off the stone face, onto the spur.

~

Past the overlook trailhead, the trail slowly descended for the return hike.

Spiritual Fruit

Below the ridge, Jack said. "*Fruit* in the Greek means 'the fruit of trees, vines or what's grown in the fields.' *Fruit* also means 'progeny and things that originate from something, an effect or result.'[615]

Spiritual fruit are attributes the Holy Spirit cultivates in us as we grow in Christ."

"Okay, what are these spiritual fruit?" Sam asked.

"When Paul wrote to the Galatians, he listed nine spiritual fruit: love, joy, peace, patience, kindness, goodness, faithfulness, gentleness and self-control."[450]

"I feel all of those after taking communion," Sam observed. "How do you know which fruit to pursue?"

"All of them. As they grow, they complement each other. Patience and self-control yield peace. Love yields joy, kindness, gentleness and goodness. As they grow, so does faithfulness and so on. My grandfather cultivated blueberries. His berries were always big and full of flavor. He said it was because he grew different varieties. He said if all the bushes had all been the same variety, the bees would get bored and the crop would be poor. When the bees find different varieties, they were happy; we always got buckets of berries. He even had high and low bushes."

"I have blueberry bushes at my home. They are happier and more productive when they cross pollinate. Mixing varieties adds different harvest times extending the harvest. When spiritual fruit cross-pollinate, they provide superior yields."

"Let's talk about spiritual fruit."

"Let's walk down Paul's list," Jack replied.

LOVE

"**L**OVE IS THE linchpin. John said God is love. The person who does not love does not know God.[616] The Greek word Paul used for love is *agapé* which means 'benevolence, charity, good will and brotherly love.' [617] Jesus said that we should love each other as He loved us. Our love for others should be our outward sign of being His disciples."[618]

"Love should be an attitude?" Sam asked.

"Love is patient. True love has tolerance without getting angry. Love is kind, gentle and compassionate. Love is content and thankful, not envious of others. Love is humble, never proud or boastful. Love is respectful. Love is selfless and thoughtful, not inconsiderate. Love is calm, maintaining a clarity of mind. True love does the right thing, checking itself to make sure it does not do the wrong thing. Love rejoices in truth. Love protects, trusts, hopes and preserves."[619]

Jack did not hear Sam's steps on the gravel trail. Turning, he saw Sam using the touchpad of his phone. "Jack, can you repeat that list?" Sam asked.

"I'll do you better. Paul's list is found it in I Corinthians 13:4-7."

"Thanks."

Jack said, "When Jesus was asked what was the greatest of all the commandments, He told them the first is to love the Lord their God with all our hearts, minds and soul.[238] The second is to love our neighbors as ourselves."[239]

"That condenses the don'ts of the Ten Commandments into two do's." Sam commented.

"If you love your spouse, you will not be shopping around for another. If you love your God, you will not be shopping other gods. If you love your neighbor, you are not going to do bad things to your neighbor."

"Do not do unto others what you do not want them to do to you." Sam commented.

"That is not what Jesus said! What you quoted is from a far-Eastern religion. The perspective is pre-reactive. It may be one of Confucius' sayings and only shows how deeply Eastern philosophy has permeated Western culture."

"I thought that was from the Bible…" Sam responded.

"Jesus was proactive. *'Do unto others what you wish others would do unto you.'*[245] As Christians, our behaviors should be motivated out of love for others, with respect and thoughtfulness. That Eastern phrase is diametrically opposed to what Jesus taught and is based on a self-preservation motivation."

"Actions do speak louder than words," Sam commented.

"Love must be sincere, never hypocritical."[620]

Jack continued, "Being proactive is the easier approach. It takes less effort to be kind and considerate of others than to second guess their reaction to something you may or may not do."

Sam laughed. "Yeah, second-guessing people's actions and reactions can be a real energy drain. I have to agree that being considerate and thoughtful frees up a lot of mental energy for other things."

"There is a freedom and joy with not being self-absorbed."

Joy

"Joy is one of the spiritual fruit?" Sam asked.

"Joy and gladness[621] are their own fruit. The kingdom of God is righteousness, peace and joy.[622] That promised joy in part sustained Jesus through His ordeal on the cross."[623]

"How do I get that kind of joy?" Sam asked.

"Jesus told us to abide in Him and have His words abide in us. If we keep His commandments, we will abide in His love. His joy will remain in us that our joy may be complete. It's God's glory that we bear fruit, showing ourselves to be His disciples."[624]

"I see a fork ahead. We stay to the right?" Jack asked.

"The left fork would take us somewhere inland." On cue, three backpackers appeared hiking from the left fork trail.

Approaching Sam, the first backpacker asked, "How's the view?"

"It couldn't be clearer. A perfect day for the dome," Sam replied.

"What's down that trail?" Jack asked.

Approaching Jack, the second backpacker said, "Last night, we camped at Lily Lake. We're making a weekend out of it."

The third backpacker who passed Jack simply waved and smiled.

As quickly as the backpackers appeared, they passed. Sam took the right fork, and the trail began to descend.

PEACE

"**J**ACK, I BELIEVE you said that peace is an attribute of God's kingdom."[211]

"The Greek word for *peace* means 'tranquility, harmony, felicity or the happiness that comes from security.'[625] God's Word says that to be carnally minded leads to death. Being spiritually minded leads to life and peace."[81]

"How do we attain that kind of peace?" Sam asked.

Jack replied. "Be spiritually minded,[81] be reasonable,[626] do not let yourself be anxious. Present your petitions to God with thankfulness,[191] and the peace of God will protect your heart and mind."[494]

"That would take patience," Sam commented.

PATIENCE

"**A**ND THE FOURTH listed spiritual fruit happens to be patience," Jack replied. "*Patience* in the Greek is 'endurance, steadfastness, longsuffering and perseverance.' [627] Think of longsuffering as having a long fuse. As Christians, we are to cloth ourselves in kindness, humility, meekness and patience.[628] This will allow us to bear with each other, resolve quarrels and forgive as Christ has forgiven us.[138] Growing patience will allow the peace of God to rule in our hearts."[211]

Sam commented, "Spiritual fruit really does cross-pollinate."

The steep descent leveled at a bridge over a mountain stream. "Let's stop. My legs feel like they are cramping," Jack said as he stopped in the middle of the bridge. He dropped his pack and commenced stroking his left thigh downward to the knee. After five strokes, he lifted his leg onto the rail and stroked his calf from the knee downward. "Always stroke away from the heart. It could be a blood clot."

"Yeah, I've heard that before; makes sense." Sam looked up the rapidly flowing stream. "I'm thankful someone built a bridge here. I'm not up for fording that stream."

"Neither am I with these cramping legs. Jack laughed as he switched to stroke his right leg.

Sam looked at Jack. "Do you have a headache?"

Jack looked up at Sam. "Yeah, its dull. I can almost ignore it."

"When did you begin to notice the headache?"

Jack lifted his right leg onto the rail and proceeded with a series of calf strokes. "About halfway through the switchbacks."

"When was the last time you had any water?" Sam asked.

"Up at the dome. I finished that electrolyte mix bottle. I thought that I had a couple more waters in my pack. They must be in the cooler in the truck." Jack bravely smiled through his pain.

"Been there, done that." Sam dropped his pack and pulled out an unopened bottle of water. Handing the bottle to Jack, he said, "Drink. I usually bring more than I drink."

Jack took the bottle and took a long drink. "Oh, yeah, exactly what I needed!"

"More than you may have thought. Common early signs of dehydration are a dull headache and muscle cramping. Of course, everybody's body is different. But if you have not been drinking enough, have a headache and are experiencing leg cramping, your body is probably telling you to drink some water. I diagnose you as showing early signs of being dehydrated." Sam raised his bottle to meet Jack's in a dull thud of water-filled plastic.

"We will have cold waters when we get back to the truck. I had planned for us to have some cold ones after the hike. I guess the cooler has a couple more than I had planned." Jack took another long drink, taking the bottle to half-empty. Jack stood straight, took another drink of water and proceeded to do a series of calf and hamstring stretches.

"Feeling better?" Sam asked.

"That was quick."

"Diagnosis confirmed." Sam sealed his bottle and put it in the beverage pocket of his pack.

"When it's warmer, like today, our bodies need more water." Sam picked up and re-shouldered his pack.

Jack took another sip. Making sure to leave more than half the volume, he slipped the half-full bottle into the beverage pocket of his pack, re-shouldered his pack and patted the bandanna he had tied as a sweat rag around his head. "I was sweating heavily earlier. Now my bandanna is mostly dry."

"Yep, dehydration. On hot days like this, it's quite common." Sam shook his head.

"I've had this combo before. Your diagnosis makes sense. Today, I learned a lesson."

"All hikers and athletes get it at some time. The question is learning from the experience." Sam turned and led the way off the bridge. "We'll plan another break somewhere between here and there."

"It didn't take long for my whole system to feel happier after some water," Jack commented.

"Our bodies are about half water. On a day like this, it's easy to lose more than you put in. Bring more water next time." Sam stopped and turned around to look at Jack.

"Yes, sir." Jack gave his best boot-camp reply.

The trail quickly crested with a bend. Beyond the bend, it made a gentle descent along the mountainside.

"Sam, it was kind of you to share your water."

"That's okay. You needed some, and I had a surplus."

KINDNESS AND GOODNESS

"KINDNESS IS ANOTHER of the spiritual fruit. The Greek word for *kindness* also means 'moral goodness, integrity, gracious and harmless.'[629] The word is derived from another word that means 'fit for use, useful, virtuous, good, pleasant and benevolent.'"[630]

Sam said, "I've never thought of kindness as being useful."

"A kindness is useful to the person to whom you are being kind. Thanks again for the water, that was kind and the water was useful."

"Growing the spiritual fruit of kindness grows your moral goodness and integrity." Sam condensed the attributes of kindness.

"The spiritual gift of goodness[631] is very similar to kindness. The root word in Greek for goodness means 'useful, good, pleasant. upright and honorable.'[632]

"Goodness and kindness almost sound interchangeable. Being kind to be kind and being good to be good without seeking a benefit or a return?" Sam commented.

"Christians ought to be living the gospel. They will know us by our fruit.[477] This pleases God who tests our hearts to discern our motivation. People who act to impress other people for their own purpose are misguided.[633] Kindness and goodness are attributes God desires for us to retain and grow in our lives. At the end of the day, our relationship with God is all that matters. Besides, God knows all[11]—even the motivation of our hearts."[634]

Sam stopped halfway across the second bridge. "I love the sound. How are you doing?"

"I'm feeling better than I was. Let's plan on a break at that big rock."

"Works for me." Sam followed Jack off the bridge.

MEEKNESS

"ALONG WITH KINDNESS and goodness, meekness, gentleness and mildness[635] should become a Christian's second nature. Christ said that we will be known by our fruit.[636]

"Meekness?" Sam paused.

"Meekness should never be confused with weakness. Although they may appear similar, weakness and meekness are diametrically opposed to each other. Meekness has confidence and is strength in gentleness."

"That makes me think of a trained elephant. While they are immensely powerful, they are also humble and gentle," Sam replied.

"Strength with a tender touch," Jack commented. "Kindness, goodness and gentleness are the trilogy of passive spiritual fruits. Joy and peace come when we practice *agapé* love for our neighbors. Practicing genuine Christian love toward others is done meekly in goodness and gentleness with kindness.[637] Practicing love toward others should never hypocritical.[620] Hypocritical acts done with the intent of making them appear to be loving acts lead to pride. Pride is incompatible with goodness and meekness."

Sam asked, "Isn't pride the original sin?"

"Satan's pride, which made him think we was greater than God,[30] led to rebellion and got him thrown out of heaven.[19] Pride is how Satan turned Eve against God.[638] Unchecked pride can be invasive. In the southeast, a fast-growing Asian vine called kudzu looks pretty in the summer. This invasive green blanket suffocates the vegetation it covers, leaving forests dead and only fit to be cut down and burned."

To the right, the steep hillside thinned. Through the tree trunks and over the lower treetops, the thinner forest permitted views of the Strait of Juan de Fuca, reminding them of how close they were to the ocean.

FAITHFULNESS AND SELF-CONTROL

"FAITHFULNESS AND SELF-CONTROL are the final two spiritual fruit on Paul's list,"[450] Jack continued. "Faith is the substance of things hoped for and not yet seen.[160] Faithfulness[639] is confidently holding onto the faith."

Sam commented, "I remember you saying that we grow our faith in God by reading His Word and building a relationship with Him."

Jack mused, "When I met my wife, I chose to be faithful to her. It was easy because I lost interest in everyone else. Over time, when she proved herself to be faithful, my faithfulness grew. I don't like being away from her, but I have faith that she will be there and still be my wife when I return."

"Did I tell you that my ex-wife and I have been speaking? Last weekend we did the exchange with the girls at a playground. She told the girls, 'The adults have adult business to discuss.' Then she directed them to go off and play. When they were busy, she turned to me and told me that she had kicked out the guy with whom she was living. I think he may be the guy who was the catalyst to our breakup."

"That's great news. Good for your girls too," Jack remarked. "Did she say why?"

"I could tell it all upset her, so I remained extra calm and quiet. When she calmed down, she confided that he had been unfaithful to her."

"Oh, boy!" Jack muttered under his breath.

"I do not know how I did it, but I remained silent. Oh, boy, that was hard. I had words I needed to restrain myself from releasing. I know because I bit my lip so hard that my mouth filled with that metallic blood taste. It took some silence for her to realize there wasn't going to be a deluge of ugly words or toxic scene. She didn't move. She looked up at me and asked my forgiveness for all the pain she has been the cause of. Hearing her words, I flashed on the terrible words I had angrily showered her with in the past."

"And?" Jack broke Sam's pause.

Sam choked up. "I told her the three words every woman wants to hear: 'I am sorry.' I am sorry for the terrible things I said while we were fighting. Please forgive me." A tear escaped from Sam's eye and ran down his cheek.

Sam dropped his pack and bent down. With one smooth move, he pulled out his water bottle and a bandanna. In the process of standing up, he discreetly wiped the tear and stuffed the bandanna into the cargo pocket of his shorts.

Jack kindly said, "God heals the brokenhearted."[343]

"Ever since talking about the power of words at the Discovery Park overlook, I've been praying to God for the opportunity to make right for what I had said."

"How did she take it?"

"She was stunned. My ex-wife literally stood silent as she slowly shook her head. Then she turned and walked off to be with the girls. It was over, so I left. This week she called me, informed me that she had a sitter for the girls and asked me for a date tomorrow afternoon."

"It sounds like you are being rewarded for your self-control and choosing to ask forgiveness over vengeance," Jack commented.

"The only way this is happening is by my showing self-control. I am certain we will be on a healthier track. If she and I get together or not, we will be better, and that is what is best for the girls." Sam returned the bottle to his pack, re-shouldered his pack and resumed walking.

"God is working on you. His goal is to make a new man out of you— a man in His likeness."[640]

"I'm not the same guy I was last summer. I like this new me." *Thank You, Jesus.*

"Exercising self-control[641] pours water on the fires of the self-induced storms in our lives."

"Oh, bring out the hose!" Sam remarked. "I literally saw its power."

A FORMULA FOR GROWING SPIRITUAL FRUIT

"THE APOSTLE PETER gave a formula for growing spiritual fruit: to our faith, we should add goodness. To goodness, add knowledge. To knowledge, add self-control. To self-control, add patience. To patience, add godliness.[642] To godliness, add kindness and to kindness, add love. God's divine power has given us everything we need for a godly knowledge of Him complete with great and precious promises. These things abiding and abounding in us will keep us from being unfruitful.[643] Don't just take someone's word that what they say is a scriptural truth. Look it up for yourself in the Bible.[337] Look at the verses their context and verify.[3] Use the concordance to verify content. With modern technology, we have Greek and Hebrew lexicons at our fingertips. Curious about what some specific word meant as it was used by the author? Look it up. Pretty cool, eh?"

The trail had been climbing since the fork for the Samish Bay Connector. Sam heard Jack using the breathing technique. Stopping at a big rock, he pulled out his water and waited for Jack to catch up. "You've been doing great. Did you feel any heart strain?" Sam said to Jack as he stepped up panting.

"Honestly, no. I thought I felt something earlier on the way up to the dome. Those switchbacks were brutal. Nitro crossed my mind. I decided to focus on my breathing, and before I knew it, we crested the rise. After that, it was easy. I feel okay, but I am still a little thirsty."

"Drink up! We're almost done."

Jack retrieved the bottle from his pack and took a long drink. "The next ones will be cold."

"How about hiking the Cascades next time?" Sam asked. "I know a trail that follows the track bed of the first railroad to cross the Cascades. They call it the Iron Horse Trail. It's a loop trail that starts with a climb to span one of the railroad's great switchbacks. Once we climb up to the old railroad bed, it's a railroad grade descent through the railroad's switchback down to the parking lot. The first part is a challenge with lots of climbing switchbacks followed by a leisurely and scenic stroll."

"I like the idea of doing all the altitude gain at the beginning of the hike. I like the idea of having a scenic view all the way back down."

"The trail is cut into the side of a mountain."

"Cool," Jack remarked.

"We'll pack in more water next time." Sam smiled.

They laughed and drank up.

A LIFE REDEEMED

THE CANOPY OPENED as the trail climbed. A vehicle could be heard be pulling into the gravel lot.

"How's the headache?" Sam asked.

"What headache?" Jack smiled. "Thanks for the hydration lesson."

"Oh, you did that to yourself. I just provided the footnotes and a way out." Sam laughed.

"Up the ramp ahead, I see the trail map."

"Bummer, I could have kept walking and talking."

"We still have the ride back," Jack replied.

Sam crested the trailhead first. At the entrance to the parking lot, he stopped and used the map board for some standing stretches while he waited for Jack to catch up.

"There's that guy we saw at the dome," Sam said.

"Yeah, same guy," Jack replied.

"You can't mistake that beard. It looks like a Persian cat hanging on his chin."

Jack burst out laughing, and Sam joined in.

The bearded guy turned around to see where the laughter was coming from.

"You know, we're going to have to pass him to get to the truck," Sam commented.

"He seems harmless but don't scare the cat," Jack added.

Together they began to walk the length of the parking lot.

The bearded guy sat with his sandaled feet hanging off the tailgate of his truck. Jack and Sam were only a few steps from passing when he raised his hand, clearly wanting to make contact. "Beautiful day for a hike," he called.

"Sure is," Jack replied.

"I saw you guys up on the dome. Can I ask you a question?"

Jack stopped, looked at him and said, "Sure, what's up?"

"Were you guys doing communion?"

"Yes, we were," Sam replied. "Why do you ask?"

"I used to do communion. I miss it," the bearded guy replied.

"Do you know Jesus?" Jack asked.

"I used to, but now I don't know anymore."

"Would you like to talk about it?" Jack asked.

"If you guys are in a hurry..." the bearded guy provided an escape for Jack and Sam.

"Don't worry about it. We just want to get out of these boots and have some cold water. That blue truck is mine. Come with us, and we'll talk. My name is Jack and..."

"I'm Sam," Sam greeted as he extended his hand.

"My name is Tony." With a hop off of the tailgate, Tony reached out and took Sam's offered hand.

Jack extended his hand to Tony, and they shook. "That's a firm grip, Tony."

"I'm a carpenter and a part-time mechanic," Tony replied.

"I'm an engineer; I design mechanical stuff," Jack offered.

"I'm the programmer who gives that mechanical stuff life," Sam said.

"Then I'm the technician who puts it all together," Tony added.

"That works for me. Let's get some of those cold waters." Jack turned and headed toward his truck. Sam and Tony followed.

Sam commented. "You said that you knew Jesus but now you don't? Did communion, but now you don't?"

"Are you guys saved?" Tony asked.

"By the grace[111] and the mercy[644] of the Almighty God, yes, I am saved." Jack smiled from ear to ear.

"Amen, me too!" Sam added with a big smile.

"I was, but now I'm not sure," Tony replied. "I know Jesus is the Son of God and that He died for my sins and three days later God raised Him from the dead.[120] Everything else seems out of sync though."

"Tell us about it," Jack suggested.

"I'm listening too," Sam added.

"I grew up in Christian family and we attended church regularly. Growing up, my parents always complained about the ministers, but I enjoyed the activities and had friends there. When I got into high school, I took a bad turn, got into drugs, and 'Trouble' became my middle name. One weekend some of my friends asked me to join them at a concert. I liked the music, and when it was over, the drummer got up and started talking. He had put on a very good performance, so I felt like he had earned a few minutes of my attention." Tony paused, and Jack could tell he was gathering his thoughts.

"That night my life changed. The drummer said I needed Jesus, and every fiber of my being agreed. When he gave the altar call, I was up there on my knees crying to God to forgive me for my sins and promising to live in repentance. I was saved that night, and I knew I was a new person. I completely lost interest in doing the bad stuff that I had previously enjoyed doing." Tony paused again to gather his thoughts.

"I was a sophomore that year. At the end of my junior year, my school guidance counselor told me that he had heard a lot of kids say they had met Jesus. He went on to say that he had not seen a life transformed like he saw in mine. In my freshman year, only my shop teachers had faith that I'd do more than follow a life of crime." Tony chuckled.

Before reaching the truck, Jack clicked the doors open. "Tony, yours sounds like a good story so far," he commented.

Tony continued. "I had a hunger for God. I was baptized in the Holy Spirit and was never without my pocket Bible that I read every day. All I wanted to do was tell other people about what I had found."

Jack opened the rear driver's side door, threw in his pack and grabbed three ice-cold waters from the cooler.

Sam commented, "It sounds like God reached down and transformed you."[492]

"Yes, He did," Tony replied as he accepted the water bottle from Jack.

"Jack, I'll take one of those too," Sam held out his hand.

Jack handed Sam a bottle before he opened his own. "I needed that."

"I did too," Sam chimed in.

"Thanks," Tony said.

Jack stepped to the front of the truck, opened the driver's door, grabbed his Chuckies and returned to the back of the truck, dropped the tailgate and hopped up to sit on it. Sam had gotten his shoes and had joined Jack on the other end of the tailgate. Tony stood away from the back of the truck, sipping his water.

"It sounds like you know that you were saved and that your life was evidence of your salvation.[645] Why would you question that now?" Jack asked.

"A girl." Tony lowered his head.

"Adam had that problem too,"[636] Sam added. "We are guys; we all have woman stories. What's yours?"

"When I got saved, I really wanted to find other Christians like me who were on fire for Christ. I was just told to find a church and get involved. I already had the church that I had grown up in, so I just went there. Nobody felt the same way I did, and eventually, I just had to conform. I tried teaching Sunday school and being a scout leader, but that just wasn't me."

"Yeah, a lot of churches think that if they plug you into something, they will have you," Jack commented.

"They should have focused on real Bible teaching. All the other kids were either Bible illiterate, didn't care or just didn't want to talk about it. The only thing the minister wanted to talk about was grace and prosperity."

"So where did the girl come in?" Sam asked.

"She was in the youth group. She had a thing for me, but I didn't for her. I didn't even think she was a Christian. After graduation, I went off to the university. After two years, I returned, and she looked me up. We went out and before I knew it, we were going steady. I guess the flame within me had dimmed to the point where she looked better than the rest of the girls who were available. That was my last semester at the university. We were hip, and nobody said anything when we moved in together."

"Your church?" Jack asked.

"We'd both lost interest. Besides, they were open-minded about couples living together."

"One day when I came home, she was sitting in the dark. I asked her what was wrong, and she said she was pregnant. I just said, 'Oh,' but I thought to myself, *I don't want to spend my future with this girl.* I asked her what she thought we should do, and she shrugged. I asked, 'Should we get married?' She shrugged again, and we didn't talk any more about it that night. After a couple of days, I came home ready to make an honest couple out of us. I had even shopped for rings. When I got home, there she was again sitting in the dark. I told her that I thought we should get married. I even had a bouquet of roses. She said that we didn't have to because she had taken care of the issue. I still remember the shock I felt. All I could say was 'What?' She then said the abortion still hurt and asked me to fix her a strong drink. I asked, 'Why?' We had not talked about abortion as an option. She said it was her body, her decision and she made the decision. I felt sick like a knife had been driven through my heart. That feeling has never gone away."

"I'm so sorry," Jack said.

"Bummer. I'm so sorry you had to go through that," Sam added.

"A thick heavy dark curtain fell between us, and it wasn't long before we parted ways. I've not heard anything from her since nor do I ever want to."

"How did you cope?" Sam asked.

"I left town," Tony replied, "I needed a change of scenery."

"What about her?" Jack asked.

"She said that it hurt, but that she felt okay about all of it. She told me that abortions are okay. Her life had more value than the life of the fetus.[646] Then she said a bunch of rhetoric about how a fetus is not really a person until it has exited the womb and taken its first breath.[647] Her reasoning was that it was for the best for everyone involved. So, she put an end to the fetus before it started breathing. Thinking about her words still makes me nauseous."

Jack looked out across the parking lot. "She got that reasoning from the Talmud. The Talmud teaches that the baby 'is not [considered] a soul, and [so] it is possible to kill it and to save its mother.'[647] Is she Jewish?" Jack added.

"Was her life at risk?" Sam asked.

"No," Tony was quick to reply. "She always was in great shape." Tony blushed. "That's mostly what drew me to her."

"Saving the mother can be broadly interpreted," Jack replied. "Is there a health issue? Would the baby cause financial or educational hardship for the mother? Is the baby inconvenient?" Jack paused. "You can justify anything if you really want to."

"And no, she is not Jewish. I know because I have a Jewish heritage, and we had talked about our heritages," Tony replied, paused and continued. "The church where we met and attended had a big thing for Jewish stuff. There were always people traveling to Israel and supporting causes in Israel. The minister liked referencing his sermons in the Torah with occasional quotes from the Talmud. By the way, isn't the Talmud just an extension of the Torah? I know Christianity grew out of Judaism. The Torah and the Talmud are both Jewish holy books. Aren't they both okay and of equal weight?"

Jack nodded. "Oh, I get it. She was mixing up apples and walnuts. Even though both grow on trees and are both edible, they are both completely different."

Tony's face wore a quizzical look. "I'm not following."

"The Torah and the Talmud are both Jewish holy books, but that's where it ends," Jack replied. "The Torah forbids murder.[74] The Tanakh says God hates the shedding of innocent blood.[93] The early Church

Fathers specifically forbade abortion,[648] and the Talmud teaches that abortion is acceptable.[646, 647] This highlights a difference between living in a Christian culture versus living in a Judeo-Christian culture."

"What's the Torah? What's the Talmud?" Sam asked.

"What is the Tanakh?" Tony asked.

Jack replied, "The Torah is the five books of Moses. It's where God, through Moses, lays down the law. The Torah is the very beginning of every Christian Bible. Centuries after Christ, the Talmud was compiled as a record of rabbinical discussion on Jewish law.[649] The Talmud postdates the Christian Bible. The very end of the Christian Bible is very clear. '*Do not add or take away from this book.*'[32] Even earlier, in the Old Testament, Moses made it very clear that no one should add to or subtract from God's law."[507] The Talmud is an extra book developed by Jews after Christ had already fulfilled the law.[59] For that reason alone, the Talmud, by default, is not recognized by Christianity. The other reason is that the Talmud is a book of rabbinical commentary and is very different from the Old and New Testaments, which are the inspired Word of God.[166]

"I just accepted what she said. In my gut, I knew something was wrong. But I could not put my finger on it." Tony looked up in that way of someone who was digesting something they had just heard for the first time. He slowly added, "I just surrendered and allowed the condemnation to sink in."

Jack looked over at Sam. "Chalk that one up to adding to or subtracting from the Bible. In this case, a whole book was added, and that church gave it the same weight as God's Word.

"So long as we're talking Scripture, I should add that the Tanakh is the other Jewish holy book. The Torah is the core of the Tanakh. The Tanakh's content is what Christians know as the Old Testament. The books of Moses, Psalms, Proverbs, prophets, kings, etc. The Tanakh is the Scriptures that the Jews studied in Jesus' time, which led to its becoming the Old Testament in the Christian Bible."

"Bible teaching was surely not one of our church's strengths," Tony commented.

"That's what Bible illiteracy gets you," Jack replied.

Sam looked at Jack. "Everything I've read in the Bible has been pretty crisp and clear. I never felt like I needed to read a bunch of commentary to understand what the Bible was saying. I did look at one commentary but found it over-flavored by the commentator's own perspective."

"Commentary can be helpful or lead you down a rabbit hole. Whatever, it never has the weight of the Word itself," Jack added.

"Whenever I want to dig deeper, I go into the original Greek or Hebrew." Sam pointed at Jack and said, "He taught me that trick."

"I can't disagree with you on the flaw of commentaries or the importance of using a concordance. I guess you guys do know what you're talking about," Tony replied.

Jack sat on the tailgate, wiggling the toes of his bare feet. "People respond to sin in two ways: they either deny they did it or justify what they did. She justified sin. What did you do?"

"I felt really bad about it, and I mean really bad. I quit that church and ran away. I never denied what happened. I'll admit that I'm glad not to have been saddled with her for the rest of my life, but there is no justification I can accept for what happened. I feel such condemnation for my part in all of it."

Jack looked at Sam then back at Tony. "Were you feeling condemnation? Or were you feeling conviction?"

"Both, I guess. What's the difference?"

"Condemnation is a state of being declared worthy of punishment.[650] Satan uses condemnation to bring us down. When we do something wrong, Satan wants us to feel like the sentence has already been passed, and we are less than dirt. We are so low that we cannot even look up to get up. On the other hand, the Holy Spirit convicts[651] us of our wrongdoing. The conviction is so we acknowledge what we have done and drive us to repentance."[49]

"But I didn't do it. I was in the process of proposing marriage to her when she stopped me and told me about the abortion." The pain showed in Tony's eyes.

"That's like using the defense that you were only driving the getaway car used in a bank heist. You may not have pulled the trigger, but you were involved with committing the crime. Sin happened, and you bear participatory guilt. Satan is the accuser[652] and is making you feel like burnt toast. However, there is no condemnation in Christ, providing you are walking in the spirit and not walking after the flesh.[653] God's Holy Spirit is trying to convict you to bring you to repentance so He can see you restored."[654]

"I thought I was walking in the spirit; obviously, I was walking in the flesh," Tony replied. "But we have grace; our church was all about grace."

Jack said, "Grace is about doing God's will,[73] not a 'get-out-of-jail-free' card or a carte blanche to continue sinning.[655]

Tony looked stunned.

Sam sensed the awkward silence and expected Tony to walk away.

Jack continued, "As Christians we are directed not to be conformed to this world, but to be transformed by the renewing of our minds that we may prove what is the good, acceptable and perfect will of God.[492] We renew our minds by washing it regularly with God's Word."[490]

Sam felt certain Tony was about to walk away, but he stood still.

"It keeps coming back to the Bible, eh?" Tony looked at the ground.

"Yes, it does. God gave us His Word for our teaching, correcting our ways and for our instruction in righteousness so that we might be thoroughly equipped to do His good works."[166]

"I think I'm going to have to dust off my Bible. I'll admit to not reading it much while we were living together or since. We did go to church and heard about grace in a hundred different flavors. We felt okay about life and forgot about what the speaker had said when we exited the church."

"And where did that get you?" Jack asked.

"Here, I guess," Tony paused. "Standing here with you guys, getting a dose of truth."

"Then I guess it was the Holy Spirit drawing us together?"[2] Jack commented.

I guess we'll be seeing more of this beard, Sam thought. "How are you feeling?"

"Like I'm having a divine appointment,"[149] Tony replied.

Jack smiled. "Here's a couple of thoughts to chew on. *Grace*[656] is getting what we don't deserve.[644] It would be a shame to squander it and turn off the spigot.[657] *Mercy*[658] is not getting what we do deserve."[644]

"Yeah, I think I should probably appeal to God for mercy," Tony admitted shoving his hands deep into his pockets.

"We all should. King David often asked God for His mercy[659] as he acknowledged his own sin and asked for mercy."[660]

Tony smiled. "My grandmom used to say that 'God likes a good repenter.'"

"Yes, He does. It sounds like you have a good grandmother."

"She was a treasure, and she loved Him. She wanted us to know Him. She is with Him now." Tony looked up. "I loved her."

Sam sensed a stillness in the air.

"Would you like to pray?" Jack asked. "God can wipe away sins.[335] Redemption comes through Jesus' blood. That's the real act of grace.[661]

"Yes, I would." Tony bowed his head.

"Dear Heavenly Father, I thank You for life and breath. I thank You for sending Your one and only Son to be the atonement for my sins. Jesus' body was broken, and His blood was shed that I might be redeemed.[58] I thank You that on the third day, You raised Him from the dead.[662] After proving He is alive,[329] You brought Him up to heaven[391] and sent down Your Holy Spirit to be our guide and comforter.[227] I know that John the Baptist recognized Jesus while they were still in their mothers' wombs.[663] You called and ordained Jeremiah while He was still in His mother's womb.[664] I was involved in breaking a commandment[74] and doing what You hate.[93] I am sorry, God. Please forgive me. I want to return to fellowship with You.[665] I pray this in Jesus' name."[197]

"Amen," Jack added. "You sound like you know how to pray."

Tony replied, "When I approach the Creator of life, the universe and everything, I want to do so with reverence and respect, thankful for what He has blessed me with. I always start my prayers with thanksgiving. This time I needed some forgiveness, and I feel like I got it. I feel lighter." Tony looked up at the sky. "Thank You, God."

Sam jumped off the tailgate. "Do you work in the city?" he asked.

"All over the greater north end."

Jack asked, "Would you like to meet for lunch sometime next week?"

"To talk about God stuff?" Tony pulled his cell phone from the cargo pocket in his shorts. "I'd like that."

Jack jumped off the tailgate and went to his pack in the cab and returned with his cell phone. "Let's exchange numbers."

Tony's phone dinged twice. "Which one of these is which?"

Sam replied. "I was first. I don't want to miss out on the opportunity to talk God stuff in the middle of the day."

Jack looked at Sam as he continued, "My work is up and down. I've been swamped for months, but I know that I have a lull this coming week and talking God stuff for lunch gives me an appetite."

"Okay, we're on!" Jack smiled.

"It's a date," Tony confirmed.

ENDNOTES

1 *mystērion*, "a hidden or secret thing, not obvious to the understanding" (Strong's G3466).

2 *No man can come to me, except the Father which hath sent me draw him* (John 6:44a KJV).

3 *Prove all things; hold fast that which is good* (1 Thessalonians 5:21 KJV).

4 *Jesus saith unto him, I am the way, the truth, and the life: no man cometh unto the Father, but by me* (John 14:6 KJV).

5 *And the Word was made flesh, and dwelt among us, (and we beheld his glory, the glory as of the only begotten of the Father,) full of grace and truth* (John 1:14 KJV).

6 *Ye are of your father the devil, and the lusts of your father ye will do. He was a murderer from the beginning, and abode not in the truth, because there is no truth in him. When he speaketh a lie, he speaketh of his own: for he is a liar, and the father of it* (John 8:44 KJV).

7 *In the beginning God created the heaven and the earth* (Genesis 1:1 KJV).

8 *So God created man in his own image, in the image of God created he him; male and female created he them* (Genesis 1:27 KJV).

9 *For where two or three are gathered together in my name, there am I in the midst of them* (Matthew 18:20 KJV).

10 *Where there is no vision, the people perish* (Proverbs 29:18a KJV).

11 *You have searched me, LORD, and you know me. You know when I sit and when I rise; you perceive my thoughts from afar. You discern my going out and my lying down; you are familiar with all my ways. Before a word is on my tongue you, LORD, know it completely* (Psalm 139:1-4 NIV).

12 *The mind governed by the flesh is hostile to God; it does not submit to God's law, nor can it do so* (Romans 8:7 NIV).

13 *But as it is written, Eye hath not seen, nor ear heard, neither have entered into the heart of man, the things which God hath prepared for them that love him. But God hath revealed them unto us by his Spirit: for the Spirit searcheth all things, yea, the deep things of God. For what man knoweth the things of a man, save the spirit of man which is in him? even so the things of God knoweth no man, but the Spirit of God. Now we have received, not the spirit of the world, but the spirit which is of God; that we might know the things that are freely given to us of God* (1 Corinthians 2:9-12 KJV).

14 *sōtēria*, "deliverance from the molestation of enemies, preservation, safety, salvation" (Strong's G4991).

15 *yesha`*, "deliverance, salvation, rescue, safety, welfare, prosperity" (Strong's H3468).

16 *yĕshuw`ah*, "deliverance, salvation, rescue, safety, welfare, prosperity" (Strong's H3444).

17 *tĕshuw`ah*, "deliverance (usually by God through human agency), salvation (spiritual in sense) (Strong's H8668).

18 *Be sober, be vigilant; because your adversary the devil, as a roaring lion, walketh about, seeking whom he may devour* (1 Peter 5:8 KJV).

19 *And the great dragon was cast out, that old serpent, called the Devil, and Satan, which deceiveth the whole world: he was cast out into the earth, and his angels were cast out with him* (Revelation 12:9 KJV).

20 *But if our gospel be hid, it is hid to them that are lost: In whom the god of this world hath blinded the minds of them which believe not, lest the light of the glorious gospel of Christ, who is the image of God, should shine unto them* (2 Corinthians 4:3-4 KJV).

21 *Wherefore we would have come unto you, even I Paul, once and again; but Satan hindered us* (1 Thessalonians 2:18 KJV).

22 *Now unto the King eternal, immortal, invisible, the only wise God, be honour and glory for ever and ever. Amen* (1 Timothy 1:17 KJV).

23 *But Jesus beheld them, and said unto them, With men this is impossible; but with God all things are possible* (Matthew 19:26 KJV).

24 *And I heard as it were the voice of a great multitude, and as the voice of*

many waters, and as the voice of mighty thunderings, saying, Alleluia: for the Lord God omnipotent reigneth (Revelation 19:6 KJV).

25 *I am Alpha and Omega, the beginning and the ending, saith the Lord, which is, and which was, and which is to come, the Almighty* (Revelation 1:8 KJV).

26 *In the beginning was the Word, and the Word was with God, and the Word was God. The same was in the beginning with God. All things were made by him; and without him was not any thing made that was made.* (John 1:1-3 KJV)

27 *For by him were all things created, that are in heaven, and that are in earth, visible and invisible, whether they be thrones, or dominions, or principalities, or powers: all things were created by him, and for him* (Colossians 1:16 KJV).

28 *Thou art worthy, O Lord, to receive glory and honour and power: for thou hast created all things, and for thy pleasure they are and were created* (Revelation 4:11 KJV).

29 *Thou hast been in Eden the garden of God; every precious stone was thy covering, the sardius, topaz, and the diamond, the beryl, the onyx, and the jasper, the sapphire, the emerald, and the carbuncle, and gold: the workmanship of thy tabrets and of thy pipes was prepared in thee in the day that thou wast created* (Ezekiel 28:13 KJV).

30 *How art thou fallen from heaven, O Lucifer, son of the morning! how art thou cut down to the ground, which didst weaken the nations! For thou hast said in thine heart, I will ascend into heaven, I will exalt my throne above the stars of God: I will sit also upon the mount of the congregation, in the sides of the north: I will ascend above the heights of the clouds; I will be like the most High* (Isaiah 14:12-14 KJV).

31 *Yet thou shalt be brought down to hell, to the sides of the pit* (Isaiah 14:15 KJV).

32 *For I testify unto every man that heareth the words of the prophecy of this book, If any man shall add unto these things, God shall add unto him the plagues that are written in this book: And if any man shall take away from the words of the book of this prophecy, God shall take away his part out of the book of life, and out of the holy city, and from the things which are written in this book* (Revelation 22:18-19 KJV).

33 *And the devil that deceived them was cast into the lake of fire and brimstone, where the beast and the false prophet are, and shall be tormented day and night for ever and ever* (Revelation 20:10 KJV).

34 *The* LORD *shall preserve thee from all evil: he shall preserve thy soul. The* LORD *shall preserve thy going out and thy coming in from this time forth, and even for evermore* (Psalm 121:7-8 KJV).

35 *Be strong and of a good courage, fear not, nor be afraid of them: for the* LORD *thy God, he it is that doth go with thee; he will not fail thee, nor forsake thee* (Deuteronomy 31:6 KJV).

36 *Let your conduct be without covetousness; be content with such things as you have. For He Himself has said, "I will never leave you nor forsake you"* (Hebrews 13:5 KJV).

37 *Submit yourselves therefore to God. Resist the devil, and he will flee from you* (James 4:7 KJV).

38 *There hath no temptation taken you but such as is common to man: but God is faithful, who will not suffer you to be tempted above that ye are able; but will with the temptation also make a way to escape, that ye may be able to bear it* (1 Corinthians 10:13 KJV).

39 *Therefore put on the full armor of God, so that when the day of evil comes, you may be able to stand your ground, and after you have done everything, to stand* (Ephesians 6:13 NIV).

40 *Every good gift and every perfect gift is from above, and cometh down from the Father of lights, with whom is no variableness, neither shadow of turning* (James 1:17 KJV).

41 *And God said, Let us make man in our image, after our likeness: and let them have dominion over the fish of the sea, and over the fowl of the air, and over the cattle, and over all the earth, and over every creeping thing that creepeth upon the earth* (Genesis 1:26 KJV).

42 *I call heaven and earth to record this day against you, that I have set before you life and death, blessing and cursing: therefore choose life, that both thou and thy seed may live* (Deuteronomy30:19 KJV).

43 *The counsel of the* LORD *standeth for ever, the thoughts of his heart to all generations* (Psalm 33:11 KJV).

44 *God is faithful, by whom ye were called unto the fellowship of his Son Jesus Christ our Lord* (1 Corinthians 1:9).

45 *For we wrestle not against flesh and blood, but against principalities, against powers, against the rulers of the darkness of this world, against spiritual wickedness in high places* (Ephesians 6:12 KJV).

46 *And having disarmed the powers and authorities, he made a public spectacle of them, triumphing over them by the cross* (Colossians 2:15 NIV).

47 *We proclaim to you what we have seen and heard, so that you also may have fellowship with us. And our fellowship is with the Father and with his Son, Jesus Christ* (1 John 1:3 NIV).

48 *And God saw every thing that he had made, and, behold, it was very good. And the evening and the morning were the sixth day* (Genesis 1:31 KJV).

49 *And the LORD God called unto Adam, and said unto him, Where art thou? And he said, I heard thy voice in the garden, and I was afraid, because I was naked; and I hid myself* (Genesis 3:9-10 KJV).

50 *Now the serpent was more subtil than any beast of the field which the LORD God had made. And he said unto the woman, Yea, hath God said, Ye shall not eat of every tree of the garden?* (Genesis 3:1 KJV).

51 *But of the fruit of the tree which is in the midst of the garden, God hath said, Ye shall not eat of it, neither shall ye touch it, lest ye die* (Genesis 3:3 KJV).

52 *But I fear, lest by any means, as the serpent beguiled Eve through his subtilty, so your minds should be corrupted from the simplicity that is in Christ* (2 Corinthians 11:3 KJV).

53 *And the man said, The woman whom thou gavest to be with me, she gave me of the tree, and I did eat* (Genesis 3:12 KJV).

54 *And thou, even thyself, shalt discontinue from thine heritage that I gave thee; and I will cause thee to serve thine enemies in the land which thou knowest not: for ye have kindled a fire in mine anger, which shall burn for ever. Thus saith the LORD; Cursed be the man that trusteth in man, and maketh flesh his arm, and whose heart departeth from the LORD* (Jeremiah 17:4-5 KJV).

55 *Wherefore, as by one man sin entered into the world, and death by sin; and so death passed upon all men, for that all have sinned: (For until the law sin was in the world: but sin is not imputed when there is no*

law. Nevertheless death reigned from Adam to Moses, even over them that had not sinned after the similitude of Adam's transgression (Romans 5:12-14a KJV).

56 *And Moses called all Israel, and said unto them, Hear, O Israel, the statutes and judgments which I speak in your ears this day, that ye may learn them, and keep, and do them* (Deuteronomy 5:1 KJV).

57 *This book of the law shall not depart out of thy mouth; but thou shalt meditate therein day and night, that thou mayest observe to do according to all that is written therein: for then thou shalt make thy way prosperous, and then thou shalt have good success* (Joshua 1:8 KJV).

58 *He was wounded for our transgressions, he was bruised for our iniquities: the chastisement of our peace was upon him; and with his stripes we are healed* (Isaiah 53:5 KJV).

59 *Think not that I am come to destroy the law, or the prophets: I am not come to destroy, but to fulfil. For verily I say unto you, Till heaven and earth pass, one jot or one tittle shall in no wise pass from the law, till all be fulfilled* (Matthew 5:17 KJV).

60 *For as many as are led by the Spirit of God, they are the sons of God. For ye have not received the spirit of bondage again to fear; but ye have received the Spirit of adoption, whereby we cry, Abba, Father. The Spirit itself beareth witness with our spirit, that we are the children of God* (Romans 8:14-16 KJV).

61 *For I know the thoughts that I think toward you, saith the LORD, thoughts of peace, and not of evil, to give you an expected end* (Jeremiah 29:11 KJV).

62 *Behold, the LORD's hand is not shortened, that it cannot save; neither his ear heavy, that it cannot hear: But your iniquities have separated between you and your God, and your sins have hid his face from you, that he will not hear* (Isaiah 59:1-2 KJV).

63 *for by the law is the knowledge of sin* (Romans 3:20b KJV).

64 *Grace to you and peace from God our Father, and the Lord Jesus Christ* (Romans 1:7b KJV).

65 *And these words, which I command thee this day, shall be in thine heart: And thou shalt teach them diligently unto thy children, and shalt talk of them when thou sittest in thine house, and when thou walkest by the way,*

and when thou liest down, and when thou risest up. And thou shalt bind them for a sign upon thine hand, and they shall be as frontlets between thine eyes. And thou shalt write them upon the posts of thy house, and on thy gates (Deuteronomy 6:6-9 KJV).

66 *The grass withereth, the flower fadeth: but the word of our God shall stand for ever* (Isaiah 40:8 KJV).

67 *In fact, this is love for God: to keep his commands. And his commands are not burdensome* (1 John 5:3 NIV).

68 *The law of the LORD is perfect, converting the soul: the testimony of the LORD is sure, making wise the simple* (Psalm 19:7 KJV).

69 *The fear of the LORD is the beginning of wisdom: a good understanding have all they that do his commandments: his praise endureth for ever* (Psalm 111:10 KJV).

70 *And he gave unto Moses, when he had made an end of communing with him upon mount Sinai, two tables of testimony, tables of stone, written with the finger of God* (Exodus 31:18 KJV).

71 *The LORD said to Moses, "Chisel out two stone tablets like the first ones, and I will write on them the words that were on the first tablets, which you broke* (Exodus 34:1 NIV).

72 *Honour thy father and thy mother: that thy days may be long upon the land which the LORD thy God giveth thee* (Exodus 20:12 KJV).

73 *And God is able to make all grace abound toward you; that ye, always having all sufficiency in all things, may abound to every good work* (2 Corinthians 9:8 KJV).

74 *Thou shalt not kill* (Exodus 20:13 KJV).

75 *Thou shalt not steal* (Exodus 20:15 KJV).

76 *ratsach*, "to murder, slay, kill, assassinate (Strong's H7523).

77 *The thief cometh not, but for to steal, and to kill, and to destroy* (John 10:10a KJV).

78 *Thou shalt not commit adultery* (Exodus 20:14 KJV).

79 *Thou shalt not covet thy neighbour's house, thou shalt not covet thy neighbour's wife, nor his manservant, nor his maidservant, nor his ox, nor his ass, nor any thing that is thy neighbour's* (Exodus 20:17 KJV).

80 *For as he thinketh in his heart, so is he* (Proverbs 23:7a KJV).

81 *For to be carnally minded is death; but to be spiritually minded is life and peace* (Romans 8:6 KJV).

82 *When I was a child, I spake as a child, I understood as a child, I thought as a child: but when I became a man, I put away childish things* (1 Corinthians 13:11 KJV).

83 *leb*, "inner man, mind, will, heart, understanding, inclination, resolution, determination (of will), as seat of appetites, as seat of emotions and passions, as seat of courage" (Strong's H3820).

84 *Wherefore God also gave them up to uncleanness through the lusts of their own hearts, to dishonor their own bodies between themselves* (Romans 1:24 KJV).

85 *nous*, "the mind, comprising alike the faculties of perceiving and understanding and those of feeling, judging, determining, the intellectual faculty, the understanding" (Strong's G3563).

86 *Thou shalt not bear false witness against thy neighbour* (Exodus 20:16 KJV).

87 *And thou shalt love the Lord thy God with all thy heart, and with all thy soul, and with all thy mind, and with all thy strength: this is the first commandment. And the second is like, namely this, Thou shalt love thy neighbour as thyself. There is none other commandment greater than these* (Mark 12:30-31 KJV).

88 *I will go before thee, and make the crooked places straight: I will break in pieces the gates of brass, and cut in sunder the bars of iron: And I will give thee the treasures of darkness, and hidden riches of secret places, that thou mayest know that I, the LORD, which call thee by thy name, am the God of Israel* (Isaiah 45:2-3 KJV).

89 *chata*, "to sin, to miss, to miss the goal, to incur penalty, to bring into guilt or condemnation or punishment, forfeit" (Strong's H2398).

90 *But every man is tempted, when he is drawn away of his own lust, and enticed. Then when lust hath conceived, it bringeth forth sin: and sin, when it is finished, bringeth forth death* (James 1:14-15 KJV).

91 *He is the Rock, his work is perfect: for all his ways are judgment: a God of truth and without iniquity, just and right is he* (Deuteronomy 32:4 KJV).

92 *Jesus Christ the same yesterday, and to day, and for ever* (Hebrews 13:8 KJV).

93 *These six things doth the* LORD *hate: yea, seven are an abomination unto him: A proud look, a lying tongue, and hands that shed innocent blood, An heart that deviseth wicked imaginations, feet that be swift in running to mischief, A false witness that speaketh lies, and he that soweth discord among brethren* (Proverbs 6:16-19 KJV).

94 *For all that is in the world, the lust of the flesh, and the lust of the eyes, and the pride of life, is not of the Father, but is of the world* (1 John 2:16 KJV).

95 *For all have sinned, and come short of the glory of God* (Romans 3:23 KJV).

96 *Know ye not that the unrighteous shall not inherit the kingdom of God? Be not deceived: neither fornicators, nor idolaters, nor adulterers, nor effeminate, nor abusers of themselves with mankind, Nor thieves, nor covetous, nor drunkards, nor revilers, nor extortioners, shall inherit the kingdom of God* (1 Corinthians 6:9-10 KJV).

97 *But the fearful, and unbelieving, and the abominable, and murderers, and whoremongers, and sorcerers, and idolaters, and all liars, shall have their part in the lake which burneth with fire and brimstone: which is the second death* (Revelation 21:8).

98 *What has been will be again, what has been done will be done again; there is nothing new under the sun* (Ecclesiastes 1:9 NIV).

99 *I am verily a man which am a Jew, born in Tarsus, a city in Cilicia, yet brought up in this city at the feet of Gamaliel, and taught according to the perfect manner of the law of the fathers, and was zealous toward God, as ye all are this day* (Acts 22:3 KJV).

100 *hamartema*, "sin, evil deed" (Strong's G265).

101 *Flee fornication. Every sin that a man doeth is without the body; but he that committeth fornication sinneth against his own body* (1 Corinthians 6:18 KJV).

102 *It is God's will that you should be sanctified: that you should avoid sexual immorality; that each of you should learn to control your own body in a way that is holy and honorable, not in passionate lust like the pagans, who do not know God* (1 Thessalonians 4:3-5 NIV).

103 *For the wages of sin is death; but the gift of God is eternal life through Jesus Christ our Lord* (Romans 6:23 KJV).

104 *For, behold, I create new heavens and a new earth: and the former shall not be remembered, nor come into mind* (Isaiah 65:17 KJV).

105 *And I saw a new heaven and a new earth: for the first heaven and the first earth were passed away; and there was no more sea. And I John saw the holy city, new Jerusalem, coming down from God out of heaven, prepared as a bride adorned for her husband* (Revelation 21:1-2 KJV).

106 *For God so loved the world, that he gave his only begotten Son, that whosoever believeth in him should not perish, but have everlasting life. For God sent not his Son into the world to condemn the world; but that the world through him might be saved* (John 3:16-17 KJV).

107 *In the sweat of thy face shalt thou eat bread, till thou return unto the ground; for out of it wast thou taken: for dust thou art, and unto dust shalt thou return* (Genesis 3:19 KJV).

108 *But there is a spirit in man: and the inspiration of the Almighty giveth them understanding* (Job 32:8 KJV).

109 *Then shall the dust return to the earth as it was: and the spirit shall return unto God who gave it* (Ecclesiastes 12:7 KJV).

110 *And as it is appointed unto men once to die, but after this the judgment* (Hebrews 9:27 KJV).

111 *For by grace are ye saved through faith; and that not of yourselves: it is the gift of God: Not of works, lest any man should boast. For we are his workmanship, created in Christ Jesus unto good works, which God hath before ordained that we should walk in them* (Ephesians 2:8-10 KJV).

112 *Verily, verily, I say unto you, He that heareth my word, and believeth on him that sent me, hath everlasting life, and shall not come into condemnation; but is passed from death unto life* (John 5:24 KJV).

113 *And the LORD God formed man of the dust of the ground, and breathed into his nostrils the breath of life; and man became a living soul* (Genesis 2:7 KJV).

114 *While we look not at the things which are seen, but at the things which are not seen: for the things which are seen are temporal; but the things which are not seen are eternal* (2 Corinthians 4:18 KJV).

115 *For God, who commanded the light to shine out of darkness, hath shined in our hearts, to give the light of the knowledge of the glory of God in the face of Jesus Christ* (2 Corinthians 4:6 KJV).

116 *But because of your stubbornness and your unrepentant heart, you are storing up wrath against yourself for the day of God's wrath, when his righteous judgment will be revealed* (Romans 2:5 NIV).

117 *I write these things to you who believe in the name of the Son of God so that you may know that you have eternal life* (1 John 5:13 NIV).

118 *The Son is the image of the invisible God, the firstborn over all creation* (Colossians 1:15 NIV).

119 *Jesus said unto her, I am the resurrection, and the life: he that believeth in me, though he were dead, yet shall he live* (John 11:25 KJV).

120 *That if thou shalt confess with thy mouth the Lord Jesus, and shalt believe in thine heart that God hath raised him from the dead, thou shalt be saved. For with the heart man believeth unto righteousness; and with the mouth confession is made unto salvation* (Romans 10:9-10 KJV).

121 *The Lord is not slow in keeping his promise, as some understand slowness. Instead he is patient with you, not wanting anyone to perish, but everyone to come to repentance* (2 Peter 3:9 NIV).

122 *Not only is this so, but we also boast in God through our Lord Jesus Christ, through whom we have now received reconciliation* (Romans 5:11 NIV).

123 *For the life of the flesh is in the blood: and I have given it to you upon the altar to make an atonement for your souls: for it is the blood that maketh an atonement for the soul* (Leviticus 17:11 KJV).

124 *And almost all things are by the law purged with blood; and without shedding of blood is no remission* (Hebrews 9:22 KJV).

125 *For it is not possible that the blood of bulls and of goats should take away sins* (Hebrews 10:4 KJV).

126 *But in those sacrifices there is a remembrance again made of sins every year* (Hebrews 10:3 KJV).

127 *And he is the propitiation for our sins: and not for ours only, but also for the sins of the whole world* (1 John 2:2 KJV).

128 *Then said he, Lo, I come to do thy will, O God. He taketh away the first, that he may establish the second. By the which will we are sanctified through the offering of the body of Jesus Christ once for all* (Hebrews 10:9-10 KJV).

129 *You must present a male without defect from the cattle, sheep or goats in order that it may be accepted on your behalf. Do not bring anything with a defect, because it will not be accepted on your behalf* (Leviticus 22:19-20 NIV).

130 *But with the precious blood of Christ, a lamb without blemish or defect* (1 Peter 1:19 NIV).

131 *Therefore the Lord himself shall give you a sign; Behold, a virgin shall conceive, and bear a son, and shall call his name Immanuel* (Isaiah 7:14 KJV).

132 *This is how the birth of Jesus the Messiah came about: His mother Mary was pledged to be married to Joseph, but before they came together, she was found to be pregnant through the Holy Spirit* (Matthew 1:18 NIV).

133 *He committed no sin, and no deceit was found in his mouth* (1 Peter 2:22 NIV).

134 *For we have not an high priest which cannot be touched with the feeling of our infirmities; but was in all points tempted like as we are, yet without sin* (Hebrews 4:15 KJV).

135 *But you know that he appeared so that he might take away our sins. And in him is no sin* (1 John 3:5 NIV).

136 *As the Father knoweth me, even so know I the Father: and I lay down my life for the sheep. And other sheep I have, which are not of this fold: them also I must bring, and they shall hear my voice; and there shall be one fold, and one shepherd. Therefore doth my Father love me, because I lay down my life, that I might take it again. No man taketh it from me, but I lay it down of myself. I have power to lay it down, and I have power to take it again. This commandment have I received of my Father* (John 10:15-18 KJV).

137 *Christ hath redeemed us from the curse of the law, being made a curse for us: for it is written, Cursed is every one that hangeth on a tree* (Galatians 3:13 KJV).

138 *Bear with each other and forgive one another if any of you has a grievance against someone. Forgive as the Lord forgave you* (Colossians 3:13 NIV).

139 *From that time Jesus began to preach, and to say, Repent: for the kingdom of heaven is at hand* (Matthew 4:17 KJV).

140 *metanoeō*, "to change one's mind, to change one's mind for better, heartily to amend with abhorrence of one's past sins. turning with contrition from sin to God" (Strong's G3340).

141 *nacham*, "to be sorry, rue, suffer grief, have compassion" (Strong's H5162).

142 *shuwb*, "to turn back, to be return, be restored, be brought back, refresh, repair, reverse" (Strong's H7725).

143 *As a dog returneth to his vomit, so a fool returneth to his folly* (Proverbs 26:11 KJV).

144 *For godly sorrow worketh repentance to salvation not to be repented of: but the sorrow of the world worketh death* (2 Corinthians 7:10 KJV).

145 *If my people, which are called by my name, shall humble themselves, and pray, and seek my face, and turn from their wicked ways; then will I hear from heaven, and will forgive their sin, and will heal their land* (2 Chronicles 7:14 KJV).

146 *Blessed is the one who always trembles before God, but whoever hardens their heart falls into trouble* (Proverbs 28:14 NIV).

147 *ra*, "bad, disagreeable, malignant, unpleasant, evil (giving pain, unhappiness, misery), worse than, worst (comparison), adversity, distress" (Strong's H7451).

148 *That the God of our Lord Jesus Christ, the Father of glory, may give unto you the spirit of wisdom and revelation in the knowledge of him: The eyes of your understanding being enlightened; that ye may know what is the hope of his calling, and what the riches of the glory of his inheritance in the saints, And what is the exceeding greatness of his power to us-ward who believe, according to the working of his mighty power* (Ephesians 1:17-19 KJV).

149 *And he that searcheth the hearts knoweth what is the mind of the Spirit, because he maketh intercession for the saints according to the will of God. And we know that all things work together for good to them that love God, to them who are the called according to his purpose. For whom he did foreknow, he also did predestinate to be conformed to the image of his Son, that he might be the firstborn among many brethren* (Romans 8:27-29 KJV).

150 *If we confess our sins, he is faithful and just to forgive us our sins, and to cleanse us from all unrighteousness* (1 John 1:9 KJV).

151 *In whom we have redemption through his blood, even the forgiveness of sins* (Colossians 1:14 KJV).

152 *Repent ye therefore, and be converted, that your sins may be blotted out, when the times of refreshing shall come from the presence of the Lord* (Acts 3:19 KJV).

153 *Because he himself suffered when he was tempted, he is able to help those who are being tempted* (Hebrews 2:18 NIV).

154 *But God commendeth his love toward us, in that, while we were yet sinners, Christ died for us* (Romans 5:8 KJV).

155 *For I delivered to you first of all that which I also received: that Christ died for our sins according to the Scriptures, And that he was buried, and that he rose again the third day according to the scriptures: and that He was seen by Cephas, then by the twelve. After that, he was seen of above five hundred brethren at once; of whom the greater part remain unto this present, but some are fallen asleep* (1 Corinthians 15:3-6 KJV).

156 Flavius Josephus, *The Antiquities of the Jews*, 18.63–18.64, c. AD 94, translated by William Whiston, A Digital Library of Classical Antiquity, 1737, https://lexundria.com/j_aj/18.55-18.84/wst.

> [63] *Now there was about this time Jesus, a wise man, if it be lawful to call him a man; for he was a doer of wonderful works, a teacher of such men as receive the truth with pleasure. He drew over to him both many of the Jews and many of the Gentiles. He was [the] Christ.* [64] *And when Pilate, at the suggestion of the principal men amongst us, had condemned him to the cross, those that loved him at the first did not forsake him; for he appeared to them alive again the third day; as the divine prophets had foretold these and ten thousand other wonderful things concerning him. And the tribe of Christians, so named from him, are not extinct at this day.*

157 *Behold, I stand at the door, and knock: if any man hear my voice, and open the door, I will come in to him, and will sup with him, and he with me* (Revelation 3:20 KJV).

158 *Jesus answered, Verily, verily, I say unto thee, Except a man be born of*

water and of the Spirit, he cannot enter into the kingdom of God. That which is born of the flesh is flesh; and that which is born of the Spirit is spirit. Marvel not that I said unto thee, Ye must be born again (John 3:5-7 KJV).

159 *That Christ may dwell in your hearts by faith; that ye, being rooted and grounded in love* (Ephesians 3:17 KJV).

160 *Now faith is the substance of things hoped for, the evidence of things not seen* (Hebrews 11:1 KJV).

161 *elpis,* "expectation of good, hope, evil, fear" (Strong's G1680).

162 *hypostasis,* "that which has foundation, is firm, confidence, firm trust, assurance, substance" (Strong's G5287).

163 *Consequently, faith comes from hearing the message, and the message is heard through the word about Christ* (Romans 10:17 NIV).

164 *Trust in the LORD forever, for the LORD, the LORD himself, is the Rock eternal* (Isaiah 26:4 NIV).

165 *Sanctify them through thy truth: thy word is truth* (John 17:17 KJV).

166 *All scripture is given by inspiration of God, and is profitable for doctrine, for reproof, for correction, for instruction in righteousness: That the man of God may be perfect, throughly furnished unto all good works* (2 Timothy 3:16-17 KJV).

167 *For the preaching of the cross is to them that perish foolishness; but unto us which are saved it is the power of God* (1 Corinthians 1:18 KJV).

168 *He hath made every thing beautiful in his time: also he hath set the world in their heart, so that no man can find out the work that God maketh from the beginning to the end* (Ecclesiastes 3:11 KJV).

169 *And one cried unto another, and said, Holy, holy, holy, is the LORD of hosts: the whole earth is full of his glory* (Isaiah 6:3 KJV).

170 *Truly I tell you, anyone who will not receive the kingdom of God like a little child will never enter it* (Mark 10:15 NIV).

171 *For I will be merciful to their unrighteousness, and their sins and their iniquities will I remember no more* (Hebrews 8:12 KJV).

172 *So that we may boldly say, The Lord is my helper, and I will not fear what man shall do unto me* (Hebrews 13:6 KJV).

173 *pantokratōr,* "almighty: God, the ruler of all, he who holds sway over all things" (Strong's G3841).

174 *Behold the fowls of the air: for they sow not, neither do they reap, nor gather into barns; yet your heavenly Father feedeth them. Are ye not much better than they?* (Matthew 6:26 KJV).

175 *Great is our LORD, and of great power: his understanding is infinite* (Psalm 147:5 KJV).

176 *But I say unto you, I will not drink henceforth of this fruit of the vine, until that day when I drink it new with you in my Father's kingdom* (Matthew 26:29 KJV).

177 *When Jesus spoke again to the people, he said, "I am the light of the world. Whoever follows me will never walk in darkness, but will have the light of life"* (John 8:12 NIV).

178 *Who will have all men to be saved, and to come unto the knowledge of the truth* (1 Timothy 2:4 KJV).

179 *Therefore if any man be in Christ, he is a new creature: old things are passed away; behold, all things are become new* (2 Corinthians 5:17 KJV).

180 *And will be a Father unto you, and ye shall be my sons and daughters, saith the Lord Almighty* (2 Corinthians 6:18 KJV).

181 *For ye are all the children of God by faith in Christ Jesus* (Galatians 3:26 KJV).

182 *Jesus answered and said unto him, Verily, verily, I say unto thee, Except a man be born again, he cannot see the kingdom of God* (John 3:3 KJV).

183 *Pray without ceasing* (1 Thessalonians 5:17 KJV).

184 *Jesus saith unto him, Thomas, because thou hast seen me, thou hast believed: blessed are they that have not seen, and yet have believed. And many other signs truly did Jesus in the presence of his disciples, which are not written in this book: But these are written, that ye might believe that Jesus is the Christ, the Son of God; and that believing ye might have life through his name* (John 20:29-31 KJV).

185 *Many have undertaken to draw up an account of the things that have been fulfilled among us, just as they were handed down to us by those who from the first were eyewitnesses and servants of the word. With this in mind, since I myself have carefully investigated everything from the beginning, I too decided to write an orderly account for you, most*

excellent Theophilus, so that you may know the certainty of the things you have been taught (Luke 1:1-4 NIV).

186 *Luke, the beloved physician, and Demas, greet you* (Colossians 4:14 KJV).

187 *There is neither Jew nor Greek, there is neither bond nor free, there is neither male nor female: for ye are all one in Christ Jesus* (Galatians 3:28 KJV).

188 *But when ye pray, use not vain repetitions, as the heathen do: for they think that they shall be heard for their much speaking* (Matthew 6:7 KJV).

189 *And it came to pass, that, as he was praying in a certain place, when he ceased, one of his disciples said unto him, Lord, teach us to pray, as John also taught his disciples* (Luke 11:1 KJV).

190 *"This, then, is how you should pray: "Our Father in heaven, hallowed be your name, your kingdom come, your will be done, on earth as it is in heaven. Give us today our daily bread. And forgive us our debts, as we also have forgiven our debtors. And lead us not into temptation, but deliver us from the evil one"'* (Matthew 6:9-13 NIV).

191 *Do not be anxious about anything, but in every situation, by prayer and petition, with thanksgiving, present your requests to God* (Philippians 4:6 NIV).

192 *In every thing give thanks: for this is the will of God in Christ Jesus concerning you* (1 Thessalonians 5:18 KJV).

193 *For if ye forgive men their trespasses, your heavenly Father will also forgive you: But if ye forgive not men their trespasses, neither will your Father forgive your trespasses* (Matthew 6:14-15 KJV).

194 *Praise be to the Lord, to God our Savior, who daily bears our burdens* (Psalm 68:19 NIV).

195 *And all things, whatsoever ye shall ask in prayer, believing, ye shall receive* (Matthew 21:22 KJV).

196 *The angel of the LORD encampeth round about them that fear him, and delivereth them* (Psalm 34:7 KJV).

197 *And whatsoever ye shall ask in my name, that will I do, that the Father may be glorified in the Son. If ye shall ask any thing in my name, I will do it* (John 14:13-14 KJV).

198 *But as many as received him, to them gave he power to become the sons*

of God, even to them that believe on his name: Which were born, not of blood, nor of the will of the flesh, nor of the will of man, but of God (John 1:12-13 KJV).

199 *And this is the confidence that we have in him, that, if we ask any thing according to his will, he heareth us: And if we know that he hear us, whatsoever we ask, we know that we have the petitions that we desired of him* (1 John 5:14-15 KJV).

200 *The tongue has the power of life and death, and those who love it will eat its fruit* (Proverbs 18:21 NIV).

201 *I have planted, Apollos watered; but God gave the increase* (1 Corinthians 3:6 KJV).

202 *And he spake many things unto them in parables, saying, Behold, a sower went forth to sow; And when he sowed, some seeds fell by the way side, and the fowls came and devoured them up: Some fell upon stony places, where they had not much earth: and forthwith they sprung up, because they had no deepness of earth: And when the sun was up, they were scorched; and because they had no root, they withered away. And some fell among thorns; and the thorns sprung up, and choked them: But other fell into good ground, and brought forth fruit, some an hundredfold, some sixtyfold, some thirtyfold* (Matthew 13:3-8 KJV).

203 *And on the seventh day God ended his work which he had made; and he rested on the seventh day from all his work which he had made. And God blessed the seventh day, and sanctified it: because that in it he had rested from all his work which God created and made* (Genesis 2:2-3 KJV).

204 *And he said unto them, The Sabbath was made for man, and not man for the Sabbath* (Mark 2:27 KJV).

205 *Therefore everyone who hears these words of mine and puts them into practice is like a wise man who built his house on the rock. The rain came down, the streams rose, and the winds blew and beat against that house; yet it did not fall, because it had its foundation on the rock. But everyone who hears these words of mine and does not put them into practice is like a foolish man who built his house on sand. The rain came down, the streams rose, and the winds blew and beat against that house, and it fell with a great crash* (Matthew 7:24-27 NIV).

206 *Is not this the carpenter, the son of Mary, the brother of James, and*

Joses, and of Juda, and Simon? and are not his sisters here with us? And they were offended at him (Mark 6:3 KJV).

207 *A sound heart is the life of the flesh: but envy the rottenness of the bones* (Proverbs 14:30 KJV).

208 *Resentment kills a fool, and envy slays the simple* (Job 5:2 NIV).

209 *What causes fights and quarrels among you? Don't they come from your desires that battle within you? You desire but do not have, so you kill. You covet but you cannot get what you want, so you quarrel and fight* (James 4:1-2a NIV).

210 *Let us therefore follow after the things which make for peace, and things wherewith one may edify another* (Romans 14:19 KJV).

211 *And let the peace of God rule in your hearts, to the which also ye are called in one body; and be ye thankful* (Colossians 3:15 KJV).

212 *Thou shalt have no other gods before me* (Exodus 20:3 KJV).

213 *Know therefore this day, and consider it in thine heart, that the LORD he is God in heaven above, and upon the earth beneath: there is none else* (Deuteronomy 4:39 KJV).

214 *You were shown these things so that you might know that the LORD is God; besides him there is no other* (Deuteronomy 4:35 NIV).

215 *Remember the former things of old: for I am God, and there is none else; I am God, and there is none like me* (Isaiah 46:9 KJV).

216 *Wherefore he is able also to save them to the uttermost that come unto God by him, seeing he ever liveth to make intercession for them* (Hebrews 7:25 KJV).

217 *O LORD, there is none like thee, neither is there any God beside thee, according to all that we have heard with our ears* (1 Chronicles 17:20 KJV).

218 *'elohiym*, "rulers, judges, divine ones, godlike one" (Strong's H430).

219 *And no wonder, for Satan himself masquerades as an angel of light. It is not surprising, then, if his servants also masquerade as servants of righteousness. Their end will be what their actions deserve* (2 Corinthians 11:14-15 NIV).

220 *For the LORD thy God is a consuming fire, even a jealous God* (Deuteronomy 4:24 KJV).

221 *"You shall not make for yourself an image in the form of anything in heaven above or on the earth beneath or in the waters below. You shall*

not bow down to them or worship them; for I, the LORD your God, am a jealous God, punishing the children for the sin of the parents to the third and fourth generation of those who hate me, but showing love to a thousand generations of those who love me and keep my commandments (Exodus 20:4-6 NIV).

222 *They that forsake the law praise the wicked: but such as keep the law contend with them. Evil men understand not judgment: but they that seek the LORD understand all things* (Proverbs 28:4-5 KJV).

223 *Thou shalt not take the name of the LORD thy God in vain; for the LORD will not hold him guiltless that taketh his name in vain* (Exodus 20:7 KJV).

224 *Neither is there salvation in any other: for there is none other name under heaven given among men, whereby we must be saved* (Acts 4:12 KJV).

225 *Don't you see that whatever enters the mouth goes into the stomach and then out of the body? But the things that come out of a person's mouth come from the heart, and these defile them* (Matthew 15:17-18 NIV).

226 *The soothing tongue is a tree of life, but a perverse tongue crushes the spirit* (Proverbs 15:4 NIV).

227 *But the Advocate, the Holy Spirit, whom the Father will send in my name, will teach you all things and will remind you of everything I have said to you* (John 14:26 NIV).

228 *For you, God, tested us; you refined us like silver* (Psalm 66:10 NIV).

229 *And herein do I exercise myself, to have always a conscience void of offence toward God, and toward men* (Acts 24:16 KJV).

230 *And when ye stand praying, forgive, if ye have ought against any: that your Father also which is in heaven may forgive you your trespasses* (Mark 11:25 KJV).

231 *then hear from heaven, your dwelling place. Forgive and act; deal with everyone according to all they do, since you know their hearts (for you alone know every human heart)* (1 Kings 8:39 NIV).

232 *Likewise, the tongue is a small part of the body, but it makes great boasts. Consider what a great forest is set on fire by a small spark* (James 3:5 NIV).

233 *Remember the Sabbath day, to keep it holy. Six days shalt thou labour,*

and do all thy work: But the seventh day is the Sabbath of the Lord thy God: in it thou shalt not do any work, thou, nor thy son, nor thy daughter, thy manservant, nor thy maidservant, nor thy cattle, nor thy stranger that is within thy gates (Exodus 20:8-10 KJV).

234 *For in six days the Lord made heaven and earth, the sea, and all that in them is, and rested the seventh day: wherefore the Lord blessed the sabbath day, and hallowed it* (Exodus 20:11 KJV).

235 *qadash*, "to be set apart or separate, be consecrated, to regard or treat as sacred or hallowed" (Strong's H6942).

236 *chodesh*, "the new moon, month, monthly, the first day of the month, the lunar month" (Strong's H2320).

237 Codex Justinianus lib. 3, tit. 12, 3; trans. in Philip Schaff, *History of the Christian Church*, Vol. 3, [http://www.ccel.org/s/schaff/hcc3/cache/hcc3.pdf pg. 324, note 692] Given the 7th day of March, Crispus and Constantine being consuls each of them for the second time [A.D. 321].

On the venerable Day of the Sun let the magistrates and people residing in cities rest, and let all workshops be closed. In the country, however, persons engaged in agriculture may freely and lawfully continue their pursuits; because it often happens that another day is not so suitable for grain-sowing or for vine-planting; lest by neglecting the proper moment for such operations the bounty of heaven should be lost.

238 *Jesus said unto him, Thou shalt love the Lord thy God with all thy heart, and with all thy soul, and with all thy mind. This is the first and great commandment* (Matthew 22:37-38 KJV).

239 *And the second is like unto it, Thou shalt love thy neighbour as thyself. On these two commandments hang all the law and the prophets* (Matthew 22:39-40 KJV).

240 *This is the verdict: Light has come into the world, but people loved darkness instead of light because their deeds were evil. Everyone who does evil hates the light, and will not come into the light for fear that their deeds will be exposed* (John 3:19-20 NIV).

241 *This is the message we have heard from him and declare to you: God is light; in him there is no darkness at all* (1 John 1:5 NIV).

242 *Whoever conceals their sins does not prosper, but the one who confesses and renounces them finds mercy* (Proverbs 28:13 NIV).

243 *For my yoke is easy, and my burden is light* (Matthew 11:30 KJV).

244 *Lie not one to another, seeing that ye have put off the old man with his deeds; And have put on the new man, which is renewed in knowledge after the image of him that created him* (Colossians 3:9-10 KJV).

245 *Therefore all things whatsoever ye would that men should do to you, do ye even so to them: for this is the law and the prophets* (Matthew 7:12 KJV).

246 *And as ye would that men should do to you, do ye also to them likewise* (Luke 6:31 KJV).

247 *Blessed is the man that walketh not in the counsel of the ungodly, nor standeth in the way of sinners, nor sitteth in the seat of the scornful. But his delight is in the law of the LORD; and in his law doth he meditate day and night. And he shall be like a tree planted by the rivers of water, that bringeth forth his fruit in his season; his leaf also shall not wither; and whatsoever he doeth shall prosper. The ungodly are not so: but are like the chaff which the wind driveth away. Therefore the ungodly shall not stand in the judgment, nor sinners in the congregation of the righteous. For the LORD knoweth the way of the righteous: but the way of the ungodly shall perish* (Psalm 1:1-6 KJV).

248 *My son, pay attention to what I say; turn your ear to my words, Do not let them out of your sight, keep them within your heart; for they are life to those who find them and health to one's whole body* (Proverbs 4:20-22 NIV).

249 *And it shall come to pass afterward, that I will pour out my spirit upon all flesh; and your sons and your daughters shall prophesy, your old men shall dream dreams, your young men shall see visions* (Joel 2:28 KJV).

250 *In a dream, in a vision of the night, when deep sleep falleth upon men, in slumberings upon the bed; Then he openeth the ears of men, and sealeth their instruction. That he may withdraw man from his purpose, and hide pride from man. He keepeth back his soul from the pit, and his life from perishing by the sword* (Job 33:15-18 KJV).

251 *And God spake unto Israel in the visions of the night, and said, Jacob, Jacob. And he said, Here am I* (Genesis 46:2 KJV).

252 *And Joseph dreamed a dream, and he told it his brethren: and they*

hated him yet the more. And he said unto them, Hear, I pray you, this dream which I have dreamed: For, behold, we were binding sheaves in the field, and, lo, my sheaf arose, and also stood upright; and, behold, your sheaves stood round about, and made obeisance to my sheaf (Genesis 37:6-7 KJV).

253 *In Gibeon the* LORD *appeared to Solomon in a dream by night: and God said, Ask what I shall give thee* (1 Kings 3:5 KJV).

254 *And Solomon's wisdom excelled the wisdom of all the children of the east country, and all the wisdom of Egypt. For he was wiser than all men;…And there came of all people to hear the wisdom of Solomon, from all kings of the earth, which had heard of his wisdom* (1 Kings 4:30-31a, 34 KJV).

255 *And a vision appeared to Paul in the night; There stood a man of Macedonia, and prayed him, saying, Come over into Macedonia, and help us* (Acts 16:9 KJV).

256 *Then spake the Lord to Paul in the night by a vision, Be not afraid, but speak, and hold not thy peace: For I am with thee, and no man shall set on thee to hurt thee: for I have much people in this city* (Acts 18:9-10 KJV).

257 *I will praise the* LORD, *who counsels me; even at night my heart instructs me* (Psalm 16:7 NIV).

258 *But while he thought on these things, behold, the angel of the Lord appeared unto him in a dream, saying, Joseph, thou son of David, fear not to take unto thee Mary thy wife: for that which is conceived in her is of the Holy Ghost* (Matthew 1:20 KJV).

259 *And when they were departed, behold, the angel of the Lord appeareth to Joseph in a dream, saying, Arise, and take the young child and his mother, and flee into Egypt, and be thou there until I bring thee word: for Herod will seek the young child to destroy him* (Matthew 2:13 KJV).

260 The Septuagint is the Greek translation of the Hebrew Scriptures (Old Testament) and used by the early Church. [https://www.septuagint.Bible/].

261 The Vulgate is a Latin version of the Holy Bible, and largely the result of the labors of Saint Jerome, who was commissioned by Pope Damasus I in A.D. 382.

Saint Jerome had been commissioned by Pope Damasus to re-vise the Old Latin text of the four Gospels from the best Greek texts, and by the time of Damasus' death in A.D. 384. he had thor-oughly completed this task, together with a more cursory revision from the Greek Septuagint of the Old Latin text of the Psalms.

After the death of the Pope, St. Jerome who had been the Pope's secretary, settled in Bethlehem, where he produced a new ver-sion of the Psalms, translated from the Hexaplar revision of the Septuagint. But from A.D. 390 to A.D. 405, St. Jerome translated anew all 39 books in the Hebrew Bible, including a further, third, version of the Psalms, which survives in a very few Vulgate manu-scripts. This new translation of the Psalms was labeled by him as "iuxta Hebraeos" (i.e. "close to the Hebrews," "immediately follow-ing the Hebrews"), but it was not ultimately used in the Vulgate. The translations of the other 38 books were used, however, and so the Vulgate is usually credited to have been the first translation of the Old Testament into Latin directly from the Hebrew Tanakh, rather than the Greek Septuagint. [http://vulgate.org/]

262 *Knowing this first, that no prophecy of the scripture is of any private interpretation. For the prophecy came not in old time by the will of man: but holy men of God spake as they were moved by the Holy Ghost* (2 Peter 1:20-21 KJV).

263 *At Caesarea there was a man named Cornelius, a centurion in what was known as the Italian Regiment. He and all his family were devout and God-fearing; he gave generously to those in need and prayed to God regularly* (Acts 10:1-2 NIV).

264 *And the next day we that were of Paul's company departed, and came unto Caesarea: and we entered into the house of Philip the evangelist, which was one of the seven; and abode with him* (Acts 21:8 KJV).

265 "Edict of Milan" (A.D. 313), Lactantius, De Mort. Pers., ch. 48. op-era, ed. 0. F. Fritzsche, II, p 288 sq. (Bibl Patr. Ecc. Lat. XI). [https://sourcebooks.fordham.edu/source/edict-milan.asp].

When I, Constantine Augustus, as well as I Licinius Augustus fortunately met near Mediolanurn (Milan), and were consider-ing everything that pertained to the public welfare and security, we thought-, among other things which we saw would be for the good of many, those regulations pertaining to the reverence of the Divinity ought certainly to be made first, so that we might grant to the Christians and others full authority to observe that religion which each preferred; whence any Divinity whatsoever in the seat of the heavens may be propitious and kindly disposed to us and all who are placed under our rule And thus by this wholesome counsel and most upright provision we thought to arrange that no one whatsoever should be denied the opportunity to give his heart to the observance of the Christian religion, of that religion which he should think best for himself, so that the Supreme Deity, to whose worship we freely yield our hearts) may show in all things His usual favor and benevolence. Therefore, your Worship should know that it has pleased us to remove all conditions whatsoever, which were in the rescripts formerly given to you officially, concerning the Christians and now any one of these who wishes to observe Christian religion may do so freely and openly, without molestation. We thought it fit to commend these things most fully to your care that you may know that we have given to those Christians free and unrestricted opportunity of religious worship. When you see that this has been granted to them by us, your Worship will know that we have also conceded to other religions the right of open and free observance of their worship for the sake of the peace of our times, that each one may have the free opportunity to worship as he pleases ; this regulation is made we that we may not seem to detract from any dignity or any religion.

266 *Ask, and it shall be given you; seek, and ye shall find; knock, and it shall be opened unto you (Matthew 7:7 KJV).*

267 *These things were done in Bethabara beyond Jordan, where John was baptizing (John 1:28 KJV).*

268 *although in fact it was not Jesus who baptized, but his disciples (John 4:2 NIV).*

269 *Go ye therefore, and teach all nations, baptizing them in the name of the Father, and of the Son, and of the Holy Ghost: Teaching them to observe all things whatsoever I have commanded you: and, lo, I am with*

you alway, even unto the end of the world. Amen (Matthew 28:19-20 KJV).

270 *And as they were eating, Jesus took bread, and blessed it, and brake it, and gave it to the disciples, and said, Take, eat; this is my body. And he took the cup, and gave thanks, and gave it to them, saying, Drink ye all of it; For this is my blood of the new testament, which is shed for many for the remission of sins* (Matthew 26:26-28 KJV).

271 *He that believeth and is baptized shall be saved; but he that believeth not shall be damned* (Mark 16:16 KJV).

272 *And he took bread, and gave thanks, and brake it, and gave unto them, saying, This is my body which is given for you: this do in remembrance of me. Likewise also the cup after supper, saying, This cup is the new testament in my blood, which is shed for you* (Luke 22:19-20 KJV).

273 *baptizō*, "to immerse, to submerge, to overwhelm, to make clean with water" (Strong's G907).

274 *And God said unto him, Thy name is Jacob: thy name shall not be called any more Jacob, but Israel shall be thy name: and he called his name Israel* (Genesis 35:10 KJV).

275 *And thou shalt dwell in the land of Goshen, and thou shalt be near unto me, thou, and thy children, and thy children's children, and thy flocks, and thy herds, and all that thou hast* (Genesis 45:10 KJV).

276 *and bring your father and your families back to me. I will give you the best of the land of Egypt and you can enjoy the fat of the land* (Genesis 45:18 NIV).

277 *Now the sojourning of the children of Israel, who dwelt in Egypt, was four hundred and thirty years* (Exodus 12:40 KJV).

278 *And the children of Israel were fruitful, and increased abundantly, and multiplied, and waxed exceeding mighty; and the land was filled with them* (Exodus 1:7 KJV).

279 *Then a new king, to whom Joseph meant nothing, came to power in Egypt. "Look," he said to his people, "the Israelites have become far too numerous for us. We must make a plan to keep them from growing even more. If we don't, and if war breaks out, they will join our enemies and fight against us. Then they will escape from the country." So they put slave masters over them to oppress them with forced labor, and they*

built Pithom and Rameses as store cities for Pharaoh (Exodus 1:8-11 NIV).

280 *And it will be like a sign on your hand and a symbol on your forehead that the LORD brought us out of Egypt with his mighty hand. When Pharaoh let the people go, God did not lead them on the road through the Philistine country, though that was shorter. For God said, "If they face war, they might change their minds and return to Egypt"* (Exodus 13:16-17 NIV).

281 *And it was told the king of Egypt that the people fled: and the heart of Pharaoh and of his servants was turned against the people, and they said, Why have we done this, that we have let Israel go from serving us?* (Exodus 14:5 KJV).

282 *And he made ready his chariot, and took his people with him: And he took six hundred chosen chariots, and all the chariots of Egypt, and captains over every one of them. And the LORD hardened the heart of Pharaoh king of Egypt, and he pursued after the children of Israel* (Exodus 14:6-8a KJV).

283 *But the Egyptians pursued after them, all the horses and chariots of Pharaoh, and his horsemen, and his army, and overtook them encamping by the sea, beside Pihahiroth, before Baalzephon* (Exodus 14:9 KJV).

284 *And Moses stretched out his hand over the sea; and the LORD caused the sea to go back by a strong east wind all that night, and made the sea dry land, and the waters were divided* (Exodus 14:21 KJV).

285 *And the children of Israel went into the midst of the sea upon the dry ground: and the waters were a wall unto them on their right hand, and on their left* (Exodus 14:22 KJV).

286 *And the Egyptians pursued, and went in after them to the midst of the sea, even all Pharaoh's horses, his chariots, and his horsemen* (Exodus 14:23 KJV).

287 *Then the LORD said to Moses, "Stretch out your hand over the sea so that the waters may flow back over the Egyptians and their chariots and horsemen." Moses stretched out his hand over the sea, and at daybreak the sea went back to its place. The Egyptians were fleeing toward it, and the LORD swept them into the sea. The water flowed back and*

covered the chariots and horsemen—the entire army of Pharaoh that had followed the Israelites into the sea. Not one of them survived (Exodus 14:26-28 NIV).

288 *The God of my rock; in him will I trust: he is my shield, and the horn of my salvation, my high tower, and my refuge, my saviour; thou savest me from violence. I will call on the Lord, who is worthy to be praised: so shall I be saved from mine enemies* (2 Samuel 22:3-4 KJV).

289 *Everything on dry land that had the breath of life in its nostrils died* (Genesis 7:22 NIV).

290 *And every living substance was destroyed which was upon the face of the ground, both man, and cattle, and the creeping things, and the fowl of the heaven; and they were destroyed from the earth: and Noah only remained alive, and they that were with him in the ark* (Genesis 7:23 KJV).

291 *For Christ also suffered once for sins, the righteous for the unrighteous, to bring you to God. He was put to death in the body but made alive in the Spirit. After being made alive, he went and made proclamation to the imprisoned spirits—to those who were disobedient long ago when God waited patiently in the days of Noah while the ark was being built. In it only a few people, eight in all, were saved through water, and this water symbolizes baptism that now saves you also—not the removal of dirt from the body but the pledge of a clear conscience toward God. It saves you by the resurrection of Jesus Christ* (1 Peter 3:18-21 NIV).

292 *The Lord is merciful and gracious, slow to anger, and plenteous in mercy* (Psalm 103:8 KJV).

293 *When the Lord could no longer endure your wicked actions and the detestable things you did, your land became a curse and a desolate waste without inhabitants, as it is today* (Jeremiah 44:22 NIV).

294 *The Lord is known by his acts of justice; the wicked are ensnared by the work of their hands* (Psalm 9:16 NIV).

295 *He is to put on the sacred linen tunic, with linen undergarments next to his body; he is to tie the linen sash around him and put on the linen turban. These are sacred garments; so he must bathe himself with water before he puts them on* (Leviticus 16:4 NIV).

296 *And the Lord spake unto Moses, saying, Thou shalt also make a laver of brass, and his foot also of brass, to wash withal: and thou shalt put*

it between the tabernacle of the congregation and the altar, and thou shalt put water therein. For Aaron and his sons shall wash their hands and their feet thereat: When they go into the tabernacle of the congregation, they shall wash with water, that they die not; or when they come near to the altar to minister, to burn offering made by fire unto the LORD: *So they shall wash their hands and their feet, that they die not: and it shall be a statute for ever to them, even to him and to his seed throughout their generations* (Exodus 30:17-21 KJV).

297 *"He himself bore our sins" in his body on the cross, so that we might die to sins and live for righteousness; "by his wounds you have been healed"* (1 Peter 2:24 NIV).

298 *And now why tarriest thou? arise, and be baptized, and wash away thy sins, calling on the name of the Lord* (Acts 22:16 KJV).

299 *Or don't you know that all of us who were baptized into Christ Jesus were baptized into his death? We were therefore buried with him through baptism into death in order that, just as Christ was raised from the dead through the glory of the Father, we too may live a new life* (Romans 6:3-4 NIV).

300 *Likewise the Spirit also helpeth our infirmities: for we know not what we should pray for as we ought: but the Spirit itself maketh intercession for us with groanings which cannot be uttered* (Romans 8:26 KJV).

301 *Likewise, I say unto you, there is joy in the presence of the angels of God over one sinner that repenteth* (Luke 15:10 KJV).

302 *Open thou mine eyes, that I may behold wondrous things out of thy law* (Psalm 119:18 KJV).

303 *But the anointing which ye have received of him abideth in you, and ye need not that any man teach you: but as the same anointing teacheth you of all things, and is truth, and is no lie, and even as it hath taught you, ye shall abide in him* (1 John 2:27 KJV).

304 *And the angel of the Lord spake unto Philip, saying, Arise, and go toward the south unto the way that goeth down from Jerusalem unto Gaza, which is desert* (Acts 8:26 KJV).

305 *The Spirit told Philip, "Go to that chariot and stay near it"* (Acts 8:29 NIV).

306 *And he arose and went: and, behold, a man of Ethiopia, an eunuch of*

great authority under Candace queen of the Ethiopians, who had the charge of all her treasure, and had come to Jerusalem for to worship, Was returning, and sitting in his chariot read Esaias the prophet (Acts 8:27-28 KJV).

307 *And the LORD shall be king over all the earth: in that day shall there be one LORD, and his name one* (Zechariah 14:9 KJV).

308 *Rejoice greatly, Daughter Zion! Shout, Daughter Jerusalem! See, your king comes to you, righteous and victorious, lowly and riding on a donkey, on a colt, the foal of a donkey* (Zechariah 9:9 NIV).

309 *Bless the LORD, O my soul, and forget not all his benefits: Who forgiveth all thine iniquities; who healeth all thy diseases; Who redeemeth thy life from destruction; who crowneth thee with loving kindness and tender mercies; Who satisfieth thy mouth with good things; so that thy youth is renewed like the eagle's* (Psalm 103:2-5 KJV).

310 *And I saw heaven opened, and behold a white horse; and he that sat upon him was called Faithful and True, and in righteousness he doth judge and make war* (Revelation 19:11 KJV).

311 *And he hath on his vesture and on his thigh a name written, KING OF KINGS, AND LORD OF LORDS* (Revelation 19:16 KJV).

312 *Then Philip ran up to the chariot and heard the man reading Isaiah the prophet. "Do you understand what you are reading?" Philip asked. "How can I," he said, "unless someone explains it to me?" So he invited Philip to come up and sit with him* (Acts 8:30-31 NIV).

313 *We want each of you to show this same diligence to the very end, so that what you hope for may be fully realized* (Hebrews 6:11 NIV).

314 *This is the passage of Scripture the eunuch was reading: "He was led like a sheep to the slaughter, and as a lamb before its shearer is silent, so he did not open his mouth. In his humiliation he was deprived of justice. Who can speak of his descendants? For his life was taken from the earth"* (Acts 8:32-33 NIV).

315 *And the eunuch answered Philip, and said, I pray thee, of whom speaketh the prophet this? of himself, or of some other man?* (Acts 8:34 KJV).

316 *Then Philip began with that very passage of Scripture and told him the good news about Jesus* (Acts 8:35 NIV).

317   *As they traveled along the road, they came to some water and the eunuch said, "Look, here is water. What can stand in the way of my being baptized?" (Acts 8:36 NIV).*

318   *And Philip said, If thou believest with all thine heart, thou mayest. And he answered and said, I believe that Jesus Christ is the Son of God (Acts 8:37 KJV).*

319   *And he commanded the chariot to stand still: and they went down both into the water, both Philip and the eunuch; and he baptized him (Acts 8:38 KJV).*

320   *When they came up out of the water, the Spirit of the Lord suddenly took Philip away, and the eunuch did not see him again, but went on his way rejoicing (Acts 8:39 NIV).*

321   *And so John the Baptist appeared in the wilderness, preaching a baptism of repentance for the forgiveness of sins (Mark 1:4 NIV).*

322   *Then Peter said unto them, Repent, and be baptized every one of you in the name of Jesus Christ for the remission of sins, and ye shall receive the gift of the Holy Ghost (Acts 2:38 KJV).*

323   *But in your hearts revere Christ as Lord. Always be prepared to give an answer to everyone who asks you to give the reason for the hope that you have. But do this with gentleness and respect, keeping a clear conscience, so that those who speak maliciously against your good behavior in Christ may be ashamed of their slander (1 Peter 3:15-16 NIV).*

324   *When the time came for the purification rites required by the Law of Moses, Joseph and Mary took him to Jerusalem to present him to the Lord (Luke 2:22 NIV).*

325   *And Jesus, when he was baptized, went up straightway out of the water: and, lo, the heavens were opened unto him, and he saw the Spirit of God descending like a dove, and lighting upon him: And lo a voice from heaven, saying, This is my beloved Son, in whom I am well pleased (Matthew 3:16-17 KJV).*

326   *Buried with him in baptism, wherein also ye are risen with him through the faith of the operation of God, who hath raised him from the dead (Colossians 2:12 KJV).*

327   *All your words are true; all your righteous laws are eternal (Psalm 119:160 NIV).*

328 *This is how you can recognize the Spirit of God: Every spirit that acknowledges that Jesus Christ has come in the flesh is from God* (1 John 4:2 NIV).

329 *And the angel answered and said unto the women, Fear not ye: for I know that ye seek Jesus, which was crucified. He is not here: for he is risen, as he said. Come, see the place where the Lord lay. And go quickly, and tell his disciples that he is risen from the dead; and, behold, he goeth before you into Galilee; there shall ye see him: lo, I have told you. And they departed quickly from the sepulchre with fear and great joy; and did run to bring his disciples word. And as they went to tell his disciples, behold, Jesus met them, saying, All hail. And they came and held him by the feet, and worshipped him. Then said Jesus unto them, Be not afraid: go tell my brethren that they go into Galilee, and there shall they see me* (Matthew 28:5-10 KJV).

330 *Beloved, believe not every spirit, but try the spirits whether they are of God: because many false prophets are gone out into the world* (1 John 4:1 KJV).

331 *Being confident of this very thing, that he which hath begun a good work in you will perform it until the day of Jesus Christ* (Philippians 1:6 KJV).

332 *Both the one who makes people holy and those who are made holy are of the same family. So Jesus is not ashamed to call them brothers and sisters* (Hebrews 2:11 NIV).

333 *Having a form of godliness, but denying the power thereof: from such turn away* (2 Timothy 3:5 KJV).

334 *And I saw the dead, small and great, stand before God; and the books were opened: and another book was opened, which is the book of life: and the dead were judged out of those things which were written in the books, according to their works* (Revelation 20:12 KJV).

335 *I, even I, am he that blotteth out thy transgressions for mine own sake, and will not remember thy sins* (Isaiah 43:25 KJV).

336 *As far as the east is from the west, so far hath he removed our transgressions from us* (Psalm 103:12 KJV).

337 *Now the Berean Jews were of more noble character than those in Thessalonica, for they received the message with great eagerness and examined*

the Scriptures every day to see if what Paul said was true (Acts 17:11 NIV).

338 *But the angel said to her, "Do not be afraid, Mary; you have found favor with God. You will conceive and give birth to a son, and you are to call him Jesus. He will be great and will be called the Son of the Most High. The Lord God will give him the throne of his father David, and he will reign over Jacob's descendants forever; his kingdom will never end." "How will this be," Mary asked the angel, "since I am a virgin?" The angel answered, "The Holy Spirit will come on you, and the power of the Most High will overshadow you. So the holy one to be born will be called the Son of God* (Luke 1:30-35 NIV).

339 *For he hath made him to be sin for us, who knew no sin; that we might be made the righteousness of God in him* (2 Corinthians 5:21 KJV).

340 *For as by one man's disobedience many were made sinners, so by the obedience of one shall many be made righteous* (Romans 5:19 KJV).

341 *yowm,* "day (24-hour period) as defined by evening and morning" (Strong's H3117).

342 *"Therefore everyone who hears these words of mine and puts them into practice is like a wise man who built his house on the rock* (Matthew 7:24 NIV).

343 *He healeth the broken in heart, and bindeth up their wounds* (Psalm 147:3 KJV).

344 *Put on the whole armour of God, that ye may be able to stand against the wiles of the devil* (Ephesians 6:11 KJV).

345 *Cast all your anxiety on him because he cares for you* (1 Peter 5:7 NIV).

346 *And all these blessings shall come on thee, and overtake thee, if thou shalt hearken unto the voice of the LORD thy God* (Deuteronomy 28:2 KJV).

347 *Cast thy burden upon the LORD, and he shall sustain thee: he shall never suffer the righteous to be moved* (Psalm 55:22 KJV).

348 *It is of the LORD's mercies that we are not consumed, because his compassions fail not. They are new every morning: great is thy faithfulness* (Lamentations 3:22-23 KJV).

349 *I love them that love me; and those that seek me early shall find me* (Proverbs 8:17 KJV).

350 *For as many of you as have been baptized into Christ have put on Christ* (Galatians 3:27 KJV).

351 *For it is God which worketh in you both to will and to do of his good pleasure* (Philippians 2:13 KJV).

352 *If that is how God clothes the grass of the field, which is here today and tomorrow is thrown into the fire, will he not much more clothe you—you of little faith?* (Matthew 6:30 NIV).

353 *"And why do you worry about clothes? See how the flowers of the field grow. They do not labor or spin* (Matthew 6:28 NIV).

354 *Fear ye not therefore, ye are of more value than many sparrows* (Matthew 10:31 KJV).

355 *But the very hairs of your head are all numbered* (Matthew 10:30 KJV).

356 *After this I beheld, and, lo, a great multitude, which no man could number, of all nations, and kindreds, and people, and tongues, stood before the throne, and before the Lamb, clothed with white robes, and palms in their hands* (Revelation 7:9 KJV).

357 *Live in harmony with one another. Do not be proud, but be willing to associate with people of low position. Do not be conceited* (Romans 12:16 NIV).

358 *For since by man came death, by man came also the resurrection of the dead* (1 Corinthians 15:21 KJV).

359 *Above all, you must understand that in the last days scoffers will come, scoffing and following their own evil desires. They will say, "Where is this 'coming' he promised? Ever since our ancestors died, everything goes on as it has since the beginning of creation." But they deliberately forget that long ago by God's word the heavens came into being and the earth was formed out of water and by water* (2 Peter 3:4-6 NIV).

359a *The waters rose and covered the mountains to a depth of more than fifteen cubits* (Genesis 7:20).

360 *For the time will come when people will not put up with sound doctrine. Instead, to suit their own desires, they will gather around them a great number of teachers to say what their itching ears want to hear. They will turn their ears away from the truth and turn aside to myths* (2 Timothy 4:3-4 NIV).

361 *For thus saith the* Lord *that created the heavens; God himself that formed the earth and made it; he hath established it, he created it not in vain, he formed it to be inhabited: I am the* Lord; *and there is none else* (Isaiah 45:18 KJV).

362 *And whosoever shall not receive you, nor hear your words, when ye depart out of that house or city, shake off the dust of your feet* (Matthew 10:14 KJV).

363 *But this thing commanded I them, saying, Obey my voice, and I will be your God, and ye shall be my people: and walk ye in all the ways that I have commanded you, that it may be well unto you* (Jeremiah 7:23 KJV).

364 *As newborn babes, desire the sincere milk of the word, that ye may grow thereby* (1 Peter 2:2 KJV).

365 *Call unto me, and I will answer thee, and shew thee great and mighty things, which thou knowest not* (Jeremiah 33:3 KJV).

366 *Now when all the people were baptized, it came to pass, that Jesus also being baptized, and praying, the heaven was opened, And the Holy Ghost descended in a bodily shape like a dove upon him, and a voice came from heaven, which said, Thou art my beloved Son; in thee I am well pleased* (Luke 3:21-22 KJV).

367 *Grace be unto you, and peace, from God our Father, and from the Lord Jesus Christ* (Philippians 1:2 KJV).

368 *And the earth was without form, and void; and darkness was upon the face of the deep. And the Spirit of God moved upon the face of the waters* (Genesis 1:2 KJV).

369 *Now the Lord is that Spirit: and where the Spirit of the Lord is, there is liberty* (2 Corinthians 3:17 KJV).

370 *I and my Father are one* (John 10:30 KJV).

371 *By the word of the* Lord *were the heavens made; and all the host of them by the breath of his mouth* (Psalm 33:6 KJV).

372 *Yĕhovah*, "Jehovah = 'the existing One,' the proper name of the one true God" (Strong's H3068).

373 *The Spirit of God hath made me, and the breath of the Almighty hath given me life* (Job 33:4 KJV).

374 *But they that wait upon the* Lord *shall renew their strength; they shall*

mount up with wings as eagles; they shall run, and not be weary; and they shall walk, and not faint (Isaiah 40:31 KJV).

375 *The voice of the LORD is over the waters; the God of glory thunders, the LORD thunders over the mighty waters* (Psalm 29:3 NIV).

376 *The voice of the LORD is powerful; the voice of the LORD is full of majesty* (Psalm 29:4 KJV).

377 *And he stayed yet other seven days; and again he sent forth the dove out of the ark; And the dove came in to him in the evening; and, lo, in her mouth was an olive leaf pluckt off: so Noah knew that the waters were abated from off the earth* (Genesis 8:10-11 KJV).

378 *Howbeit when he, the Spirit of truth, is come, he will guide you into all truth: for he shall not speak of himself; but whatsoever he shall hear, that shall he speak: and he will shew you things to come* (John 16:13 KJV).

379 *That he would grant you, according to the riches of his glory, to be strengthened with might by his Spirit in the inner man* (Ephesians 3:16 KJV).

380 *And when they had prayed, the place was shaken where they were assembled together; and they were all filled with the Holy Ghost, and they spake the word of God with boldness* (Acts 4:31 KJV).

381 *But you will receive power when the Holy Spirit comes on you; and you will be my witnesses in Jerusalem, and in all Judea and Samaria, and to the ends of the earth* (Acts 1:8 NIV).

382 *But we ought always to thank God for you, brothers and sisters loved by the Lord, because God chose you as firstfruits to be saved through the sanctifying work of the Spirit and through belief in the truth* (2 Thessalonians 2:13 NIV).

383 *For through him we both have access by one Spirit unto the Father* (Ephesians 2:18 KJV).

384 *Quench not the Spirit* (1 Thessalonians 5:19 KJV).

385 *You are my friends if you do what I command. I no longer call you servants, because a servant does not know his master's business. Instead, I have called you friends, for everything that I learned from my Father I have made known to you* (John 15:14-15 NIV).

386 *For the grace of God that bringeth salvation hath appeared to all men* (Titus 2:11 KJV).

387 *He that spared not his own Son, but delivered him up for us all, how shall he not with him also freely give us all things?* (Romans 8:32 KJV).

388 *For God hath not given us the spirit of fear; but of power, and of love, and of a sound mind* (2 Timothy 1:7 KJV).

389 *Then opened he their understanding, that they might understand the scriptures, And said unto them, Thus it is written, and thus it behoved Christ to suffer, and to rise from the dead the third day* (Luke 24:45-46 KJV).

390 *To whom also he shewed himself alive after his passion by many infallible proofs, being seen of them forty days, and speaking of the things pertaining to the kingdom of God* (Acts 1:3 KJV).

391 *And when he had spoken these things, while they beheld, he was taken up; and a cloud received him out of their sight. And while they looked steadfastly toward heaven as he went up, behold, two men stood by them in white apparel; Which also said, Ye men of Galilee, why stand ye gazing up into heaven? this same Jesus, which is taken up from you into heaven, shall so come in like manner as ye have seen him go into heaven* (Acts 1:9-11 KJV).

392 *And, behold, I send the promise of my Father upon you: but tarry ye in the city of Jerusalem, until ye be endued with power from on high* (Luke 24:49 KJV).

393 *And, being assembled together with them, commanded them that they should not depart from Jerusalem, but wait for the promise of the Father, which, saith he, ye have heard of me* (Acts 1:4 KJV).

394 *For John truly baptized with water; but ye shall be baptized with the Holy Ghost not many days hence* (Acts 1:5 KJV).

395 *And you also were included in Christ when you heard the message of truth, the gospel of your salvation. When you believed, you were marked in him with a seal, the promised Holy Spirit, who is a deposit guaranteeing our inheritance until the redemption of those who are God's possession—to the praise of his glory* (Ephesians 1:13-14 NIV).

396 *Who hath also sealed us, and given the earnest of the Spirit in our hearts* (2 Corinthians 1:22 KJV).

397 *Then he answered and spake unto me, saying, This is the word of the LORD unto Zerubbabel, saying, Not by might, nor by power, but by my spirit, saith the LORD of hosts* (Zechariah 4:6 KJV).

398 *Observe the month of Abib, and keep the Passover unto the* LORD *thy God: for in the month of Abib the* LORD *thy God brought thee forth out of Egypt by night* (Deuteronomy 16:1 KJV).

399 *This is a day you are to commemorate; for the generations to come you shall celebrate it as a festival to the* LORD—*a lasting ordinance* (Exodus 12:14 NIV).

400 *The animals you choose must be year-old males without defect, and you may take them from the sheep or the goats. Take care of them until the fourteenth day of the month, when all the members of the community of Israel must slaughter them at twilight* (Exodus 12:6 NIV).

401 *At the place where Jesus was crucified, there was a garden, and in the garden a new tomb, in which no one had ever been laid. Because it was the Jewish day of Preparation and since the tomb was nearby, they laid Jesus there* (John 19:41-42 NIV).

402 *Now before the feast of the passover, when Jesus knew that his hour was come that he should depart out of this world unto the Father, having loved his own which were in the world, he loved them unto the end* (John 13:1 KJV).

403 *He was oppressed and afflicted, yet he did not open his mouth; he was led like a lamb to the slaughter, and as a sheep before its shearers is silent, so he did not open his mouth* (Isaiah 53:7 NIV).

404 *Count off seven weeks from the time you begin to put the sickle to the standing grain. Then celebrate the Festival of Weeks to the* LORD *your God by giving a freewill offering in proportion to the blessings the* LORD *your God has given you* (Deuteronomy 16:9-10 KJV).

405 *And when the day of Pentecost was fully come, they were all with one accord in one place* (Acts 2:1 KJV).

406 *And suddenly there came a sound from heaven as of a rushing mighty wind, and it filled all the house where they were sitting* (Acts 2:2 KJV).

407 *And there appeared unto them cloven tongues like as of fire, and it sat upon each of them* (Acts 2:3 KJV).

408 *And they were all filled with the Holy Ghost, and began to speak with other tongues, as the Spirit gave them utterance* (Acts 2:4 KJV).

409 *And there were dwelling at Jerusalem Jews, devout men, out of every nation under heaven* (Acts 2:5 KJV).

410 *Now when this was noised abroad, the multitude came together, and were confounded, because that every man heard them speak in his own language (Acts 2:6 KJV).*

411 *(both Jews and converts to Judaism); Cretans and Arabs—we hear them declaring the wonders of God in our own tongues! (Acts 2:11 NIV).*

412 *And they were all amazed and marvelled, saying one to another, Behold, are not all these which speak Galilaeans? And how hear we every man in our own tongue, wherein we were born? (Acts 2:7-8 KJV).*

413 *Then they that gladly received his word were baptized: and the same day there were added unto them about three thousand souls (Acts 2:41 KJV).*

414 *For since the creation of the world God's invisible qualities—his eternal power and divine nature—have been clearly seen, being understood from what has been made, so that people are without excuse (Romans 1:20 NIV).*

415 *And it came to pass, that, while Apollos was at Corinth, Paul having passed through the upper coasts came to Ephesus: and finding certain disciples, He said unto them, Have ye received the Holy Ghost since ye believed? And they said unto him, We have not so much as heard whether there be any Holy Ghost. And he said unto them, Unto what then were ye baptized? And they said, Unto John's baptism (Acts 19:1-3 KJV).*

416 *Then said Paul, John verily baptized with the baptism of repentance, saying unto the people, that they should believe on him which should come after him, that is, on Christ Jesus. When they heard this, they were baptized in the name of the Lord Jesus. And when Paul had laid his hands upon them, the Holy Ghost came on them; and they spake with tongues, and prophesied (Acts 19:4-6 KJV).*

417 *And this continued by the space of two years; so that all they which dwelt in Asia heard the word of the Lord Jesus, both Jews and Greeks (Acts 19:10 KJV).*

418 *Many of them also which used curious arts brought their books together, and burned them before all men: and they counted the price of them, and found it fifty thousand pieces of silver (Acts 19:19 KJV).*

419 *About that time there arose a great disturbance about the Way (Acts 19:23 KJV).*

420 *dynamis*, "strength power, ability, natural ability, general and inherent" (Strong's G1411).

421 *My people are destroyed for lack of knowledge* (Hosea 4:6a KJV).

422 *The Spirit clearly says that in later times some will abandon the faith and follow deceiving spirits and things taught by demons* (1 Timothy 4:1 NIV).

423 *For God is not the author of confusion, but of peace, as in all churches of the saints* (1 Corinthians 14:33 KJV).

424 *For when the Gentiles, which have not the law, do by nature the things contained in the law, these, having not the law, are a law unto themselves: Which shew the work of the law written in their hearts, their conscience also bearing witness, and their thoughts the mean while accusing or else excusing one another* (Romans 2:14-15 KJV).

425 *I indeed baptize you with water unto repentance: but he that cometh after me is mightier than I, whose shoes I am not worthy to bear: he shall baptize you with the Holy Ghost, and with fire* (Matthew 3:11 KJV).

426 *I am come that they might have life, and that they might have it more abundantly* (John 10:10b KJV).

427 *for I am the LORD that healeth thee* (Exodus 15:26b KJV).

428 *But my God shall supply all your need according to his riches in glory by Christ Jesus* (Philippians 4:19 KJV).

429 *Trust in the LORD with all thine heart; and lean not unto thine own understanding. In all thy ways acknowledge him, and he shall direct thy paths* (Proverbs 3:5-6 KJV).

430 *For we know that our old self was crucified with him so that the body ruled by sin might be done away with, that we should no longer be slaves to sin* (Romans 6:6 NIV).

431 *mashach*, "to smear, anoint, spread a liquid" (Strong's H4886).

432 *That word, I say, ye know, which was published throughout all Judaea, and began from Galilee, after the baptism which John preached; How God anointed Jesus of Nazareth with the Holy Ghost and with power: who went about doing good, and healing all that were oppressed of the devil; for God was with him* (Acts 10:37-38 KJV).

433 *chriō*, "to anoint, enduing Christians with the gifts of the Holy Spirit" (Strong's G5548).

434   *Know ye not that ye are the temple of God, and that the Spirit of God dwelleth in you?* (1 Corinthians 3:16 KJV).

435   *"For everyone who asks receives; the one who seeks finds; and to the one who knocks, the door will be opened* (Matthew 7:8 NIV).

436   *For the Holy Ghost shall teach you in the same hour what ye ought to say* (Luke 12:12 KJV).

437   *O give thanks unto the* LORD, *for he is good: for his mercy endureth for ever* (Psalm 107:1 KJV).

438   *Then Simon himself believed also: and when he was baptized, he continued with Philip, and wondered, beholding the miracles and signs which were done* (Acts 8:13 KJV).

439   *And when Simon saw that through laying on of the apostles' hands the Holy Ghost was given, he offered them money, Saying, Give me also this power, that on whomsoever I lay hands, he may receive the Holy Ghost"* (Acts 8:18-19 KJV).

440   *But Peter said unto him, Thy money perish with thee, because thou hast thought that the gift of God may be purchased with money. hou hast neither part nor lot in this matter: for thy heart is not right in the sight of God* (Acts 8:20-21 KJV).

441   *"Repent of this wickedness and pray to the Lord in the hope that he may forgive you for having such a thought in your heart. For I see that you are full of bitterness and captive to sin"* (Acts 8:22-23 NIV).

442   *If ye love me, keep my commandments. And I will pray the Father, and he shall give you another Comforter, that he may abide with you for ever* (John 14:15-16 KJV).

443   *The Spirit of truth. The world cannot accept him, because it neither sees him nor knows him. But you know him, for he lives with you and will be in you* (John 14:17 NIV).

444   *The circumcised believers who had come with Peter were astonished that the gift of the Holy Spirit had been poured out even on Gentiles. For they heard them speaking in tongues and praising God. Then Peter said, "Surely no one can stand in the way of their being baptized with water. They have received the Holy Spirit just as we have"* (Acts 10:45-47 NIV).

445   *And these signs shall follow them that believe; In my name shall they cast out devils; they shall speak with new tongues* (Mark 16:17 KJV).

446 *For anyone who speaks in a tongue does not speak to people but to God. Indeed, no one understands them; they utter mysteries by the Spirit* (1 Corinthians 14:2 NIV).

447 *It is the spirit that quickeneth; the flesh profiteth nothing: the words that I speak unto you, they are spirit, and they are life* (John 6:63 KJV).

448 *For your Father knoweth what things ye have need of, before ye ask him* (Matthew 6:8b KJV).

449 *For if I pray in an unknown tongue, my spirit prayeth, but my understanding is unfruitful* (1 Corinthians 14:14 KJV).

450 *But the fruit of the Spirit is love, joy, peace, longsuffering, gentleness, goodness, faith, Meekness, temperance: against such there is no law* (Galatians 5:22-23 KJV).

451 *Praying always with all prayer and supplication in the Spirit, and watching thereunto with all perseverance and supplication for all saints* (Ephesians 6:18 KJV).

452 *And Jesus came and spake unto them, saying, All power is given unto me in heaven and in earth* (Matthew 28:18 KJV).

453 *For it is not ye that speak, but the Spirit of your Father which speaketh in you* (Matthew 10:20 KJV).

454 *So shall my word be that goeth forth out of my mouth: it shall not return unto me void, but it shall accomplish that which I please, and it shall prosper in the thing whereto I sent it* (Isaiah 55:11 KJV).

455 *Put on the whole armour of God, that ye may be able to stand against the wiles of the devil* (Ephesians 6:11 KJV).

456 *Be not overcome of evil, but overcome evil with good* (Romans 12:21 KJV).

457 *Stand therefore, having your loins girt about with truth, and having on the breastplate of righteousness* (Ephesians 6:14 KJV).

458 *Thy word is true from the beginning: and every one of thy righteous judgments endureth for ever* (Psalm 119:160 KJV).

459 *But unto the Son he saith, Thy throne, O God, is for ever and ever: a sceptre of righteousness is the sceptre of thy kingdom. Thou hast loved righteousness, and hated iniquity; therefore God, even thy God, hath anointed thee with the oil of gladness above thy fellows* (Hebrews 1:8-9 KJV).

460 *Finally, brethren, whatsoever things are true, whatsoever things are honest, whatsoever things are just, whatsoever things are pure, whatsoever*

things are lovely, whatsoever things are of good report; if there be any virtue, and if there be any praise, think on these things (Philippians 4:8 KJV).

461 *tsaddiyq*, "right, correct, lawful, just. In government, in one's cause, in conduct and character and as justified and vindicated by God" (Strong's H6662).

462 *For when ye were the servants of sin, ye were free from righteousness* (Romans 6:20 KJV).

463 *Being then made free from sin, ye became the servants of righteousness* (Romans 6:18 KJV).

464 *I came not to call the righteous, but sinners to repentance* (Luke 5:32 KJV).

465 *Blessed are they which do hunger and thirst after righteousness: for they shall be filled* (Matthew 5:6 KJV).

466 *Blessed are they which are persecuted for righteousness' sake: for theirs is the kingdom of heaven* (Matthew 5:10 KJV).

467 *For they being ignorant of God's righteousness, and going about to establish their own righteousness, have not submitted themselves unto the righteousness of God* (Romans 10:3 KJV).

468 *But we are all as an unclean thing, and all our righteousnesses are as filthy rags; and we all do fade as a leaf; and our iniquities, like the wind, have taken us away* (Isaiah 64:6 KJV).

469 *As it is written, There is none righteous, no, not one* (Romans 3:10 KJV).

470 *This righteousness is given through faith in Jesus Christ to all who believe. There is no difference between Jew and Gentile* (Romans 3:22 NIV).

471 *And he believed in the LORD; and he counted it to him for righteousness* (Genesis 15:6 KJV).

472 *This is why "it was credited to him as righteousness"* (Romans 4:22 NIV).

473 *But if we walk in the light, as he is in the light, we have fellowship one with another, and the blood of Jesus Christ his Son cleanseth us from all sin* (1 John 1:7 KJV).

474 *In your relationships with one another, have the same mindset as Christ Jesus* (Philippians 2:5 NIV).

475 *(For the fruit of the Spirit is in all goodness and righteousness and truth)* (Ephesians 5:9 KJV).

476 *For ye were sometimes darkness, but now are ye light in the Lord: walk as children of light* (Ephesians 5:8 KJV).

477 *Ye shall know them by their fruits* (Matthew 7:16a KJV).

478 *And with your feet fitted with the readiness that comes from the gospel of peace* (Ephesians 6:15 KJV).

479 *hetoimasia*, "the act of preparing, the condition of a person or thing so far forth as prepared, preparedness, readiness" (Strong's G2091).

480 *The God of peace will soon crush Satan under your feet. The grace of our Lord Jesus be with you* (Romans 16:20 NIV).

481 *In addition to all this, take up the shield of faith, with which you can extinguish all the flaming arrows of the evil one* (Ephesians 6:16 NIV).

482 *And thou shalt anoint the tabernacle of the congregation therewith, and the ark of the testimony* (Exodus 30:26 KJV).

483 *And thou shalt anoint Aaron and his sons, and consecrate them, that they may minister unto me in the priest's office. And thou shalt speak unto the children of Israel, saying, This shall be an holy anointing oil unto me throughout your generations. Upon man's flesh shall it not be poured, neither shall ye make any other like it, after the composition of it: it is holy, and it shall be holy unto you* (Exodus 30:30-32 KJV).

484 *Take the anointing oil and anoint the tabernacle and everything in it; consecrate it and all its furnishings, and it will be holy* (Exodus 40:9 NIV).

485 *And let them make me a sanctuary; that I may dwell among them* (Exodus 25:8 KJV).

486 *Do you not know that your bodies are temples of the Holy Spirit, who is in you, whom you have received from God? You are not your own* (1 Corinthians 6:19 NIV).

487 *You study the Scriptures diligently because you think that in them you have eternal life. These are the very Scriptures that testify about me* (John 5:39 NIV).

488 *The Son is the radiance of God's glory and the exact representation of his being, sustaining all things by his powerful word. After he had provided purification for sins, he sat down at the right hand of the Majesty in heaven* (Hebrews 1:3 NIV).

489 *He is before all things, and in him all things hold together* (Colossians 1:17 NIV).

490 *That he might sanctify and cleanse it with the washing of water by the word* (Ephesians 5:26 KJV).

491 *And take the helmet of salvation, and the sword of the Spirit, which is the word of God* (Ephesians 6:17 KJV).

492 *And be not conformed to this world: but be ye transformed by the renewing of your mind, that ye may prove what is that good, and acceptable, and perfect, will of God* (Romans 12:2 KJV).

493 *Keep thy heart with all diligence; for out of it are the issues of life* (Proverbs 4:23 KJV).

494 *And the peace of God, which passeth all understanding, shall keep your hearts and minds through Christ Jesus* (Philippians 4:7 KJV).

495 *And grieve not the holy Spirit of God, whereby ye are sealed unto the day of redemption* (Ephesians 4:30 KJV).

496 *When he comes, he will prove the world to be in the wrong about sin and righteousness and judgment* (John 16:8 NIV).

497 *Husbands, love your wives, even as Christ also loved the church, and gave himself for it* (Ephesians 5:25 KJV).

498 *And he saith unto me, Write, Blessed are they which are called unto the marriage supper of the Lamb. And he saith unto me, These are the true sayings of God* (Revelation 19:9 KJV).

499 *Or do you think Scripture says without reason that he jealously longs for the spirit he has caused to dwell in us?* (James 4:5 NIV).

500 *For I am jealous over you with godly jealousy: for I have espoused you to one husband, that I may present you as a chaste virgin to Christ* (2 Corinthians 11:2 KJV).

501 *And he had in his right hand seven stars: and out of his mouth went a sharp two edged sword: and his countenance was as the sun shineth in his strength* (Revelation 1:16 KJV).

502 *For the word of God is quick, and powerful, and sharper than any twoedged sword, piercing even to the dividing asunder of soul and spirit, and of the joints and marrow, and is a discerner of the thoughts and intents of the heart* (Hebrews 4:12 KJV).

503 *For bodily exercise profiteth little: but godliness is profitable unto all things, having promise of the life that now is, and of that which is to come* (1 Timothy 4:8 KJV).

504 *Therefore I endure all things for the elect's sakes, that they may also obtain the salvation which is in Christ Jesus with eternal glory* (2 Timothy 2:10 KJV).

505 *Study to shew thyself approved unto God, a workman that needeth not to be ashamed, rightly dividing the word of truth* (2 Timothy 2:15 KJV).

506 *Do nothing out of selfish ambition or vain conceit. Rather, in humility value others above yourselves, not looking to your own interests but each of you to the interests of the others* (Philippians 2:3-4 NIV).

507 *Do not add to what I command you and do not subtract from it, but keep the commands of the LORD your God that I give you* (Deuteronomy 4:2 NIV).

508 *My voice shalt thou hear in the morning, O LORD; in the morning will I direct my prayer unto thee, and will look up* (Psalm 5:3 KJV).

509 *Thy word is a lamp unto my feet, and a light unto my path* (Psalm 119:105 KJV).

510 *charisma*, "a favour with which one receives without any merit of his own" (Strong's G5486).

511 *Now to each one the manifestation of the Spirit is given for the common good* (1 Corinthians 12:7 NIV).

512 *We have different gifts, according to the grace given to each of us. If your gift is prophesying, then prophesy in accordance with your faith; ⁷if it is serving, then serve; if it is teaching, then teach; ⁸if it is to encourage, then give encouragement; if it is giving, then give generously; if it is to lead, do it diligently; if it is to show mercy, do it cheerfully* (Romans 12:6-8 NIV).

513 *To one there is given through the Spirit a message of wisdom, to another a message of knowledge by means of the same Spirit, ⁹to another faith by the same Spirit, to another gifts of healing by that one Spirit, ¹⁰to another miraculous powers, to another prophecy, to another distinguishing between spirits, to another speaking in different kinds of tongues, and to still another the interpretation of tongues. ¹¹All these are the work of one and the same Spirit, and he distributes them to each one, just as he determines. ¹²Just as a body, though one, has many parts, but all its many parts form one body, so it is with Christ.* (1 Corinthians 12:8-12 NIV).

514 *Each of you should use whatever gift you have received to serve others, as faithful stewards of God's grace in its various forms* (1 Peter 4:10 NIV).

515 *For the gifts and calling of God are without repentance* (Romans 11:29 KJV).

516 *For the kingdom of heaven is as a man travelling into a far country, who called his own servants, and delivered unto them his goods. And unto one he gave five talents, to another two, and to another one; to every man according to his several ability; and straightway took his journey. Then he that had received the five talents went and traded with the same, and made them other five talents. And likewise he that had received two, he also gained other two. But he that had received one went and digged in the earth, and hid his lord's money.*

After a long time the lord of those servants cometh, and reckoneth with them. And so he that had received five talents came and brought other five talents, saying, Lord, thou deliveredst unto me five talents: behold, I have gained beside them five talents more. His lord said unto him, Well done, thou good and faithful servant: thou hast been faithful over a few things, I will make thee ruler over many things: enter thou into the joy of thy lord. He also that had received two talents came and said, Lord, thou deliveredst unto me two talents: behold, I have gained two other talents beside them. His lord said unto him, Well done, good and faithful servant; thou hast been faithful over a few things, I will make thee ruler over many things: enter thou into the joy of thy lord.

Then he which had received the one talent came and said, Lord, I knew thee that thou art an hard man, reaping where thou hast not sown, and gathering where thou hast not strawed: And I was afraid, and went and hid thy talent in the earth: lo, there thou hast that is thine. His lord answered and said unto him, Thou wicked and slothful servant, thou knewest that I reap where I sowed not, and gather where I have not strawed: Thou oughtest therefore to have put my money to the exchangers, and then at my coming I should have received mine own with usury. Take therefore the talent from him, and give it unto him which hath ten talents. For unto every one that hath shall be given, and he shall have abundance: but from him that hath not shall be taken away even that which he hath. And cast ye the unprofitable servant into outer darkness: there shall be weeping and gnashing of teeth (Matthew 25:14-30 KJV).

517 *So Pharaoh said to Joseph, "I hereby put you in charge of the whole land of Egypt"* (Genesis 41:41 NIV).

518 *and the seven years of famine began, just as Joseph had said. There was famine in all the other lands, but in the whole land of Egypt there was food* (Genesis 41:54 NIV).

519 *But we speak the wisdom of God in a mystery, even the hidden wisdom, which God ordained before the world unto our glory: Which none of the princes of this world knew: for had they known it, they would not have crucified the Lord of glory. But as it is written, Eye hath not seen, nor ear heard, neither have entered into the heart of man, the things which God hath prepared for them that love him. But God hath revealed them unto us by his Spirit: for the Spirit searcheth all things, yea, the deep things of God. For what man knoweth the things of a man, save the spirit of man which is in him? even so the things of God knoweth no man, but the Spirit of God. Now we have received, not the spirit of the world, but the spirit which is of God; that we might know the things that are freely given to us of God. Which things also we speak, not in the words which man's wisdom teacheth, but which the Holy Ghost teacheth; comparing spiritual things with spiritual* (1 Corinthians 2:7-13 KJV).

520 *Then Jesus asked, "What is the kingdom of God like? What shall I compare it to? It is like a mustard seed, which a man took and planted in his garden. It grew and became a tree, and the birds perched in its branches* (Luke 13:18-19 NIV).

521 *Whatever you do, work at it with all your heart, as working for the Lord, not for human masters, since you know that you will receive an inheritance from the Lord as a reward. It is the Lord Christ you are serving* (Colossians 3:23-24 NIV).

522 *I can do all things through Christ which strengtheneth me* (Philippians 4:13 KJV).

523 *And my speech and my preaching was not with enticing words of man's wisdom, but in demonstration of the Spirit and of power* (1 Corinthians 2:4 KJV).

524 *And Jesus said unto them, Because of your unbelief: for verily I say unto you, If ye have faith as a grain of mustard seed, ye shall say unto this mountain, Remove hence to yonder place; and it shall remove; and nothing shall be impossible unto you* (Matthew 17:20 KJV).

525 *That your faith should not stand in the wisdom of men, but in the power of God* (1 Corinthians 2:5 KJV).

526 *But without faith it is impossible to please him: for he that cometh to God must believe that he is, and that he is a rewarder of them that diligently seek him* (Hebrews 11:6 KJV).

527 *To the faithful you show yourself faithful, to the blameless you show yourself blameless* (Psalm 18:25 NIV).

528 *When Jesus saw Nathanael approaching, he said of him, "Here truly is an Israelite in whom there is no deceit." "How do you know me?" Nathanael asked. Jesus answered, "I saw you while you were still under the fig tree before Philip called you." Then Nathanael declared, "Rabbi, you are the Son of God; you are the king of Israel"* (John 1:47-49 NIV).

529 *But Peter said, Not so, Lord; for I have never eaten any thing that is common or unclean* (Acts 10:14 KJV).

530 *One day at about three in the afternoon he had a vision. He distinctly saw an angel of God, who came to him and said, "Cornelius!" Cornelius stared at him in fear. "What is it, Lord?" he asked. The angel answered, "Your prayers and gifts to the poor have come up as a memorial offering before God. Now send men to Joppa to bring back a man named Simon who is called Peter. He is staying with Simon the tanner, whose house is by the sea." When the angel who spoke to him had gone, Cornelius called two of his servants and a devout soldier who was one of his attendants. He told them everything that had happened and sent them to Joppa* (Acts 10:3-8 NIV).

531 *About noon the following day as they were on their journey and approaching the city, Peter went up on the roof to pray. He became hungry and wanted something to eat, and while the meal was being prepared, he fell into a trance* (Acts 10:9-10 NIV).

532 *The voice spoke to him a second time, "Do not call anything impure that God has made clean"* (Acts 10:15 NIV).

533 *While Peter was still thinking about the vision, the Spirit said to*

him, "Simon, three men are looking for you. So get up and go downstairs. Do not hesitate to go with them, for I have sent them" (Acts 10:19-20 NIV).

534 *So Peter went down and said, "I'm the man you are looking for. Why have you come?"* (Acts 10:21 NIV).

535 *The following day he arrived in Caesarea. Cornelius was expecting them and had called together his relatives and close friends. As Peter entered the house, Cornelius met him and fell at his feet in reverence* (Acts 10:24-25 NIV).

536 *Immediately therefore I sent to thee; and thou hast well done that thou art come. Now therefore are we all here present before God, to hear all things that are commanded thee of God* (Acts 10:33 KJV).

537 *While Peter yet spake these words, the Holy Ghost fell on all them which heard the word* (Acts 10:44 KJV).

538 *For the LORD giveth wisdom: out of his mouth cometh knowledge and understanding* (Proverbs 2:6 KJV).

539 *If any of you lack wisdom, let him ask of God, that giveth to all men liberally, and upbraideth not; and it shall be given him* (James 1:5 KJV).

540 *If anyone speaks in a tongue, two—or at the most three—should speak, one at a time, and someone must interpret* (1 Corinthians 14:27 NIV).

541 *But If there is no interpreter, the speaker should keep quiet in the church and speak to himself and to God* (1 Corinthians 14:28 NIV).

542 *prophēteuō*, "with the idea of foretelling future events pertaining esp. to the kingdom of God, to utter forth, declare, a thing which can only be known by divine revelation" (Strong's G4395).

543 *And to know the love of Christ, which passeth knowledge, that ye might be filled with all the fulness of God. Now unto him that is able to do exceeding abundantly above all that we ask or think, according to the power that worketh in us* (Ephesians 3:19-20 KJV).

544 *Therefore, whether you eat or drink, or whatever you do, do all to the glory of God* (1 Corinthians 10:31 NKJV).

545 *Do not turn to mediums or seek out spiritists, for you will be defiled by them. I am the LORD your God* (Leviticus 19:31 NIV).

546 *prophēteia*, "a discourse emanating from divine inspiration and declaring the purposes of God, whether by reproving and admonishing

the wicked, or comforting the afflicted, or revealing things hidden; esp. by foretelling future events" (Strong's G4394).

547 *How is it then, brethren? when ye come together, every one of you hath a psalm, hath a doctrine, hath a tongue, hath a revelation, hath an interpretation. Let all things be done unto edifying* (1 Corinthians 14:26 KJV).

548 *For God does speak—now one way, now another— though no one perceives it* (Job 33:14 NIV).

549 *Do not treat prophecies with contempt* (1 Thessalonians 5:20 NIV).

550 *I marvel that ye are so soon removed from him that called you into the grace of Christ unto another gospel: Which is not another; but there be some that trouble you, and would pervert the gospel of Christ. But though we, or an angel from heaven, preach any other gospel unto you than that which we have preached unto you, let him be accursed* (Galatians 1:6-8 KJV).

551 *For the testimony of Jesus is the spirit of prophecy* (Revelation 19:10b KJV).

552 *And many false prophets shall rise, and shall deceive many* (Matthew 24:11 KJV).

553 *To the law and to the testimony: if they speak not according to this word, it is because there is no light in them* (Isaiah 8:20 KJV).

554 *Beware of false prophets, which come to you in sheep's clothing, but inwardly they are ravening wolves. Ye shall know them by their fruits* (Matthew 7:15-16a KJV).

555 *If a prophet, or one who foretells by dreams, appears among you and announces to you a sign or wonder, and if the sign or wonder spoken of takes place, and the prophet says, "Let us follow other gods" (gods you have not known) "and let us worship them," you must not listen to the words of that prophet or dreamer. The LORD your God is testing you to find out whether you love him with all your heart and with all your soul* (Deuteronomy 13:1-3 NIV).

556 *Hereby know ye the Spirit of God: Every spirit that confesseth that Jesus Christ is come in the flesh is of God: And every spirit that confesseth not that Jesus Christ is come in the flesh is not of God: and this is that spirit of antichrist, whereof ye have heard that it should come; and even now already is it in the world* (1 John 4:2-3 KJV).

557 *But he that prophesieth speaketh unto men to edification, and exhortation, and comfort* (1 Corinthians 14:3 KJV).

558 *If any thing be revealed to another that sitteth by, let the first hold his peace. For ye may all prophesy one by one, that all may learn, and all may be comforted* (1 Corinthians 14:30-31 KJV).

559 *Having then gifts differing according to the grace that is given to us, whether prophecy, let us prophesy according to the proportion of faith* (Romans 12:6 KJV).

560 *diakrinō,* "to separate, make a distinction, discriminate, to learn by discrimination, to try, decide" (Strong's G1252).

561 *For every one that useth milk is unskilful in the word of righteousness: for he is a babe. But strong meat belongeth to them that are of full age, even those who by reason of use have their senses exercised to discern both good and evil* (Hebrews 5:13-14 KJV).

562 *And this I pray, that your love may abound yet more and more in knowledge and in all judgment* (Philippians 1:9 KJV).

563 *We are of God: he that knoweth God heareth us; he that is not of God heareth not us. Hereby know we the spirit of truth, and the spirit of error* (1 John 4:6 KJV).

564 *The woman saith unto him, Sir, I perceive that thou art a prophet* (John 4:19 KJV).

565 *And she said unto her husband, Behold now, I perceive that this is an holy man of God, which passeth by us continually* (2 Kings 4:9 KJV).

566 *For there stood by me this night the angel of God, whose I am, and whom I serve* (Acts 27:23 KJV).

567 *Then a spirit passed before my face; the hair of my flesh stood up: It stood still, but I could not discern the form thereof: an image was before mine eyes, there was silence, and I heard a voice* (Job 4:15-16 KJV).

568 *For where envying and strife is, there is confusion and every evil work* (James 3:16 KJV).

569 *And whatsoever we ask, we receive of him, because we keep his commandments, and do those things that are pleasing in his sight* (1 John 3:22 KJV).

570 *And it shall come to pass in the last days, saith God, I will pour out*

of my Spirit upon all flesh: and your sons and your daughters shall prophesy, and your young men shall see visions, and your old men shall dream dreams (Acts 2:17 KJV).

571 *And, behold, the angel that talked with me went forth, and another angel went out to meet him* (Zechariah 2:3 KJV).

572 *And Jacob went on his way, and the angels of God met him. And when Jacob saw them, he said, This is God's host: and he called the name of that place Mahanaim* (Genesis 32:1-2 KJV).

573 *And Elisha prayed, and said, LORD, I pray thee, open his eyes, that he may see. And the LORD opened the eyes of the young man; and he saw: and, behold, the mountain was full of horses and chariots of fire round about Elisha* (2 Kings 6:17 KJV).

574 *And there appeared an angel unto him from heaven, strengthening him* (Luke 22:43 KJV).

575 *When the even was come, they brought unto him many that were possessed with devils: and he cast out the spirits with his word, and healed all that were sick* (Matthew 8:16 KJV).

576 *And he called unto him the twelve, and began to send them forth by two and two; and gave them power over unclean spirits* (Mark 6:7 KJV).

577 *The seventy-two returned with joy and said, "Lord, even the demons submit to us in your name"* (Luke 10:17 NIV).

578 *Once when we were going to the place of prayer, we were met by a female slave who had a spirit by which she predicted the future. She earned a great deal of money for her owners by fortune-telling. She followed Paul and the rest of us, shouting, "These men are servants of the Most High God, who are telling you the way to be saved." She kept this up for many days. Finally Paul became so annoyed that he turned around and said to the spirit, "In the name of Jesus Christ I command you to come out of her!" At that moment the spirit left her. When her owners realized that their hope of making money was gone, they seized Paul and Silas and dragged them into the marketplace to face the authorities* (Acts 16:16-19 NIV).

579 *The discerning heart seeks knowledge, but the mouth of a fool feeds on folly* (Proverbs 15:14 NIV).

580 *Fellow Israelites, listen to this: Jesus of Nazareth was a man accredited*

by God to you by miracles, wonders and signs, which God did among you through him, as you yourselves know (Acts 2:22 NIV).

581 *Verily, verily, I say unto you, He that believeth on me, the works that I do shall he do also; and greater works than these shall he do; because I go unto my Father* (John 14:12 KJV).

582 *They shall lay hands on the sick, and they shall recover* (Mark 16:18b KJV).

583 *iaomai*, "to cure, heal, to make whole, to free from errors and sins, to bring about (one's) salvation" (Strong's G2390).

584 *therapeuō*, "to heal, cure, restore to health" (Strong's G2323).

585 *Jesus saith unto him, Rise, take up thy bed, and walk. And immediately the man was made whole, and took up his bed, and walked* (John 5:8-9a KJV).

586 *The LORD sustains them on their sickbed and restores them from their bed of illness* (Psalm 41:3 NIV).

587 *For we know that if our earthly house of this tabernacle were dissolved, we have a building of God, an house not made with hands, eternal in the heavens* (2 Corinthians 5:1 KJV).

588 *In order that Satan might not outwit us. For we are not unaware of his schemes* (2 Corinthians 2:11 NIV).

589 *And Jesus looking upon them saith, With men it is impossible, but not with God: for with God all things are possible* (Mark 10:27 KJV).

590 *Jesus saith unto them, Fill the waterpots with water. And they filled them up to the brim. And he saith unto them, Draw out now, and bear unto the governor of the feast. And they bare it. When the ruler of the feast had tasted the water that was made wine, and knew not whence it was: (but the servants which drew the water knew;) the governor of the feast called the bridegroom, And saith unto him, Every man at the beginning doth set forth good wine; and when men have well drunk, then that which is worse: but thou hast kept the good wine until now* (John 2:7-10 KJV).

591 *Then he called his twelve disciples together, and gave them power and authority over all devils, and to cure diseases* (Luke 9:1 KJV).

592 *And one of the multitude answered and said, Master, I have brought unto thee my son, which hath a dumb spirit* (Mark 9:17 KJV).

593 *So went Satan forth from the presence of the LORD, and smote Job with sore boils from the sole of his foot unto his crown* (Job 2:7 KJV).

594 *And the sea gave up the dead which were in it; and death and hell delivered up the dead which were in them: and they were judged every man according to their works. And death and hell were cast into the lake of fire. This is the second death (Revelation* 20:13-14 KJV).

595 *And the* LORD *God commanded the man, saying, Of every tree of the garden thou mayest freely eat: But of the tree of the knowledge of good and evil, thou shalt not eat of it: for in the day that thou eatest thereof thou shalt surely die (Genesis* 2:16-17 KJV).

596 *All his days also he eateth in darkness, and he hath much sorrow and wrath with his sickness (Ecclesiastes* 5:17 KJV).

597 *The last enemy that shall be destroyed is death* (1 Corinthians 15:26 KJV).

598 *amēn,* "verily, truly, amen, so be it" (Strong's H543).

599 *amen,* "verily, firm, amen, so be it" (Strong's G281).

600 *For there shall arise false Christs, and false prophets, and shall shew great signs and wonders; insomuch that, if it were possible, they shall deceive the very elect (Matthew* 24:24 KJV).

601 *It is the* LORD *your God you must follow, and him you must revere. Keep his commands and obey him; serve him and hold fast to him. That prophet or dreamer must be put to death for inciting rebellion against the* LORD *your God, who brought you out of Egypt and redeemed you from the land of slavery. That prophet or dreamer tried to turn you from the way the* LORD *your God commanded you to follow. You must purge the evil from among you (Deuteronomy* 13:4-5 NIV).

602 *Behold, I send you forth as sheep in the midst of wolves: be ye therefore wise as serpents, and harmless as doves (Matthew* 10:16 KJV).

603 *eucharisteo,* "to be grateful, feel thankful, give thanks" (Strong's G2168).

604 *koinonia,* "fellowship, association, community, joint participation, a connection between persons or groups, an embodiment and proof of fellowship" (Strong's G2842).

605 *For I have received of the Lord that which also I delivered unto you, That the Lord Jesus the same night in which he was betrayed took bread: And when he had given thanks, he brake it, and said, Take, eat: this is my body, which is broken for you: this do in remembrance of me. After the same manner also he took the cup, when he had supped, saying, This cup is the new testament in my blood: this do ye, as oft as ye drink it, in*

remembrance of me. For as often as ye eat this bread, and drink this cup, ye do shew the Lord's death till he come (1 Corinthians 11:23-26 KJV).

606 *And as they did eat, Jesus took bread, and blessed, and brake it, and gave to them, and said, Take, eat: this is my body. And he took the cup, and when he had given thanks, he gave it to them: and they all drank of it. And he said unto them, This is my blood of the new testament, which is shed for many* (Mark 14:22-24 KJV).

607 *You also, like living stones, are being built into a spiritual house to be a holy priesthood, offering spiritual sacrifices acceptable to God through Jesus Christ* (1 Peter 2:5 NIV).

608 *And the sons of Aaron the priest shall put fire upon the altar, and lay the wood in order upon the fire* (Leviticus 1:7 KJV).

609 *But you are a chosen people, a royal priesthood, a holy nation, God's special possession, that you may declare the praises of him who called you out of darkness into his wonderful light* (1 Peter 2:9 NIV).

610 *So then, whoever eats the bread or drinks the cup of the Lord in an unworthy manner will be guilty of sinning against the body and blood of the Lord* (1 Corinthians 11:27 NIV).

611 *For those who eat and drink without discerning the body of Christ eat and drink judgment on themselves* (1 Corinthians 11:29 NIV).

612 *Everyone ought to examine themselves before they eat of the bread and drink from the cup. For those who eat and drink without discerning the body of Christ eat and drink judgment on themselves* (1 Corinthians 11:28 NIV).

613 *Then I acknowledged my sin to you and did not cover up my iniquity. I said, "I will confess my transgressions to the LORD." And you forgave the guilt of my sin* (Psalm 32:5 NIV).

614 *Know ye that the LORD he is God: it is he that hath made us, and not we ourselves; we are his people, and the sheep of his pasture. Enter into his gates with thanksgiving, and into his courts with praise: be thankful unto him, and bless his name. For the LORD is good; his mercy is everlasting; and his truth endureth to all generations* (Psalm 100:3-5 KJV).

615 *karpos*, "fruit of the trees, vines, of the fields. Fruit of one's loins, e.g. progeny, posterity. That which originates from something, an effect, result, work, act, deed" (Strong's G2590).

616 *He that loveth not knoweth not God; for God is love* (1 John 4:8 KJV).

617 *agapē,* "affection, good will, love, charity, benevolence brotherly love" (Strong's G26).

618 *A new commandment I give unto you, That ye love one another; as I have loved you, that ye also love one another. By this shall all men know that ye are my disciples, if ye have love one to another* (John 13:34-35 KJV).

619 *Love is patient, love is kind. It does not envy, it does not boast, it is not proud. Doth not behave itself unseemly, seeketh not her own, is not easily provoked, thinketh no evil; Love does not delight in evil but rejoices with the truth. It always protects, always trusts, always hopes, always perseveres* (1 Corinthians 13:4-7 NIV).

620 *Love must be sincere. Hate what is evil; cling to what is good* (Romans 12:9 NIV).

621 *chara,* "joy, gladness, the cause or occasion of joy, the joy received from you" (Strong's G5479).

622 *For the kingdom of God is not meat and drink; but righteousness, and peace, and joy in the Holy Ghost* (Romans 14:17 KJV).

623 *Looking unto Jesus the author and finisher of our faith; who for the joy that was set before him endured the cross, despising the shame, and is set down at the right hand of the throne of God* (Hebrews 12:2 KJV).

624 *If ye abide in me, and my words abide in you, ye shall ask what ye will, and it shall be done unto you. Herein is my Father glorified, that ye bear much fruit; so shall ye be my disciples. As the Father hath loved me, so have I loved you: continue ye in my love. If ye keep my commandments, ye shall abide in my love; even as I have kept my Father's commandments, and abide in his love. These things have I spoken unto you, that my joy might remain in you, and that your joy might be full* (John 15:7-11 KJV).

625 *eirēnē,* "tranquility, peace between individuals, e.g. harmony, concord, felicity because peace and harmony make and keep things safe and prosperous" (Strong's G1515).

626 *Let your moderation be known unto all men* (Philippians 4:5a KJV).

627 *makrothymai,* "patience, longsuffering, constancy, steadfastness, fortitude, forbearance, perseverance and slowness in avenging wrongs" (Strong's G3115).

628 *Therefore, as God's chosen people, holy and dearly loved, clothe your-selves with compassion, kindness, humility, gentleness and patience* (Colossians 3:12 NIV).

629 *chrēstotēs*, "integrity, moral goodness, kindness, benignity" (Strong's G5544).

630 *chrēstos*, "fit, fit for use, virtuous, useful, manageable, pleasant, kind, benevolent" (Strong's G5543).

631 *agathōsynē*, "uprightness of heart, goodness, kindness" (Strong's G19).

632 *agathos*, "of good constitution or nature, useful, pleasant, agreeable upright, honorable" (Strong's G18).

633 *But as we were allowed of God to be put in trust with the gospel, even so we speak; not as pleasing men, but God, which trieth our hearts* (1 Thessalonians 2:4 KJV).

634 *Shall not God search this out? for he knoweth the secrets of the heart* (Psalm 44:21 KJV).

635 *praotes*, "gentleness, meekness mildness" (Strong's G4236).

636 *Wherefore by their fruits ye shall know them* (Matthew 7:20 KJV).

637 *My little children, let us not love in word, neither in tongue; but in deed and in truth. And hereby we know that we are of the truth, and shall assure our hearts before him. For if our heart condemn us, God is greater than our heart, and knoweth all things* (1 John 3:18-20 KJV).

638 *And the serpent said unto the woman, Ye shall not surely die: For God doth know that in the day ye eat thereof, then your eyes shall be opened, and ye shall be as gods, knowing good and evil. And when the woman saw that the tree was good for food, and that it was pleasant to the eyes, and a tree to be desired to make one wise, she took of the fruit thereof, and did eat, and gave also unto her husband with her; and he did eat* (Genesis 3:4-6 KJV).

639 *pistis*, "the character of one who can be relied on, fidelity, belief with the predominate idea of trust (or confidence) whether in God or in Christ, springing from faith in the same" (Strong's G4102).

640 *And that ye put on the new man, which after God is created in righ-teousness and true holiness* (Ephesians 4:24 KJV).

641 *egkrateia*, "self-control (the virtue of one who masters his desires and passions, esp. his sensual appetites)" (Strong's G1466).

642 *eusebeia,* "reverence, respect, piety towards God, godliness" (Strong's G2150).

643 *Through these he has given us his very great and precious promises, so that through them you may participate in the divine nature, having escaped the corruption in the world caused by evil desires. For this very reason, make every effort to add to your faith goodness; and to goodness, knowledge; and to knowledge, self-control; and to self-control, perseverance; and to perseverance, godliness; and to godliness, mutual affection; and to mutual affection, love. For if you possess these qualities in increasing measure, they will keep you from being ineffective and unproductive in your knowledge of our Lord Jesus Christ* (2 Peter 1:4-8 NIV).

644 *Not by works of righteousness which we have done, but according to his mercy he saved us, by the washing of regeneration, and renewing of the Holy Ghost; Which he shed on us abundantly through Jesus Christ our Saviour; That being justified by his grace, we should be made heirs according to the hope of eternal life* (Titus 3:5-7 KJV).

645 *Let no man despise thy youth; but be thou an example of the believers, in word, in conversation, in charity, in spirit, in faith, in purity* (1 Timothy 4:12 KJV).

646 A woman who was having trouble giving birth, they cut up the fetus inside her and take it out limb by limb, because her life comes before its life. If most of it had come out already they do not touch it because we do not push off one life for another (Mishnah Oholot 7:6).

647 …as the entire time that that it has not gone out into the air of the world, it is not [considered] a soul, and [so] it is possible to kill it and to save its mother. But when its head came out, we cannot touch it to kill it, as it is like a born [baby]; and we do not push off one soul for the sake of another (Sanhedrin 72b:14).

648 …you shall not abort a child or commit infanticide (Didache 2.2).

649 Talmud. In the *New World Encyclopedia.* Retrieved March 3, 2019 from http://www.newworldencyclopedia.org/entry/Talmud.

650 *katakrinō,* "to judge worthy of punishment" (Strong's G2632).

651 *elegchō,* "to expose, to chasten, to call to account, show one his fault, demand an explanation, by conviction to bring to the light" (Strong's G1651).

652 *And I heard a loud voice saying in heaven, Now is come salvation, and strength, and the kingdom of our God, and the power of his Christ: for the accuser of our brethren is cast down, which accused them before our God day and night* (Revelation 12:10 KJV).

653 *There is therefore now no condemnation to them which are in Christ Jesus, who walk not after the flesh, but after the Spirit* (Romans 8:1 KJV).

654 *Brothers and sisters, if someone is caught in a sin, you who live by the Spirit should restore that person gently. But watch yourselves, or you also may be tempted* (Galatians 6:1 NIV).

655 *What shall we say then? Shall we continue in sin, that grace may abound? God forbid. How shall we, that are dead to sin, live any longer therein?* (Romans 6:1-2 KJV).

656 *charis,* "good will, loving-kindness, favour. of the merciful kindness by which God, exerting his holy influence upon souls, turns them to Christ, keeps, strengthens, increases them in Christian faith, knowledge, affection, and kindles them to the exercise of the Christian virtues (Strong's G5485).

657 *What then? shall we sin, because we are not under the law, but under grace? God forbid* (Romans 6:15 KJV).

658 *racham,* "to love, love deeply, have mercy, be compassionate, have tender affection, have compassion (Strong's H7355).

659 *And David said unto Gad, I am in a great strait: let me fall now into the hand of the LORD; for very great are his mercies: but let me not fall into the hand of man* (1 Chronicles 21:13 KJV).

660 *Have mercy upon me, O God, according to thy loving kindness: according unto the multitude of thy tender mercies blot out my transgressions. Wash me thoroughly from my iniquity, And cleanse me from my sin. For I acknowledge my transgressions: and my sin is ever before me* (Psalm 51:1b-3 KJV).

661 *In whom we have redemption through his blood, the forgiveness of sins, according to the riches of his grace* (Ephesians 1:7 KJV).

662 *And that he was buried, and that he rose again the third day according to the scriptures* (1 Corinthians 15:4 KJV).

663 *And Mary arose in those days, and went into the hill country with*

haste, into a city of Juda; And entered into the house of Zacharias, and saluted Elisabeth. And it came to pass, that, when Elisabeth heard the salutation of Mary, the babe leaped in her womb; and Elisabeth was filled with the Holy Ghost: And she spake out with a loud voice, and said, Blessed art thou among women, and blessed is the fruit of thy womb. And whence is this to me, that the mother of my Lord should come to me? For, lo, as soon as the voice of thy salutation sounded in mine ears, the babe leaped in my womb for joy (Luke 1:39-44 KJV).

664 *The word of the LORD came to me, saying, "Before I formed you in the womb I knew you, before you were born I set you apart; I appointed you as a prophet to the nations"* (Jeremiah 1:4-5 NIV).

665 *As the hart panteth after the water brooks, so panteth my soul after thee, O God* (Psalm 42:1 KJV).

www.ingramcontent.com/pod-product-compliance
Lightning Source LLC
Chambersburg PA
CBHW021352090426
42742CB00009B/821